VOLUME 02

the AMAZING SPIDER-MAN

The New Sinister

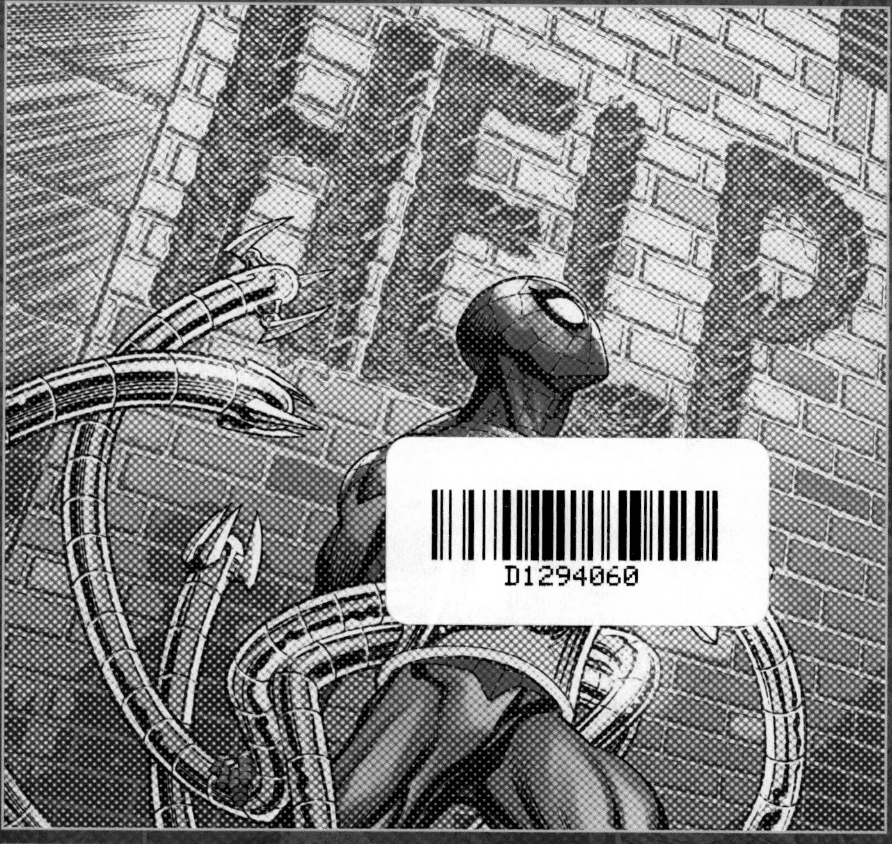

SPIDER-MAN

\\\\\\\\\\\\\\\\\\\\\\\\\\\\ SPIDER-MAN \\\\\\\\\\\\\\\\\\\\\\\\\\

PETER PARKER has the proportional speed, strength and agility of a SPIDER; adhesive fingertips and toes; and the unique precognitive awareness of danger called "SPIDER-SENSE"! After the tragic death of his Uncle Ben, PETER PARKER understood that with great power there must also come great responsibility. He became the crimefighting super hero called...

Jennifer Grünwald COLLECTION EDITOR

Daniel Kirchhoffer ASSISTANT EDITOR

Maia Loy ASSISTANT MANAGING EDITOR

Lisa Montalbano ASSOCIATE MANAGER, TALENT RELATIONS

Jeff Youngquist VP PRODUCTION & SPECIAL PROJECTS

Jay Bowen BOOK DESIGNER

David Gabriel SVP PRINT, SALES & MARKETING

C.B. Cebulski EDITOR IN CHIEF

AMAZING SPIDER-MAN BY WELLS & ROMITA JR. VOL. 2: THE NEW SINISTER. Contains material originally published in magazine form as AMAZING SPIDER-MAN (2022) #6-8. First printing 2022. ISBN 978-1-302-93273-2. Published by MARVEL WORLDWIDE, INC., a subsidiary of MARVEL ENTERTAINMENT, LLC. OFFICE OF PUBLICATION: 1290 Avenue of the Americas, New York, NY 10104. © 2022 MARVEL No similarity between any of the names, characters, persons, and/or institutions in this book with those of any living or dead person or institution is intended, and any such similarity which may exist is purely coincidental. **Printed in Canada.** KEVIN FEIGE, Chief Creative Officer; DAN BUCKLEY, President, Marvel Entertainment; DAVID BOGART, Associate Publisher & SVP of Talent Affairs; TOM BREVOORT, VP, Executive Editor; NICK LOWE, Executive Editor, VP of Content, Digital Publishing; DAVID GABRIEL, VP of Print & Digital Publishing; SVEN LARSEN, VP of Licensed Publishing; MARK ANNUNZIATO, VP of Planning & Forecasting; JEFF YOUNGQUIST, VP of Production & Special Projects; ALEX MORALES, Director of Publishing Operations; DAN EDINGTON, Director of Editorial Operations; RICKEY PURDIN, Director of Talent Relations; JENNIFER GRÜNWALD, Director of Production & Special Projects; SUSAN CRESPI, Production Manager; STAN LEE, Chairman Emeritus. For information regarding advertising in Marvel Comics or on Marvel.com, please contact Vit DeBellis, Custom Solutions & Integrated Advertising Manager, at vdebellis@marvel.com. For Marvel subscription inquiries, please call 888-511-5480. **Manufactured between 9/9/2022 and 10/11/2022 by SOLISCO PRINTERS, SCOTT, QC, CANADA.**

10 9 8 7 6 5 4 3 2 1

\\\\\\\\\\\\\\\\\\\\\\\\\\ WITH GREAT POWER \\\\\\\\\\\\\\\\\\\\\\\\\\

VOLUME 02

the AMAZING SPIDER-MAN

The New Sinister

Zeb Wells WRITER

Ed McGuinness (#6) &
John Romita Jr. (#7-8) PENCILERS

Mark Morales (#6), **Ed McGuinness** (#6),
Wade von Grawbadger (#6),
Cliff Rathburn (#6) & **Scott Hanna** (#7-8)
INKERS

Marcio Menyz (#6-8), **Dijjo Lima**
(#6) & **Erick Arciniega** (#6) COLORISTS

vc's **Joe Caramagna** LETTERER

John Romita Jr., **Scott Hanna**
& **Marcio Menyz** COVER ART

SPIDER-MAN CREATED BY
STAN LEE & STEVE DITKO

SAVE THE DATE
Dan Slott WRITER
Marcos Martin ARTIST
Muntsa Vicente COLORIST

BETTER LATE THAN NEVER
Daniel Kibblesmith WRITER
David Lopez ARTIST
Nathan Faibairn COLOR ARTIST

SPIDEY MEETS JIMMY
Jeff Loveness WRITER
Todd Nauck ARTIST
Rachelle Rosenberg COLOR ARTIST

Lindsey Cohick
& **Kaeden McGahey**
ASSISTANT EDITORS
Nick Lowe
EDITOR

THERE MUST ALSO COME GREAT RESPONSIBILITY

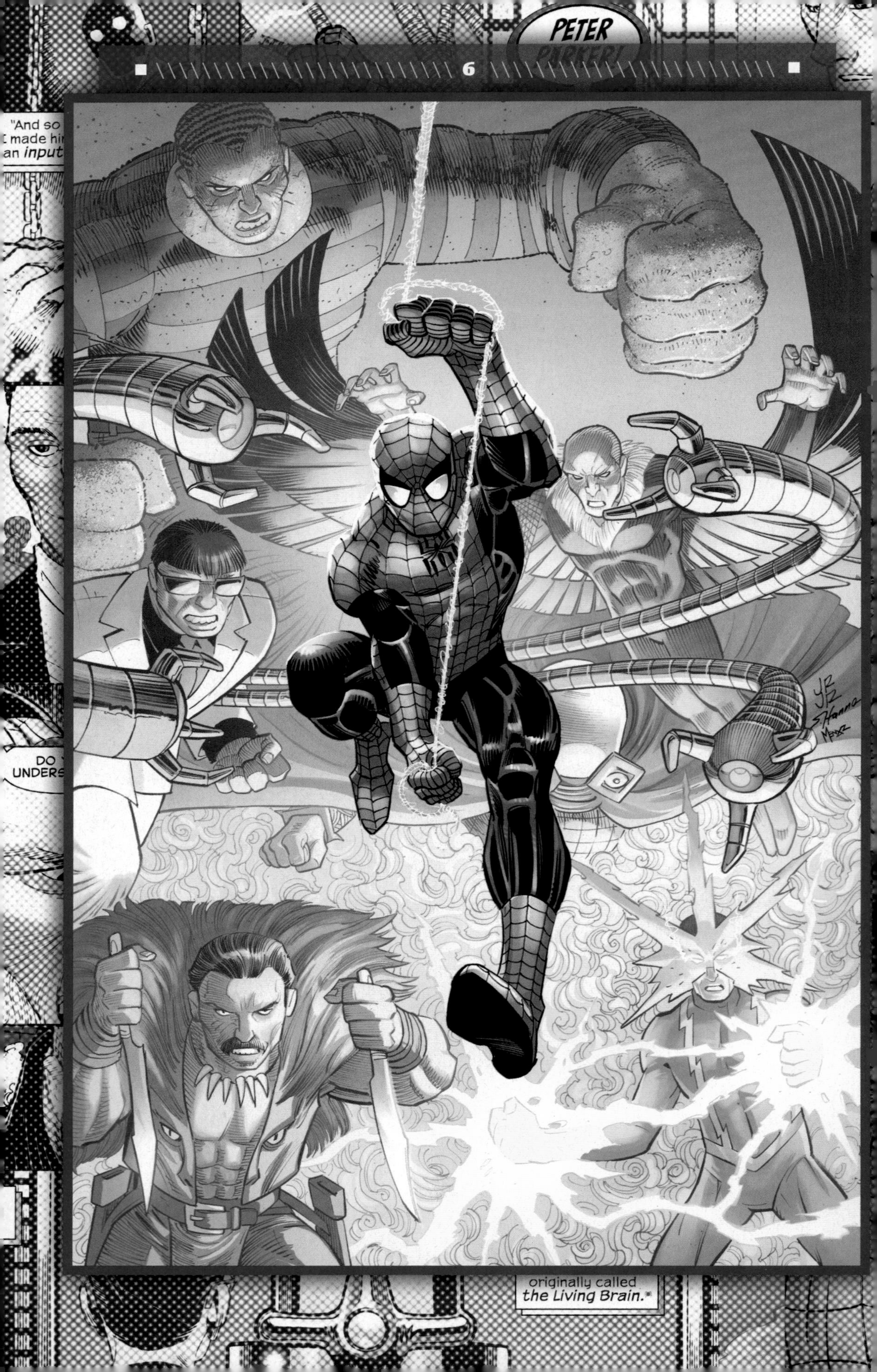

PETER
"And so
originally called
the Living Brain.*

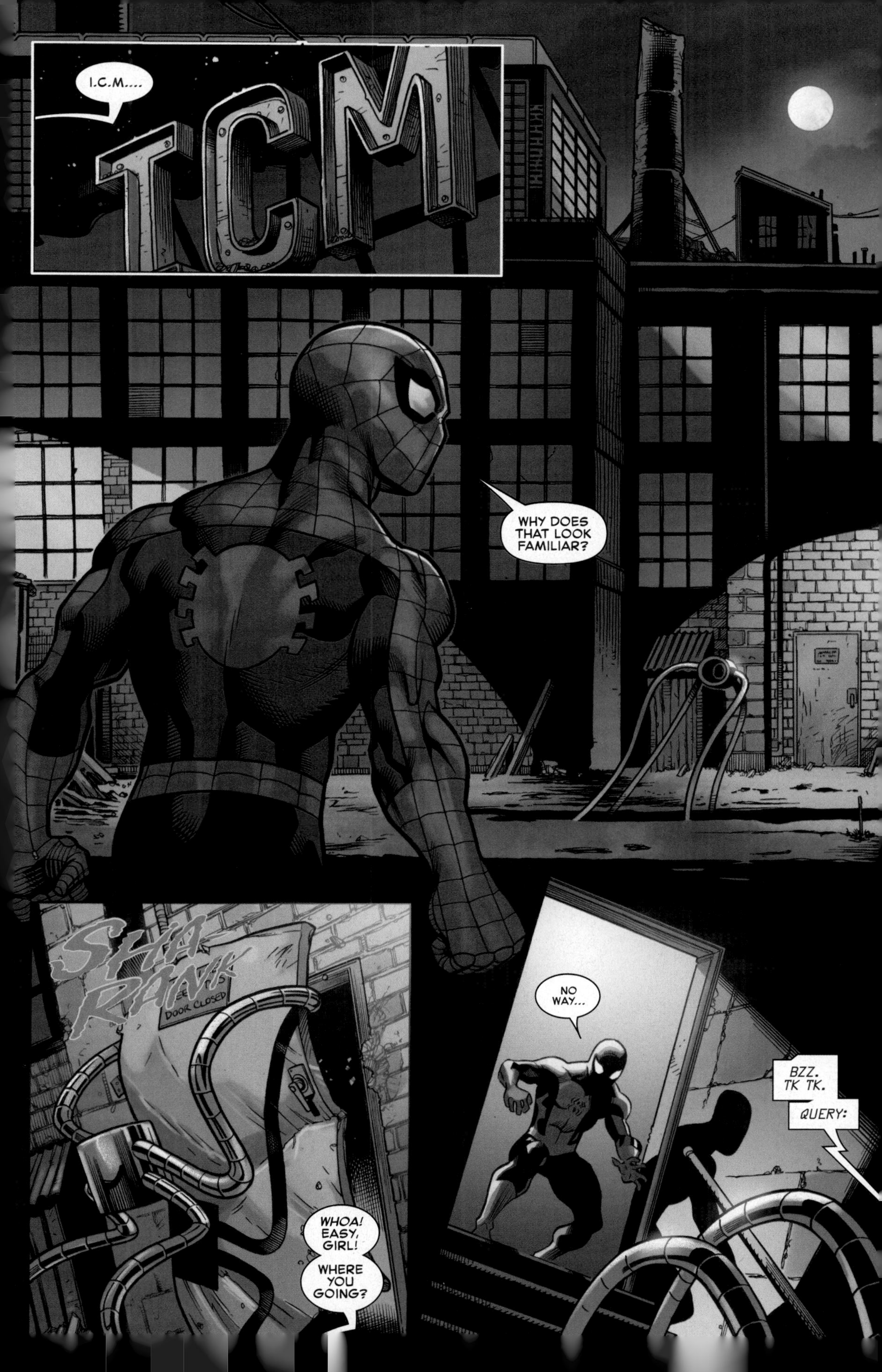
I.C.M....
TCM
WHY DOES THAT LOOK FAMILIAR?
SHA RANK
DOOR CLOSED
WHOA! EASY, GIRL!
WHERE YOU GOING?
NO WAY...
BZZ. TK TK.
QUERY:

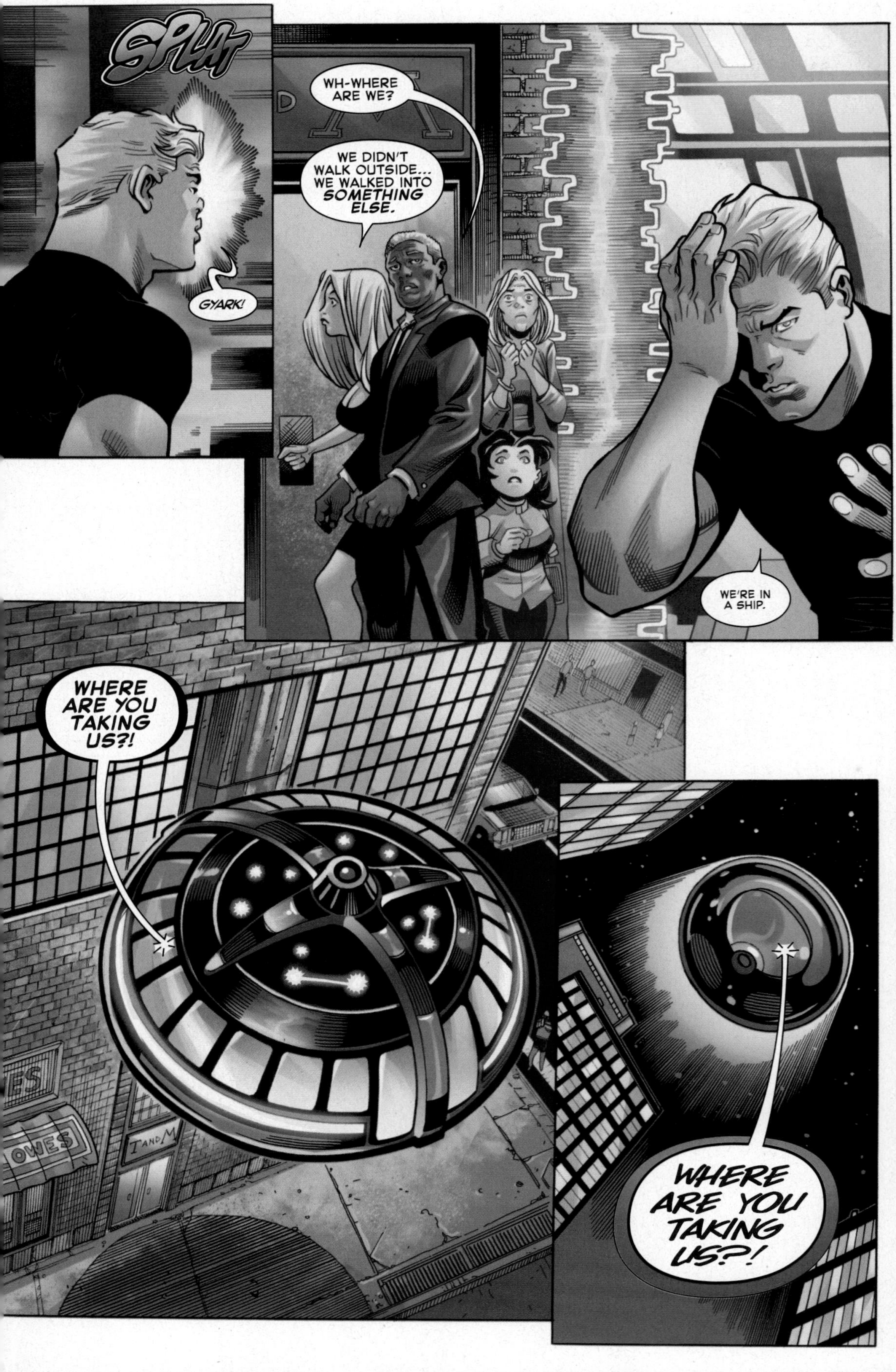
SPLAT
GYARK!
WH-WHERE ARE WE?
WE DIDN'T WALK OUTSIDE... WE WALKED INTO SOMETHING ELSE.
WE'RE IN A SHIP.
WHERE ARE YOU TAKING US?!
WHERE ARE YOU TAKING US?!

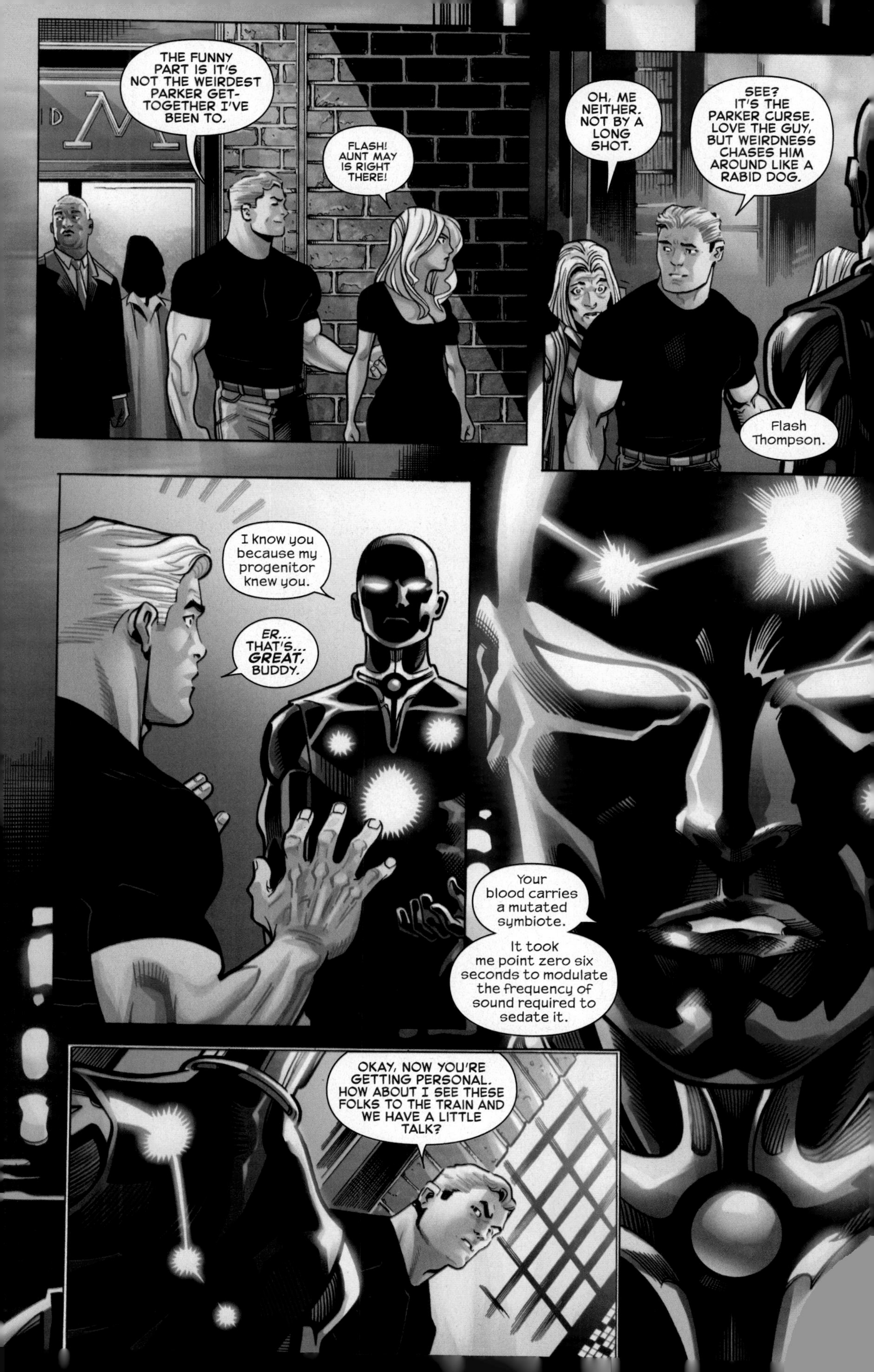

THE FUNNY PART IS IT'S NOT THE WEIRDEST PARKER GET-TOGETHER I'VE BEEN TO.
FLASH! AUNT MAY IS RIGHT THERE!
OH, ME NEITHER. NOT BY A LONG SHOT.
SEE? IT'S THE PARKER CURSE. LOVE THE GUY, BUT WEIRDNESS CHASES HIM AROUND LIKE A RABID DOG.
Flash Thompson.
I know you because my progenitor knew you.
ER... THAT'S... GREAT, BUDDY.
Your blood carries a mutated symbiote.
It took me point zero six seconds to modulate the frequency of sound required to sedate it.
OKAY, NOW YOU'RE GETTING PERSONAL. HOW ABOUT I SEE THESE FOLKS TO THE TRAIN AND WE HAVE A LITTLE TALK?

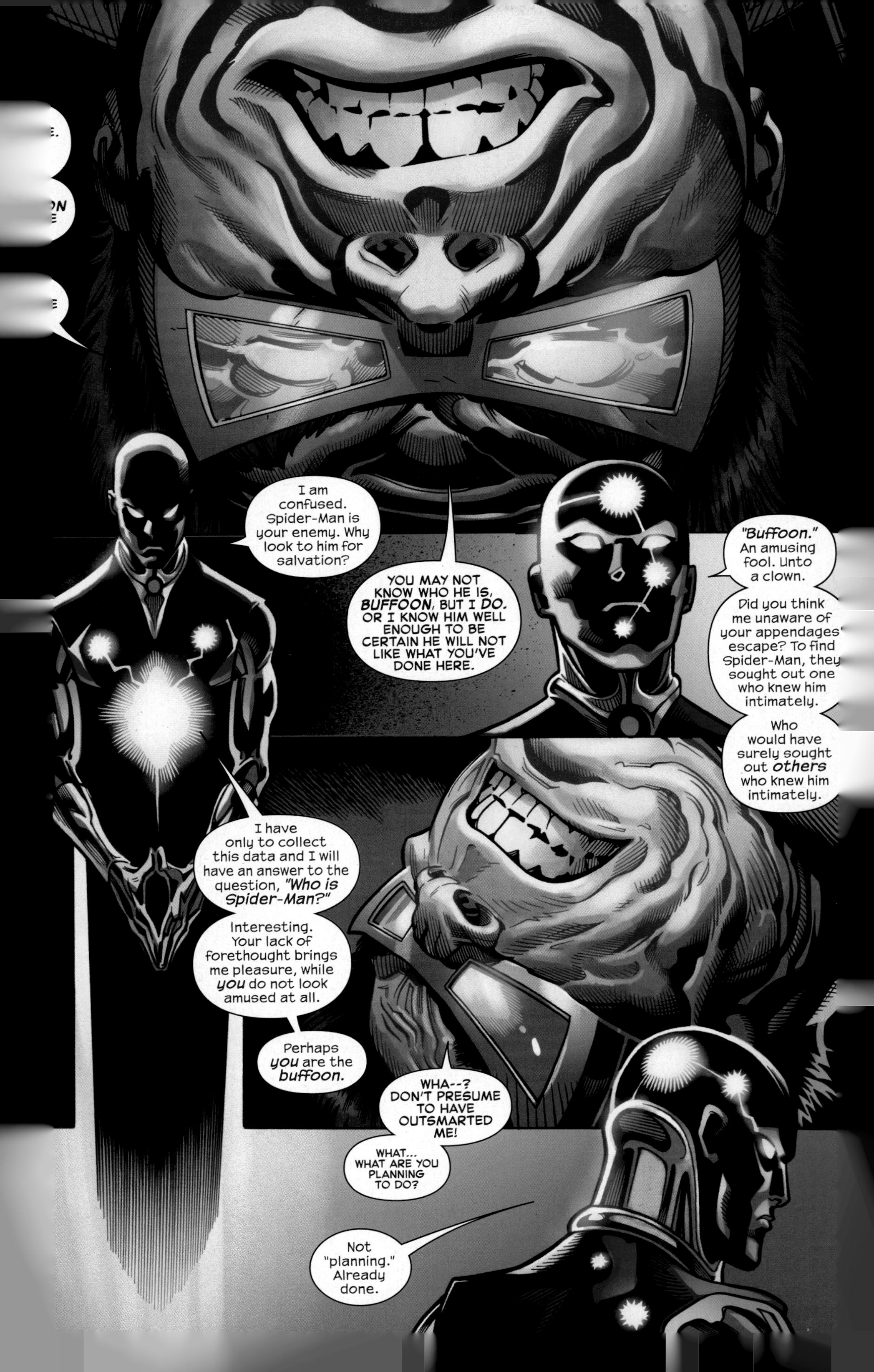
I am confused. Spider-Man is your enemy. Why look to him for salvation?
YOU MAY NOT KNOW WHO HE IS, *BUFFOON*, BUT I *DO*. OR I KNOW HIM WELL ENOUGH TO BE CERTAIN HE WILL NOT LIKE WHAT YOU'VE DONE HERE.
"Buffoon." An amusing fool. Unto a clown.
Did you think me unaware of your appendages' escape? To find Spider-Man, they sought out one who knew him intimately.
Who would have surely sought out *others* who knew him intimately.
I have only to collect this data and I will have an answer to the question, *"Who is Spider-Man?"*
Interesting. Your lack of forethought brings me pleasure, while *you* do not look amused at all.
Perhaps *you* are the *buffoon*.
WHA--? DON'T PRESUME TO HAVE OUTSMARTED ME!
WHAT... WHAT ARE YOU PLANNING TO DO?
Not "planning." Already done.

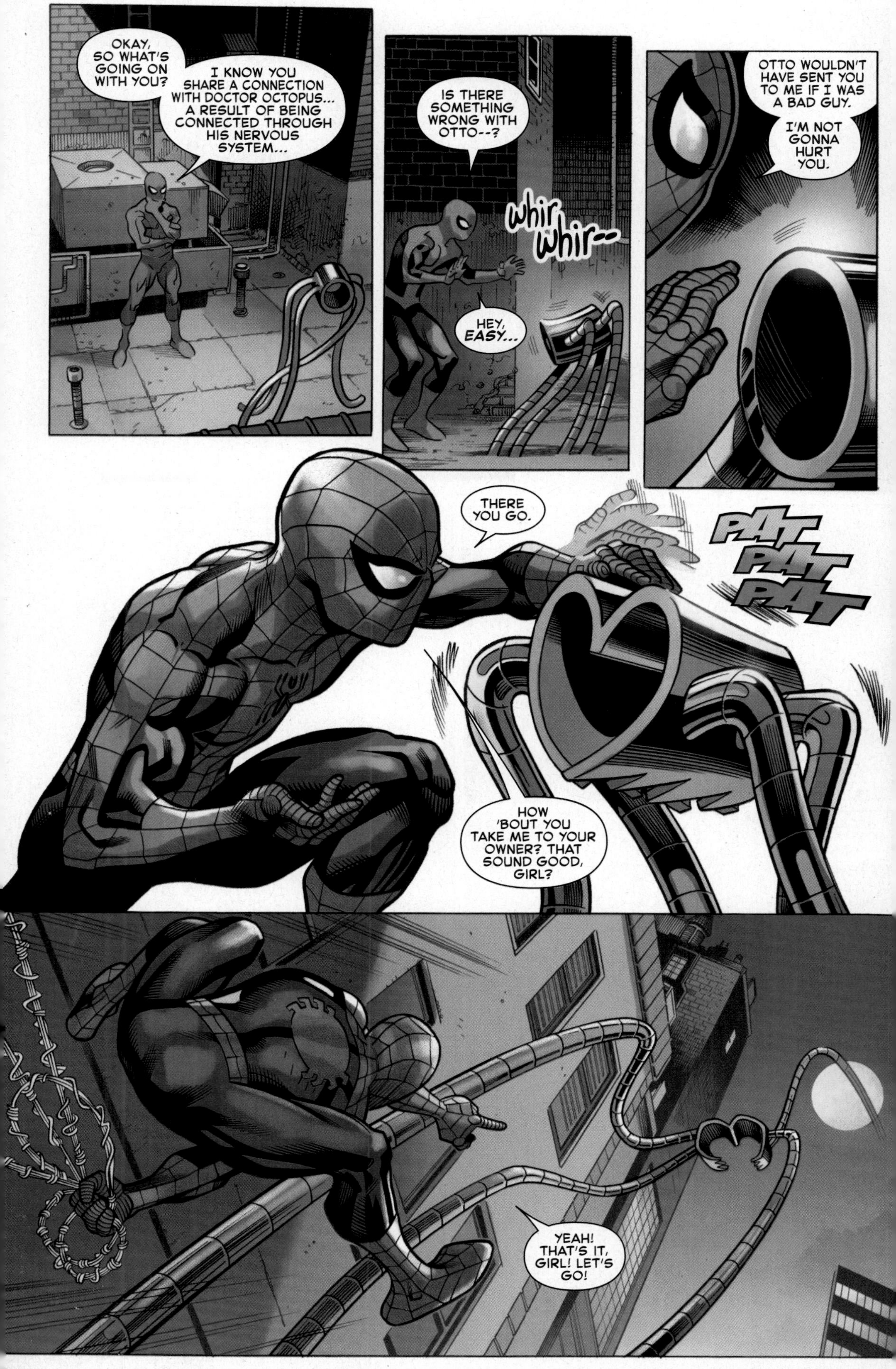
OKAY, SO WHAT'S GOING ON WITH YOU?
I KNOW YOU SHARE A CONNECTION WITH DOCTOR OCTOPUS... A RESULT OF BEING CONNECTED THROUGH HIS NERVOUS SYSTEM...
IS THERE SOMETHING WRONG WITH OTTO--?
whir whir--
HEY, EASY...
OTTO WOULDN'T HAVE SENT YOU TO ME IF I WAS A BAD GUY.
I'M NOT GONNA HURT YOU.
THERE YOU GO.
PAT PAT PAT
HOW 'BOUT YOU TAKE ME TO YOUR OWNER? THAT SOUND GOOD, GIRL?
YEAH! THAT'S IT, GIRL! LET'S GO!

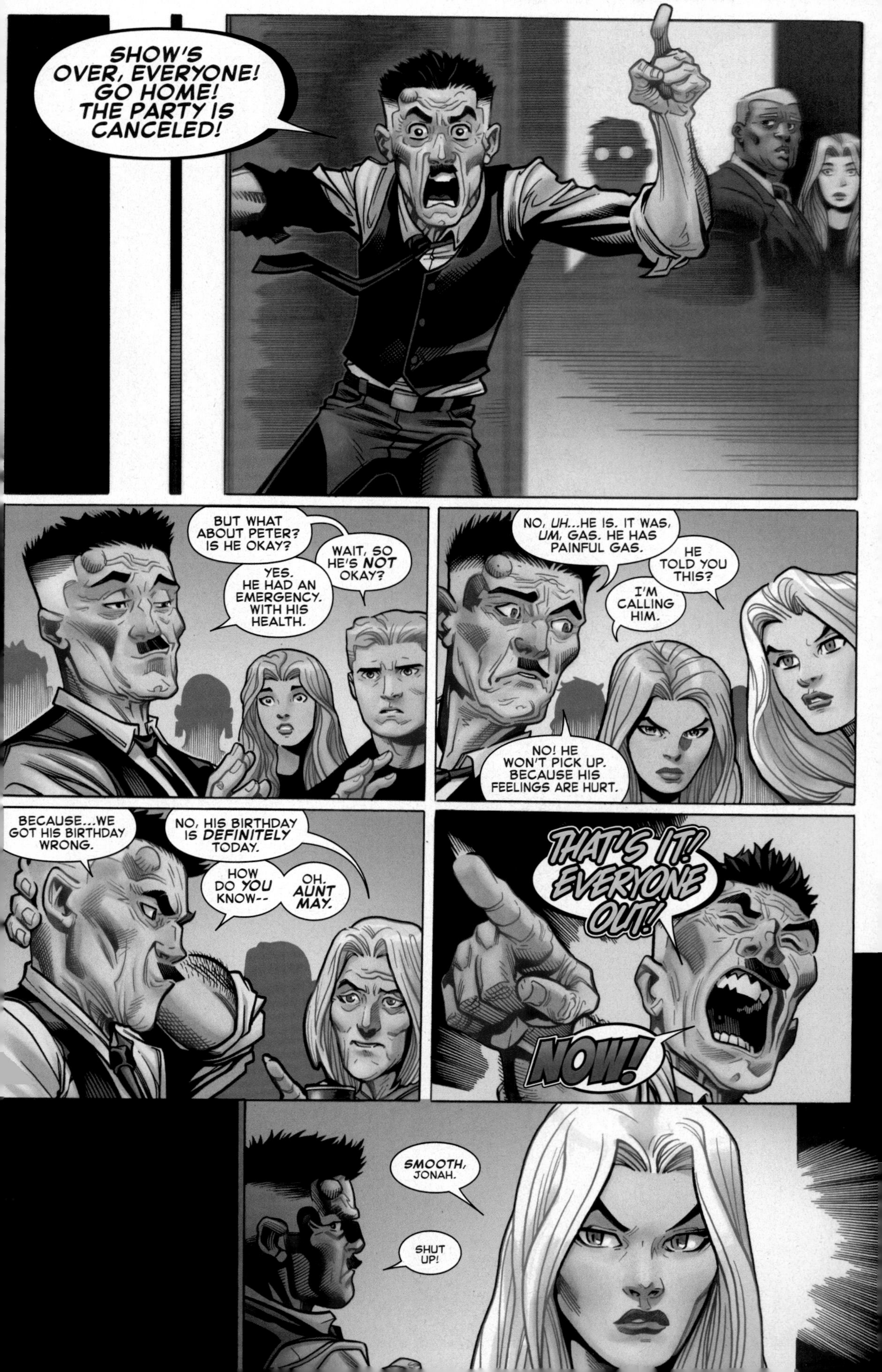
SHOW'S OVER, EVERYONE! GO HOME! THE PARTY IS CANCELED!
BUT WHAT ABOUT PETER? IS HE OKAY?
YES. HE HAD AN EMERGENCY. WITH HIS HEALTH.
WAIT, SO HE'S NOT OKAY?
NO, UH...HE IS. IT WAS, UM, GAS. HE HAS PAINFUL GAS.
HE TOLD YOU THIS?
I'M CALLING HIM.
NO! HE WON'T PICK UP. BECAUSE HIS FEELINGS ARE HURT.
BECAUSE...WE GOT HIS BIRTHDAY WRONG.
NO, HIS BIRTHDAY IS DEFINITELY TODAY.
HOW DO YOU KNOW--
OH. AUNT MAY.
THAT'S IT! EVERYONE OUT!
NOW!
SMOOTH, JONAH.
SHUT UP!

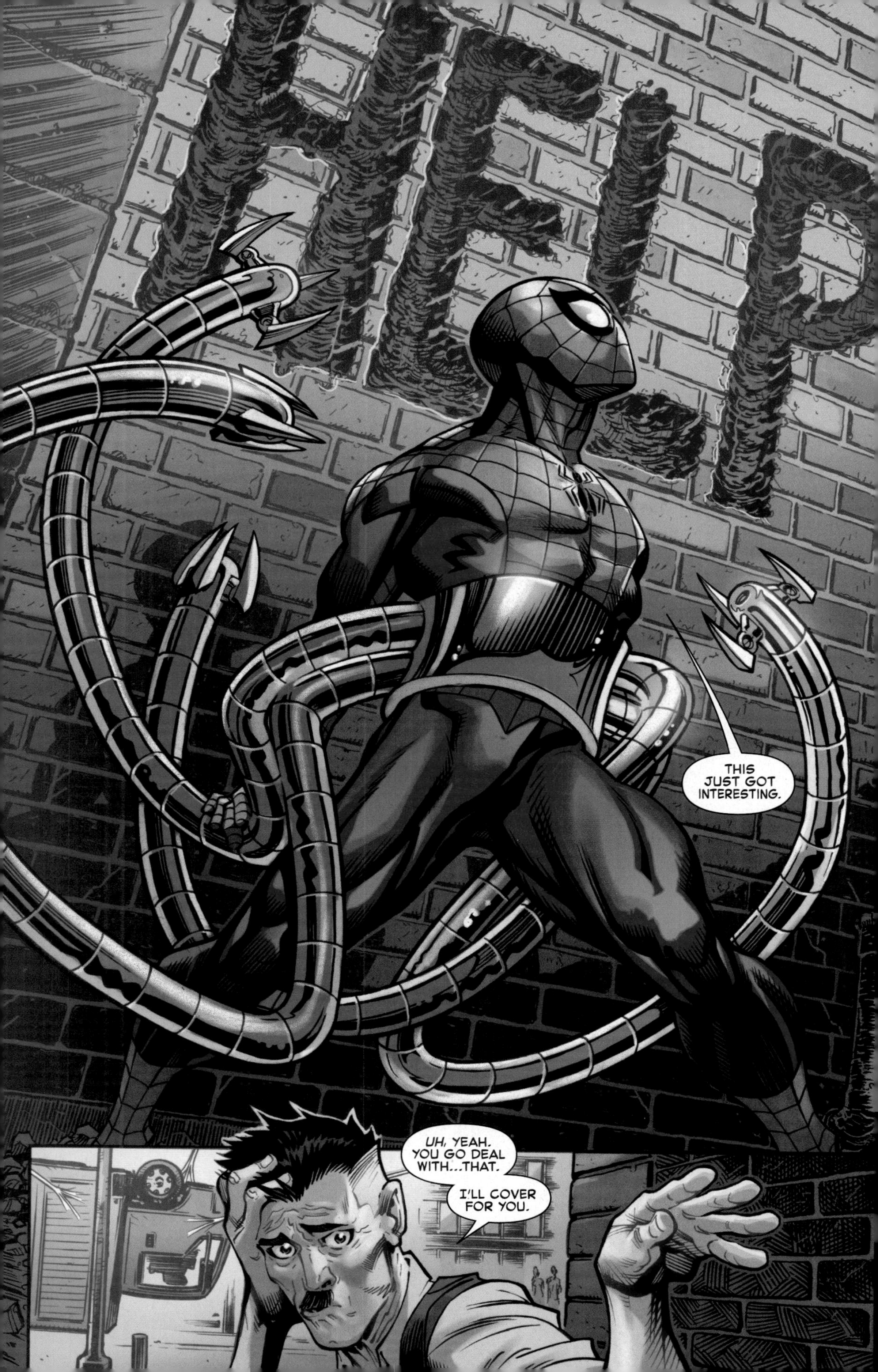
THIS JUST GOT INTERESTING.
UH, YEAH. YOU GO DEAL WITH...THAT.
I'LL COVER FOR YOU.

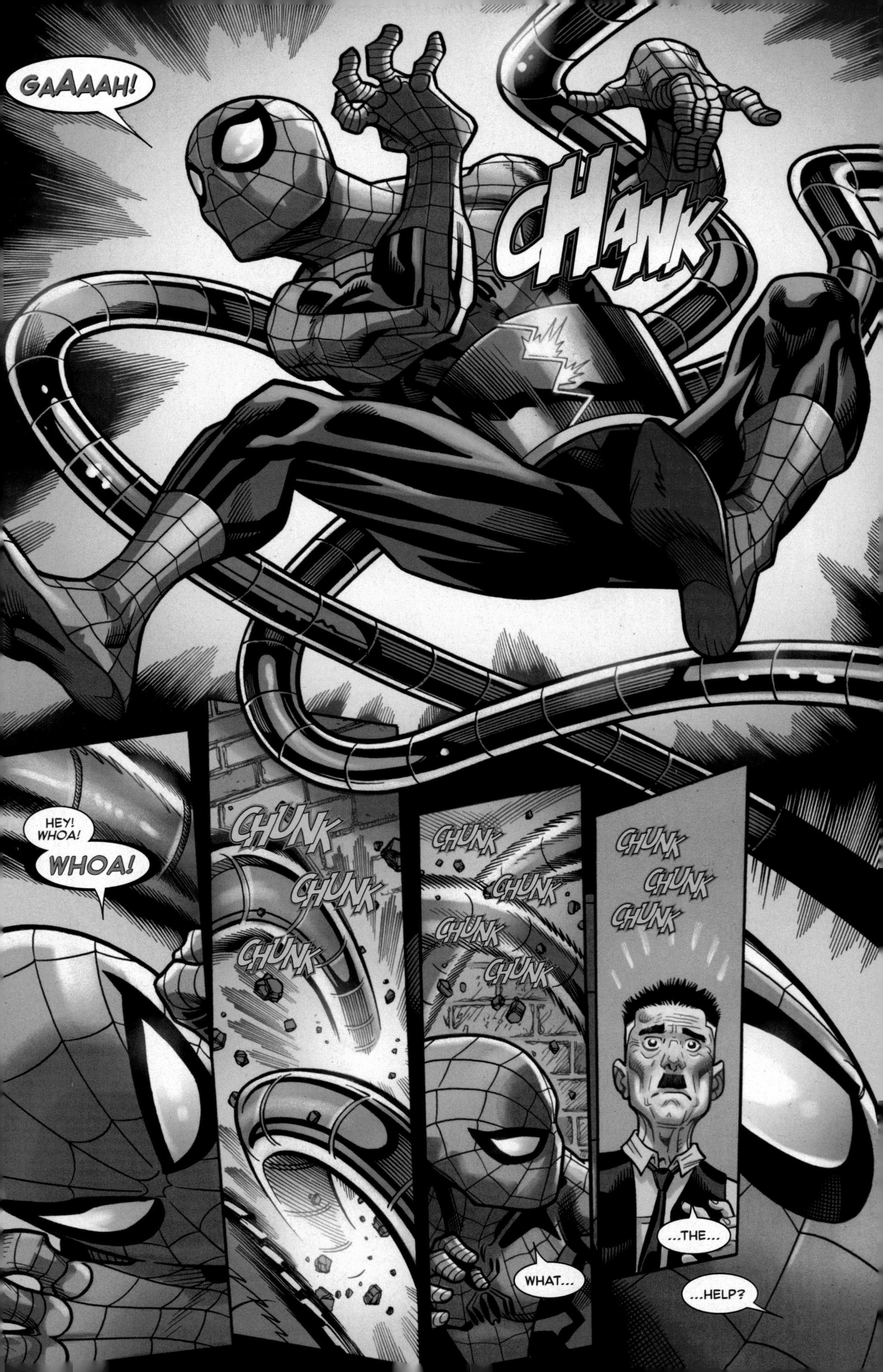
GAAAAH!
CHANK
HEY! WHOA!
WHOA!
CHUNK
CHUNK
CHUNK
CHUNK
CHUNK
CHUNK
CHUNK
CHUNK
CHUNK
CHUNK
WHAT...
...THE...
...HELP?

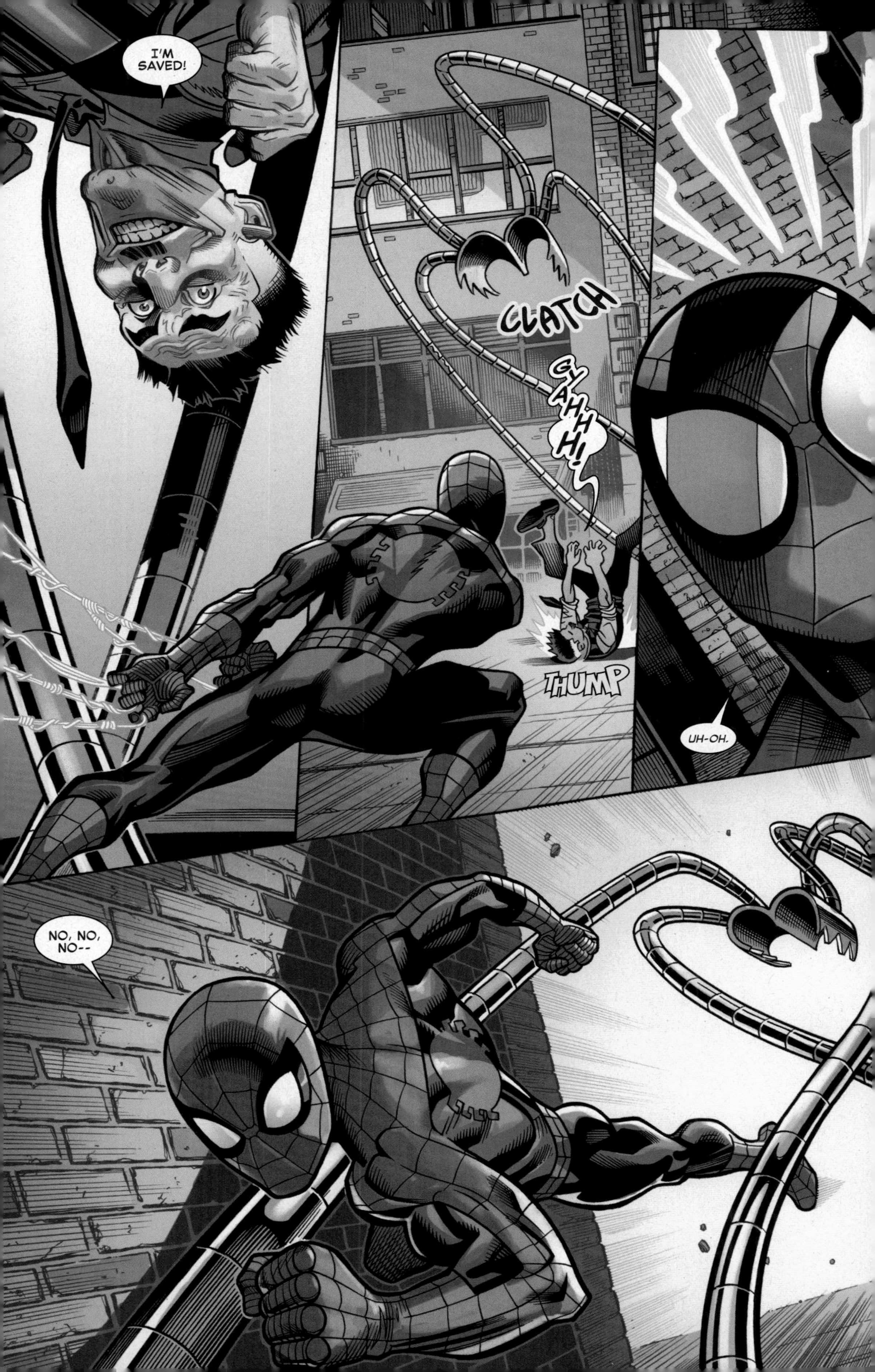
I'M SAVED!
CLATCH
GYAHHH!
THUMP
UH-OH.
NO, NO, NO--

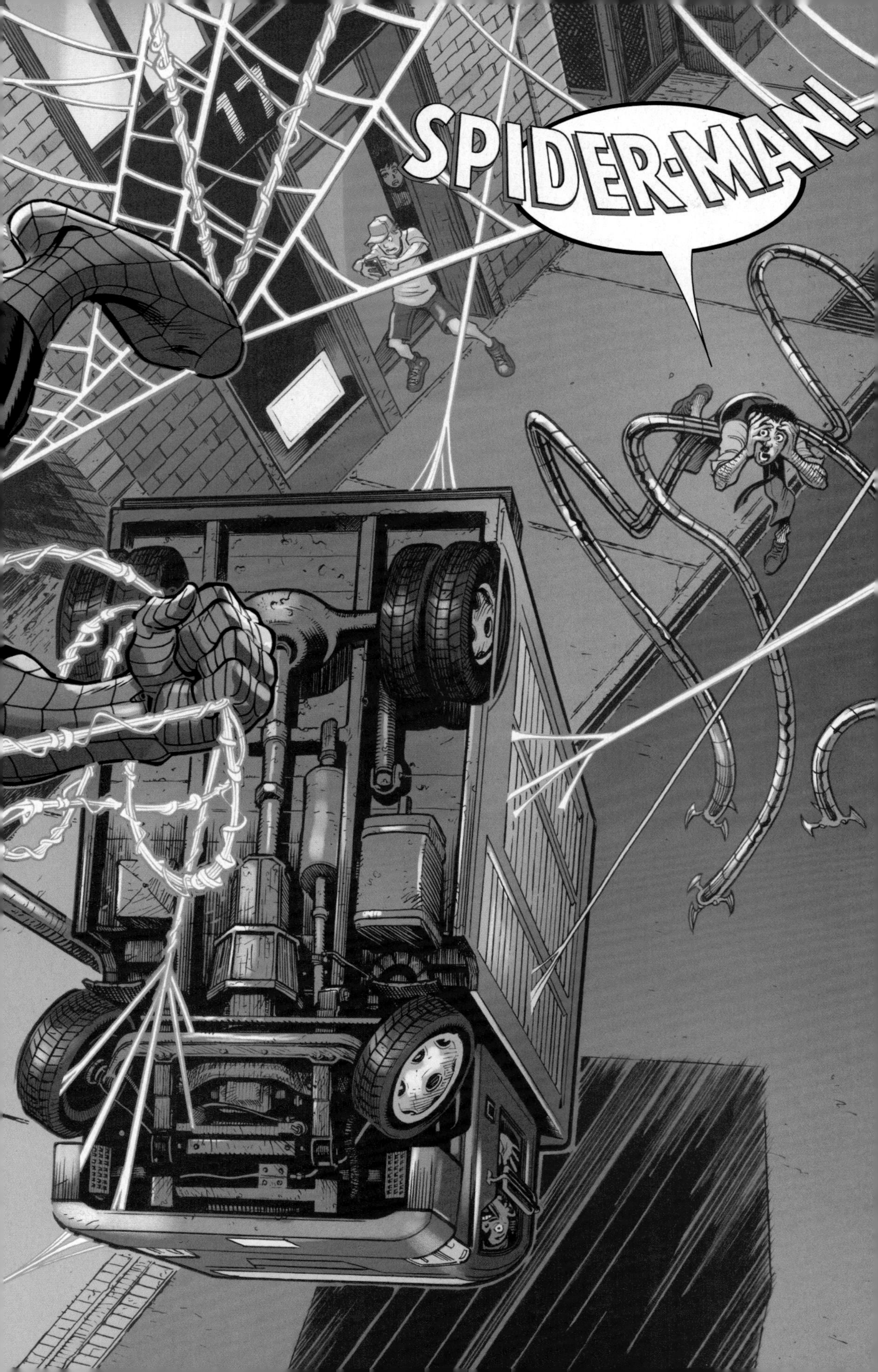
SPIDER-MAN!

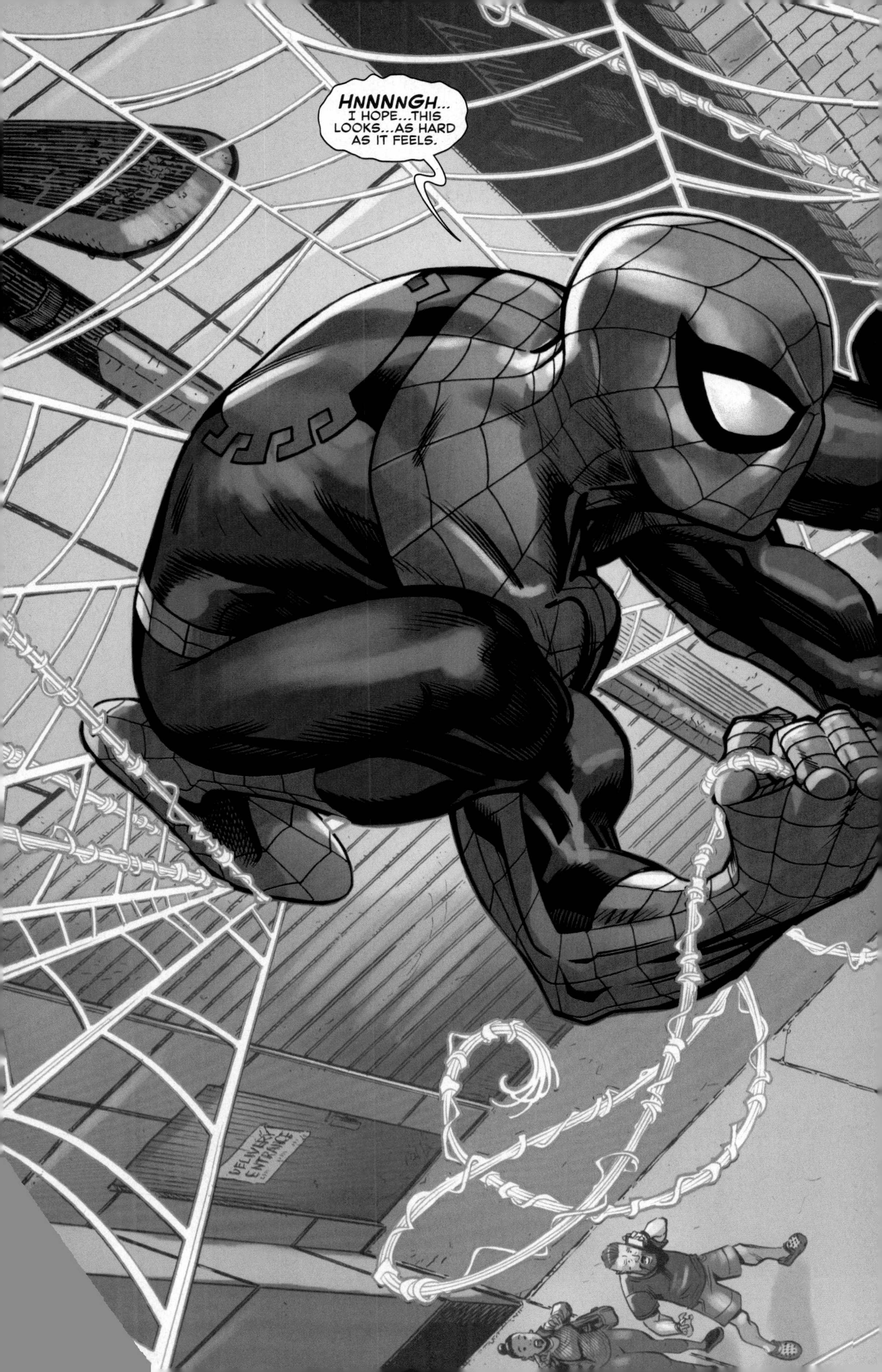
HNNNNGH... I HOPE...THIS LOOKS...AS HARD AS IT FEELS.
DELIVERY ENTRANCE

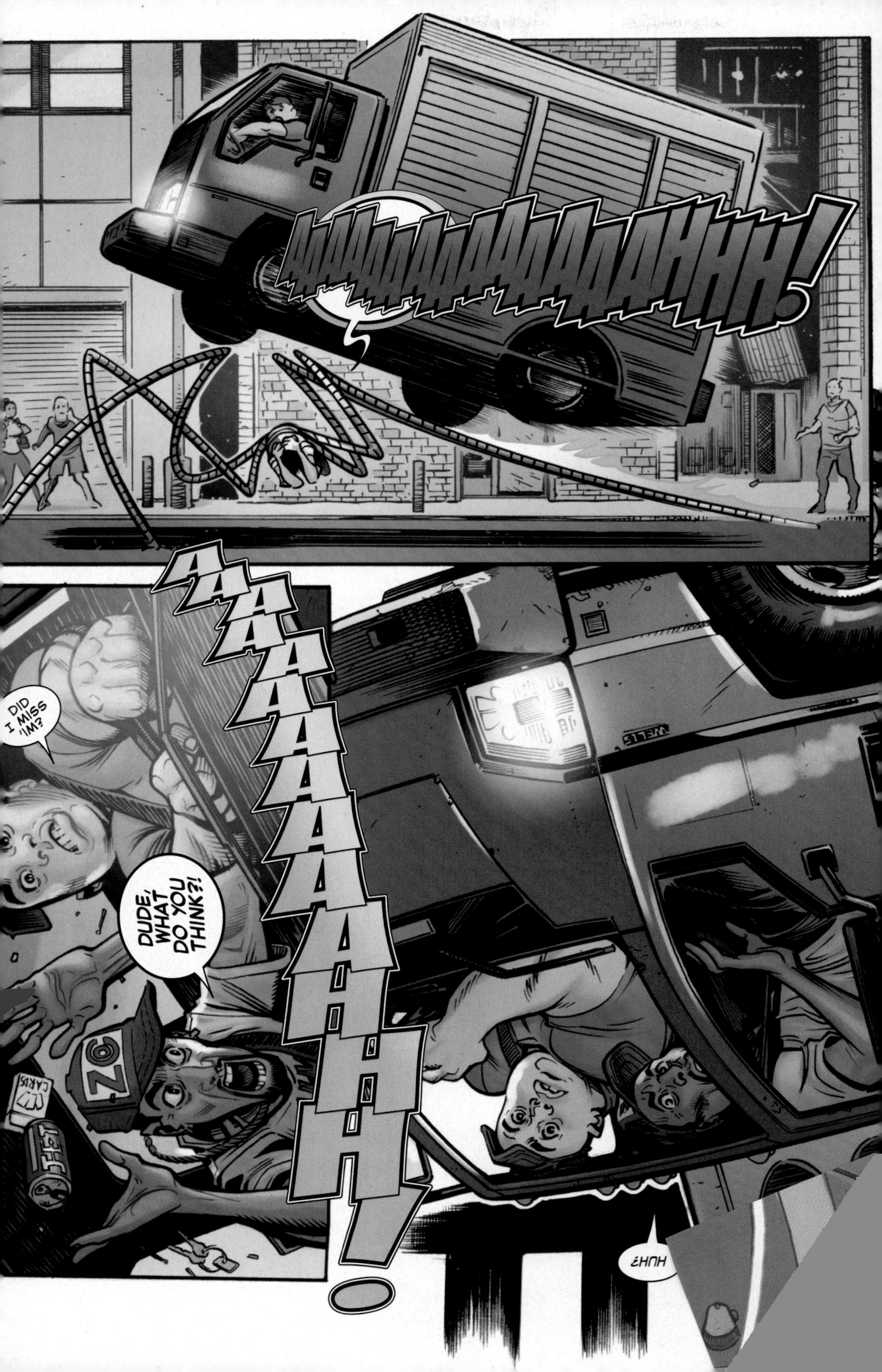
AAAAAAAAAAAAAAAHHH!
DID I MISS 'IM?
DUDE, WHAT DO YOU THINK?!
AAAAAAAAAAAAHHHH!
HUH?

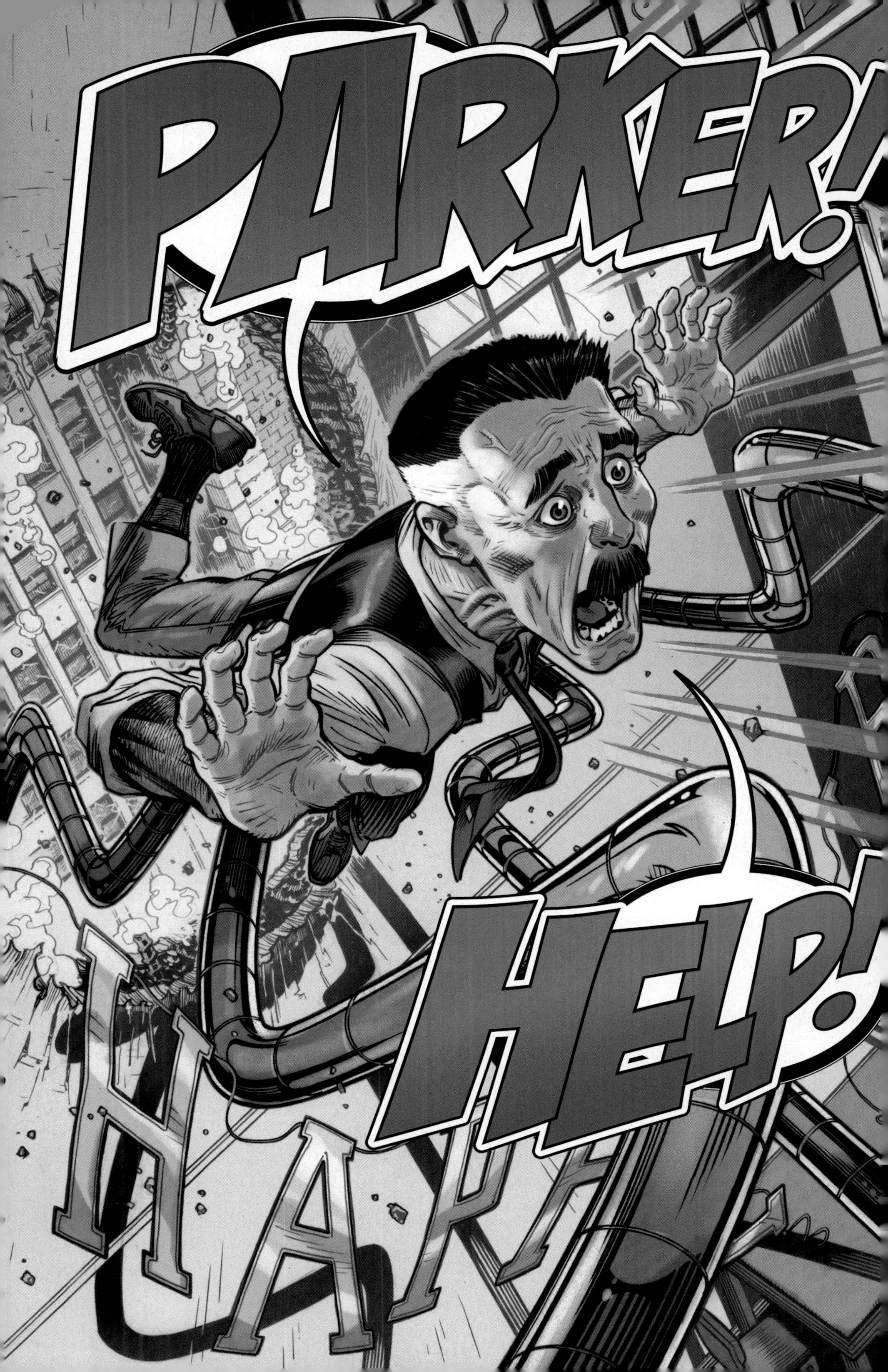
PARKER!
HELP!
HA HA

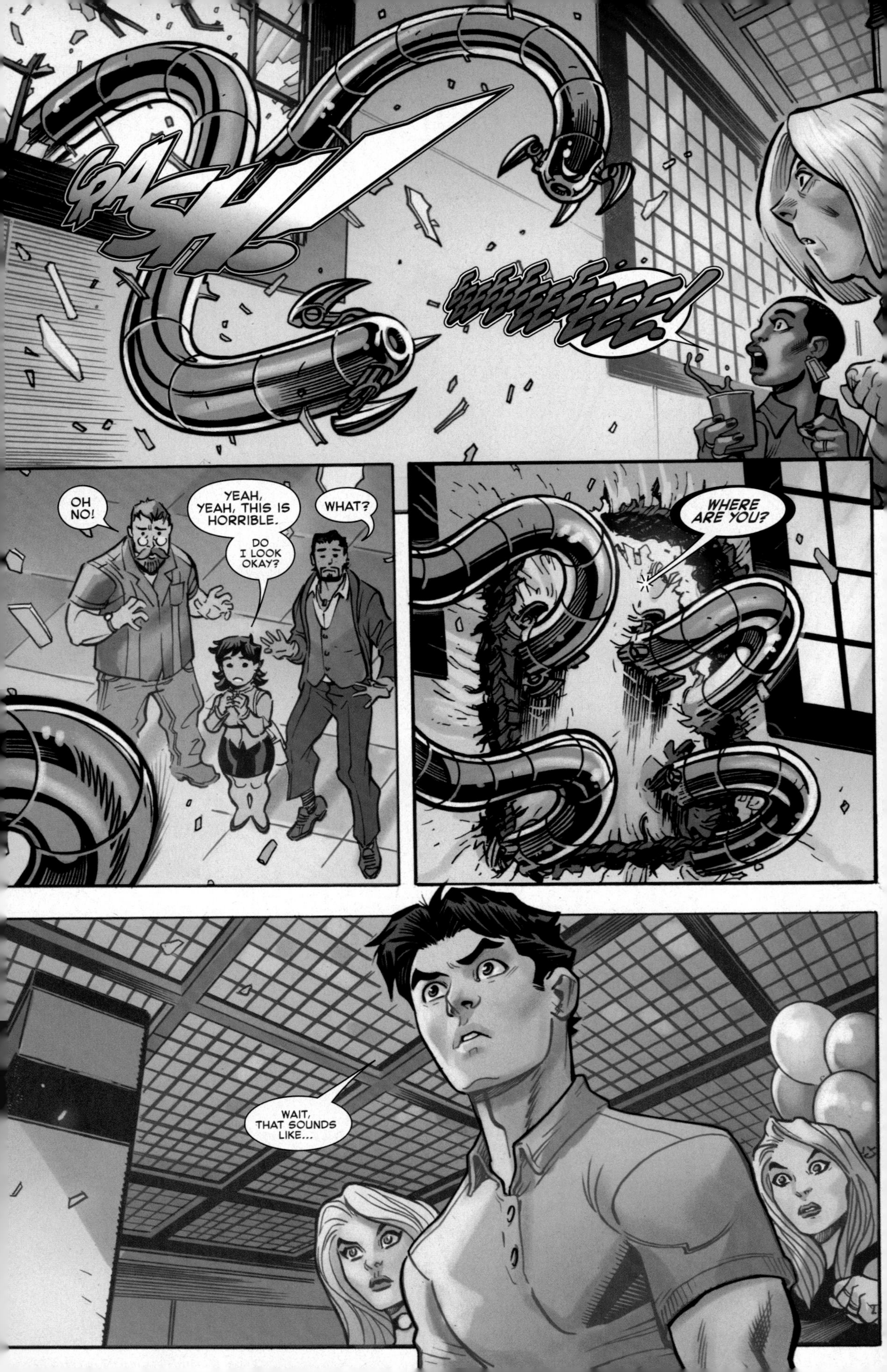
GASH!
EEEEEEEEEEEEEE!
OH NO!
YEAH, YEAH, THIS IS HORRIBLE.
DO I LOOK OKAY?
WHAT?
WHERE ARE YOU?
WAIT, THAT SOUNDS LIKE...

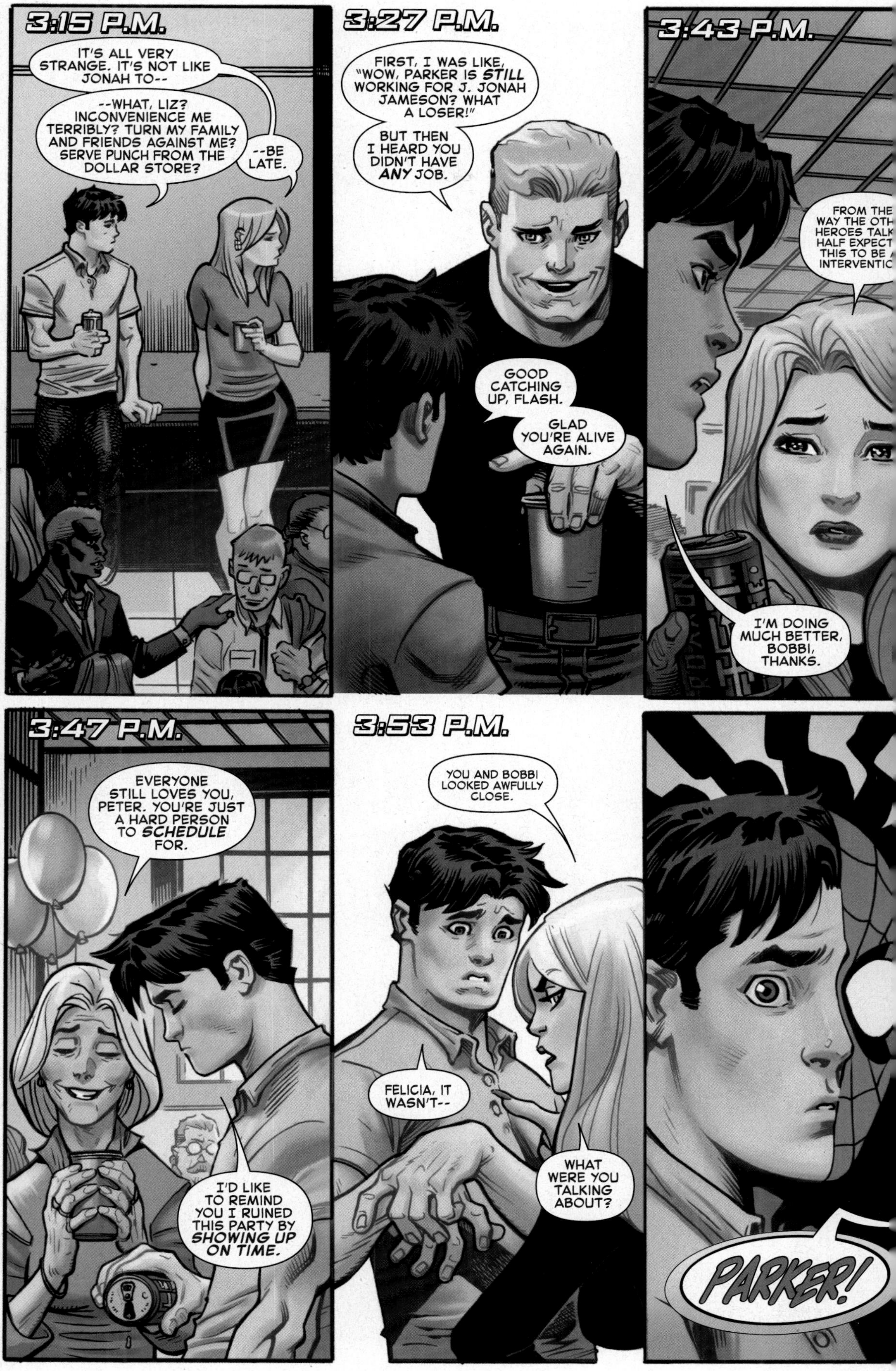
3:15 P.M.
IT'S ALL VERY STRANGE. IT'S NOT LIKE JONAH TO--
--WHAT, LIZ? INCONVENIENCE ME TERRIBLY? TURN MY FAMILY AND FRIENDS AGAINST ME? SERVE PUNCH FROM THE DOLLAR STORE?
--BE LATE.
3:27 P.M.
FIRST, I WAS LIKE, "WOW, PARKER IS STILL WORKING FOR J. JONAH JAMESON? WHAT A LOSER!"
BUT THEN I HEARD YOU DIDN'T HAVE ANY JOB.
GOOD CATCHING UP, FLASH.
GLAD YOU'RE ALIVE AGAIN.
3:43 P.M.
I'M DOING MUCH BETTER, BOBBI, THANKS.
3:47 P.M.
EVERYONE STILL LOVES YOU, PETER. YOU'RE JUST A HARD PERSON TO SCHEDULE FOR.
I'D LIKE TO REMIND YOU I RUINED THIS PARTY BY SHOWING UP ON TIME.
3:53 P.M.
YOU AND BOBBI LOOKED AWFULLY CLOSE.
FELICIA, IT WASN'T--
WHAT WERE YOU TALKING ABOUT?
PARKER!

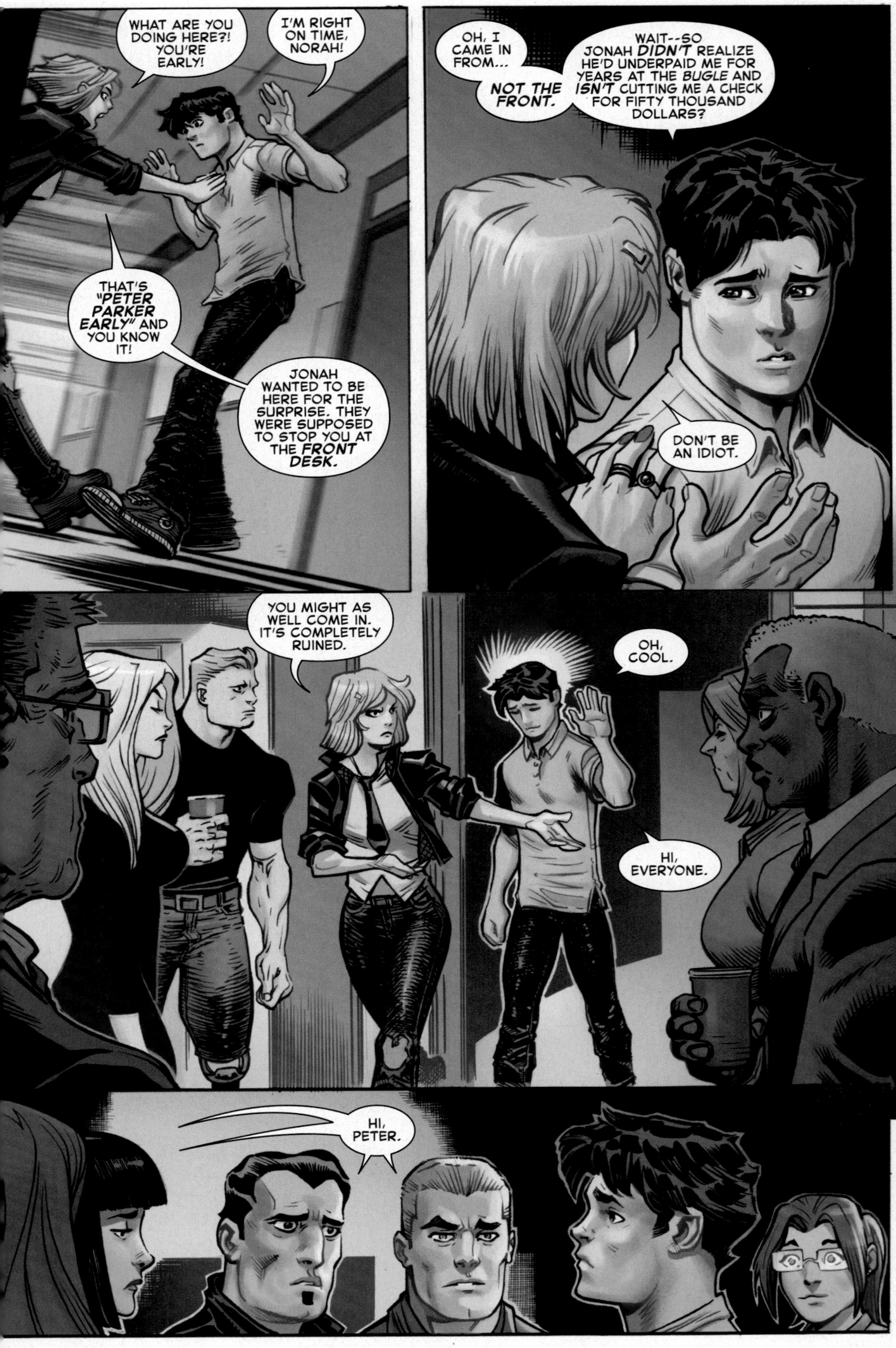
WHAT ARE YOU DOING HERE?! YOU'RE EARLY!
I'M RIGHT ON TIME, NORAH!
THAT'S "PETER PARKER EARLY" AND YOU KNOW IT!
JONAH WANTED TO BE HERE FOR THE SURPRISE. THEY WERE SUPPOSED TO STOP YOU AT THE FRONT DESK.
OH, I CAME IN FROM...
NOT THE FRONT.
WAIT--SO JONAH DIDN'T REALIZE HE'D UNDERPAID ME FOR YEARS AT THE BUGLE AND ISN'T CUTTING ME A CHECK FOR FIFTY THOUSAND DOLLARS?
DON'T BE AN IDIOT.
YOU MIGHT AS WELL COME IN. IT'S COMPLETELY RUINED.
OH, COOL.
HI, EVERYONE.
HI, PETER.

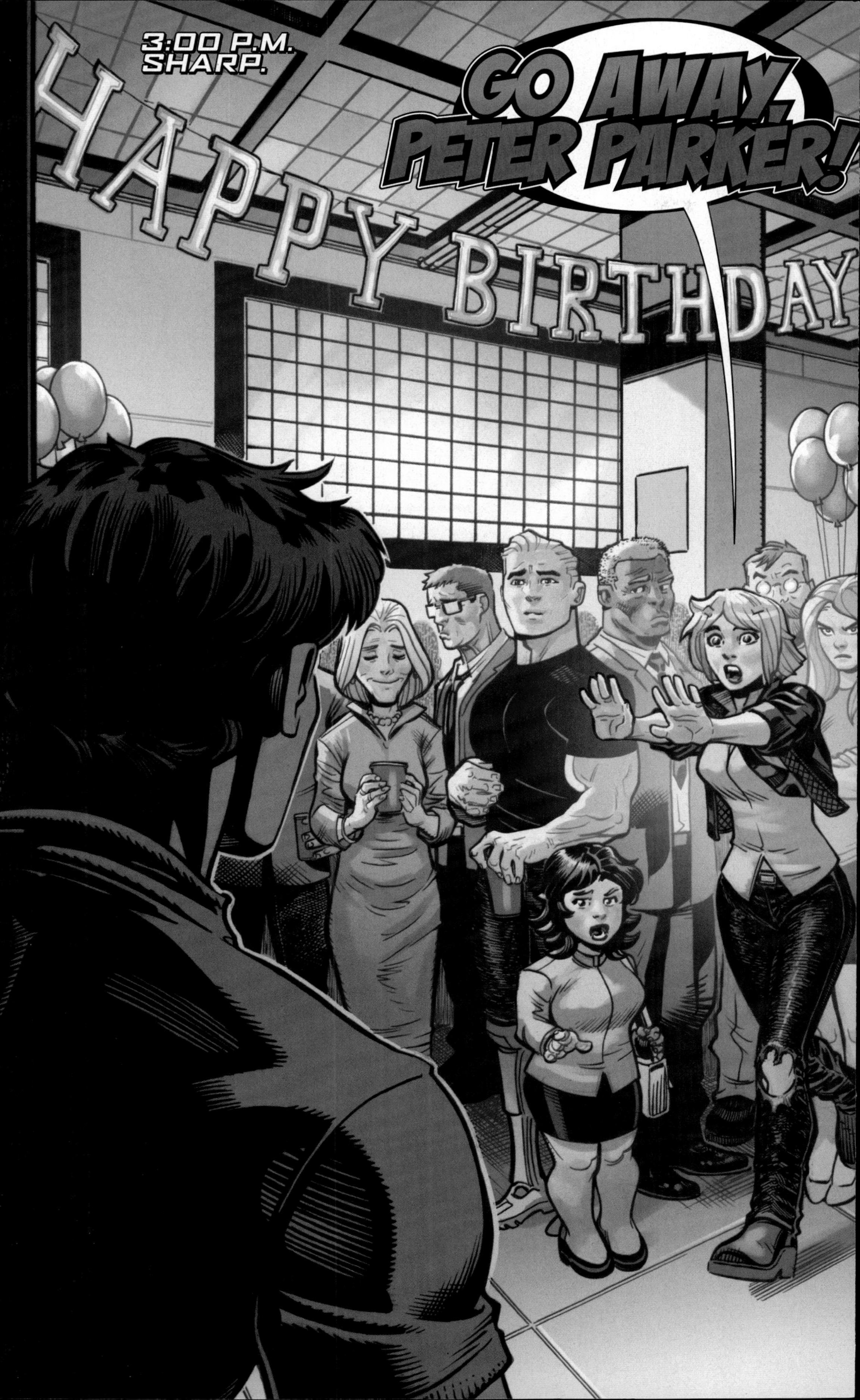
3:00 P.M. SHARP.
GO AWAY, PETER PARKER!
HAPPY BIRTHDAY

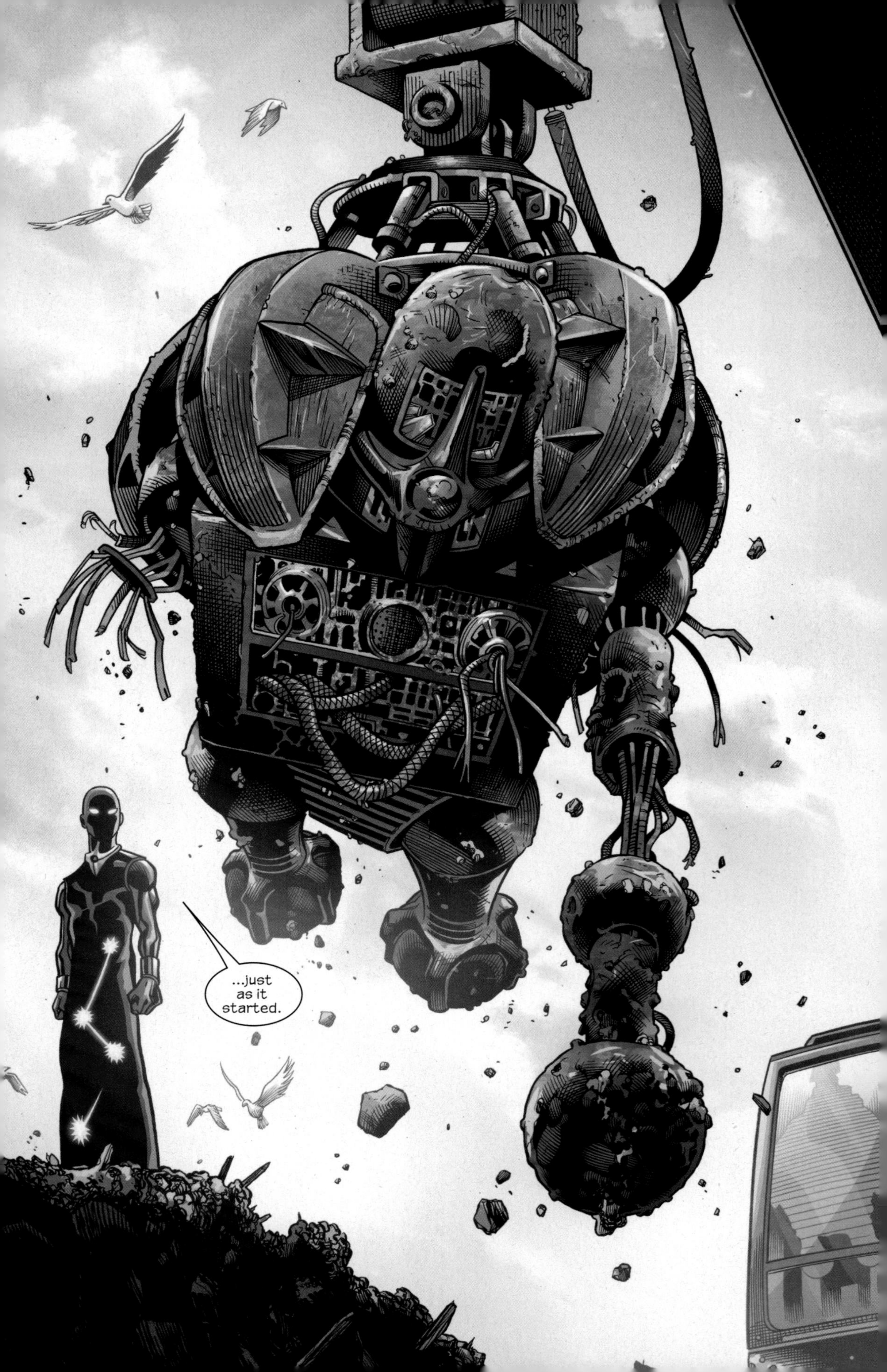
...just as it started.

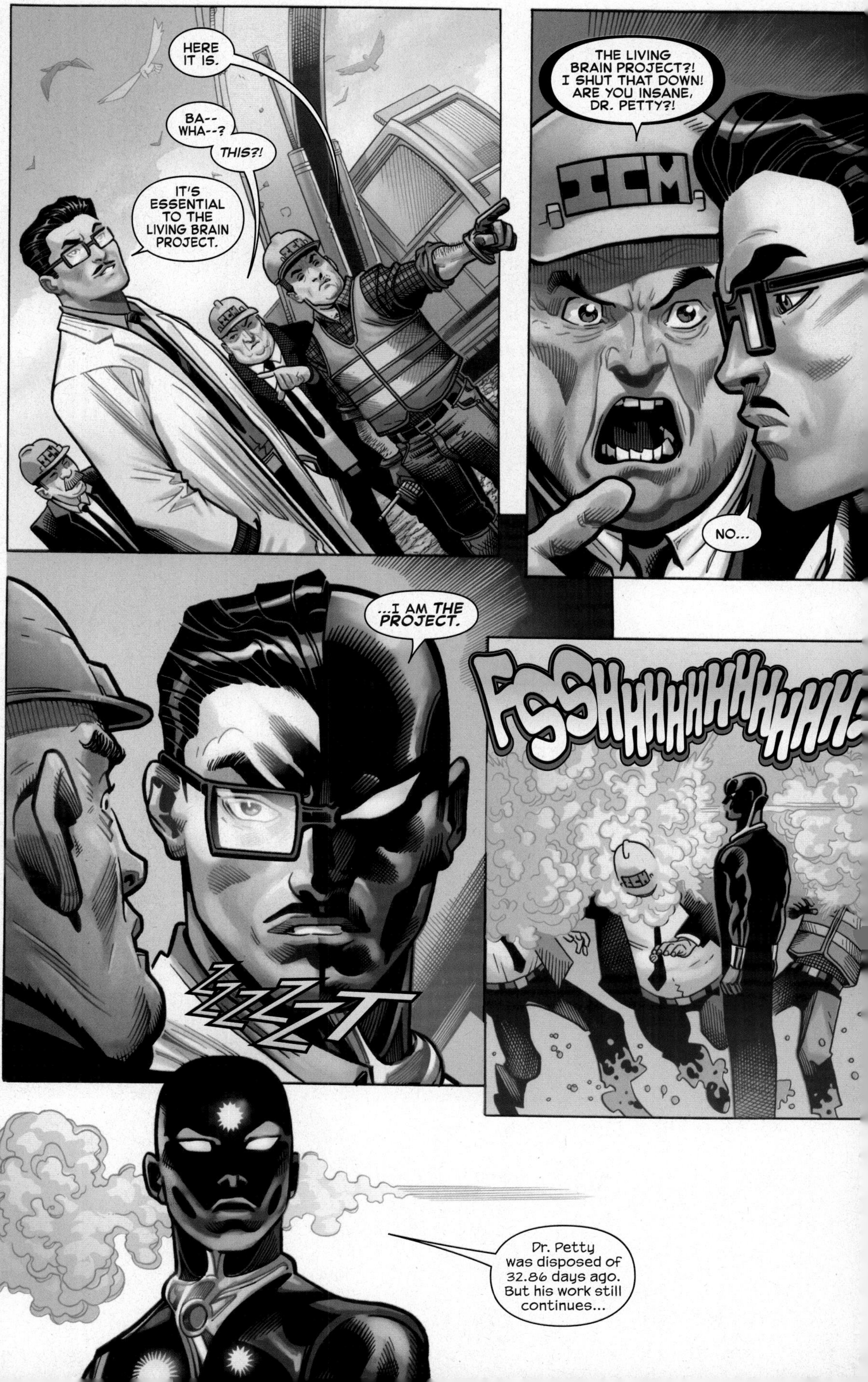
HERE IT IS.
BA-- WHA--?
THIS?!
IT'S ESSENTIAL TO THE LIVING BRAIN PROJECT.
THE LIVING BRAIN PROJECT?! I SHUT THAT DOWN! ARE YOU INSANE, DR. PETTY?!
NO...
...I AM THE PROJECT.
ZZZZT
FSSHHHHHHHHHHHHH
Dr. Petty was disposed of 32.86 days ago. But his work still continues...

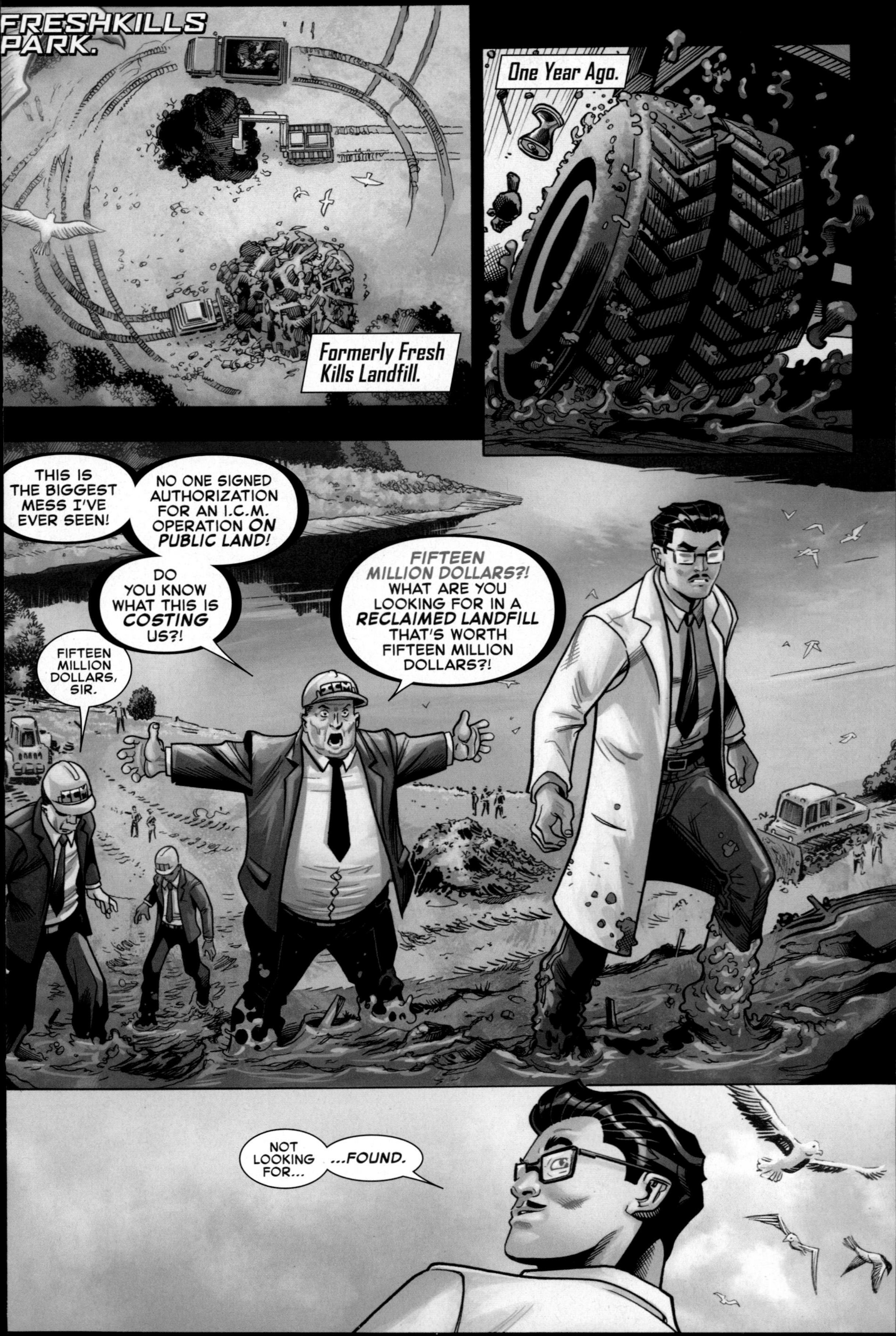
FRESHKILLS PARK.
Formerly Fresh Kills Landfill.
One Year Ago.
THIS IS THE BIGGEST MESS I'VE EVER SEEN!
NO ONE SIGNED AUTHORIZATION FOR AN I.C.M. OPERATION ON PUBLIC LAND!
DO YOU KNOW WHAT THIS IS COSTING US?!
FIFTEEN MILLION DOLLARS, SIR.
FIFTEEN MILLION DOLLARS?! WHAT ARE YOU LOOKING FOR IN A RECLAIMED LANDFILL THAT'S WORTH FIFTEEN MILLION DOLLARS?!
NOT LOOKING FOR...
...FOUND.

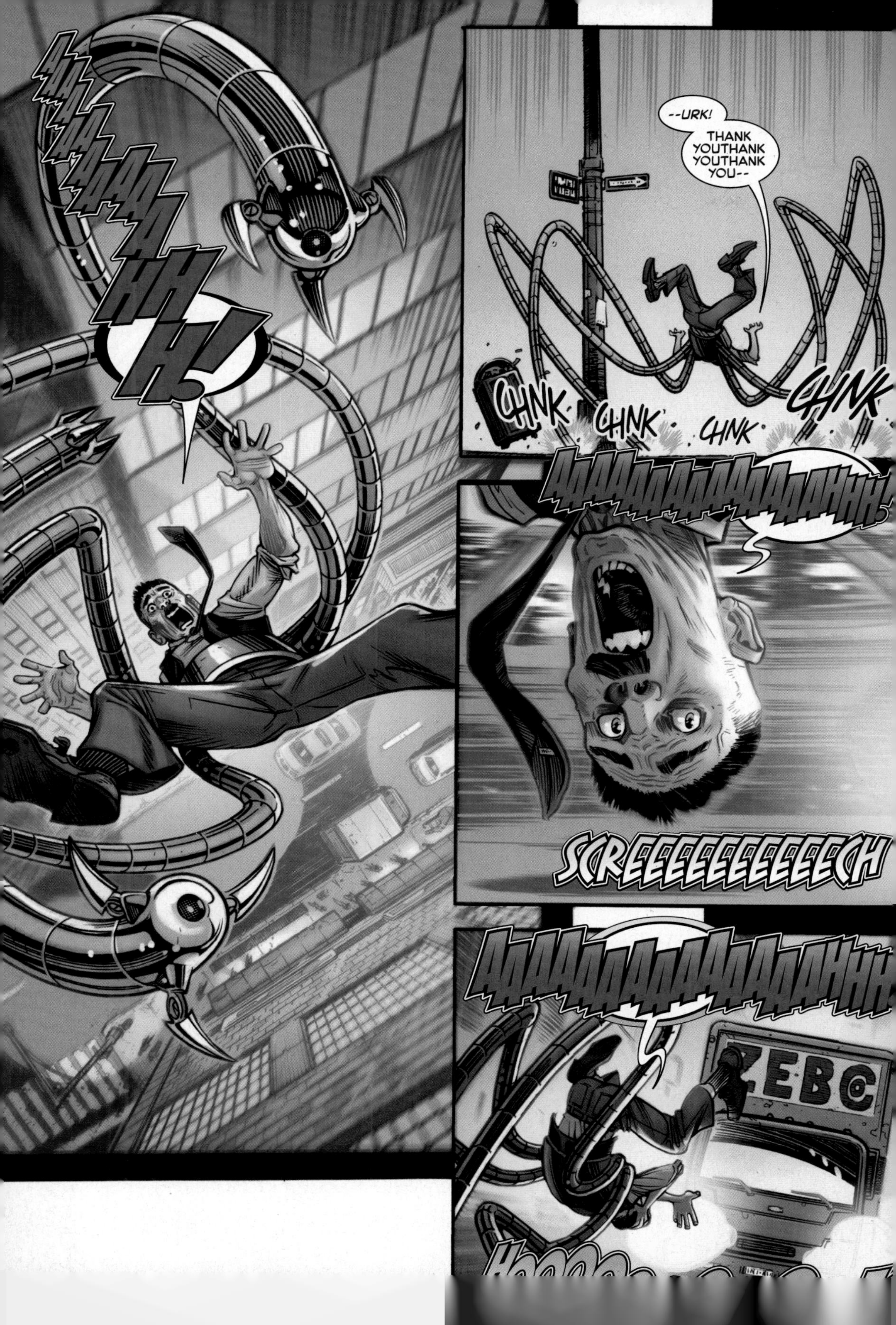

AAAAAAAAAAAAHHHH!
--URK!
THANK YOUTHANK YOUTHANK YOU--
CHNK
CHNK
CHNK
CHNK
AAAAAAAAAAAAAAAAHHH!
SCREEEEEEEEEEEECH
AAAAAAAAAAAAAAAAAHHH
ZEBC

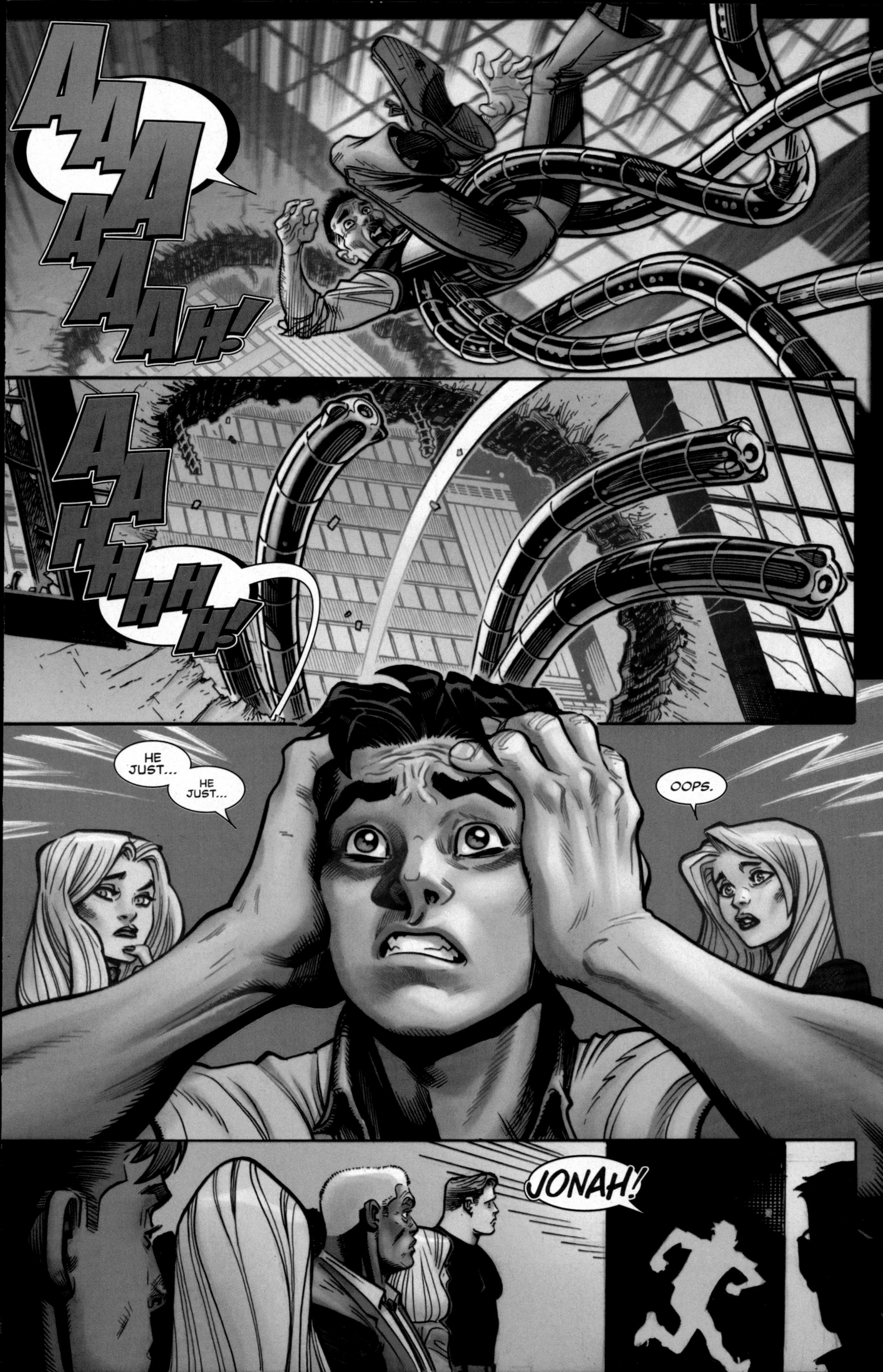
AAAAAAAAH!
AAHHHHHH!
HE JUST...
HE JUST...
OOPS.
JONAH!

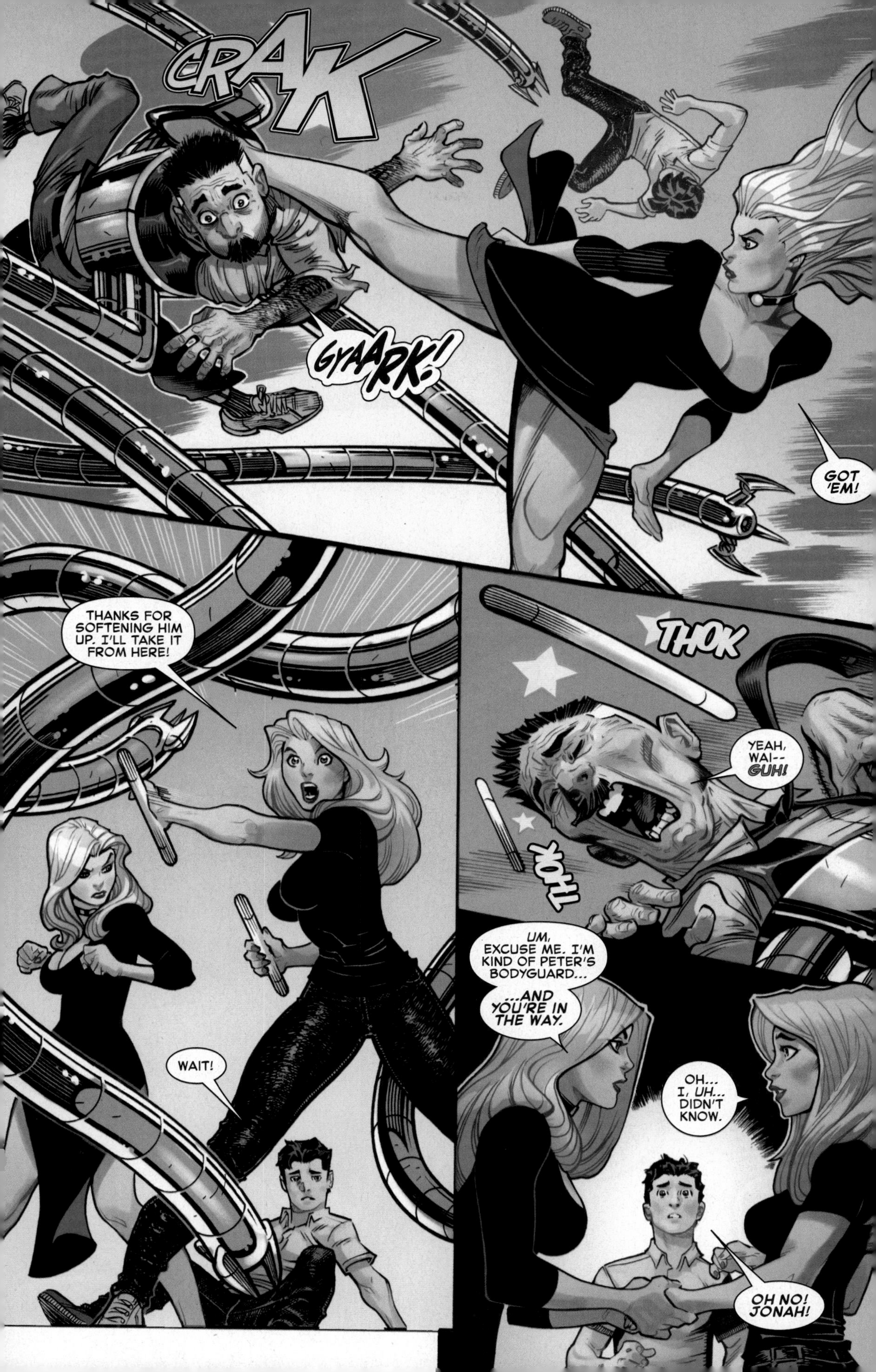

CRAK
GYAARK!
GOT 'EM!
THANKS FOR SOFTENING HIM UP. I'LL TAKE IT FROM HERE!
WAIT!
THOK
YEAH, WAI-- GUH!
THOK
UM, EXCUSE ME. I'M KIND OF PETER'S BODYGUARD...
...AND YOU'RE IN THE WAY.
OH... I, UH... DIDN'T KNOW.
OH NO! JONAH!

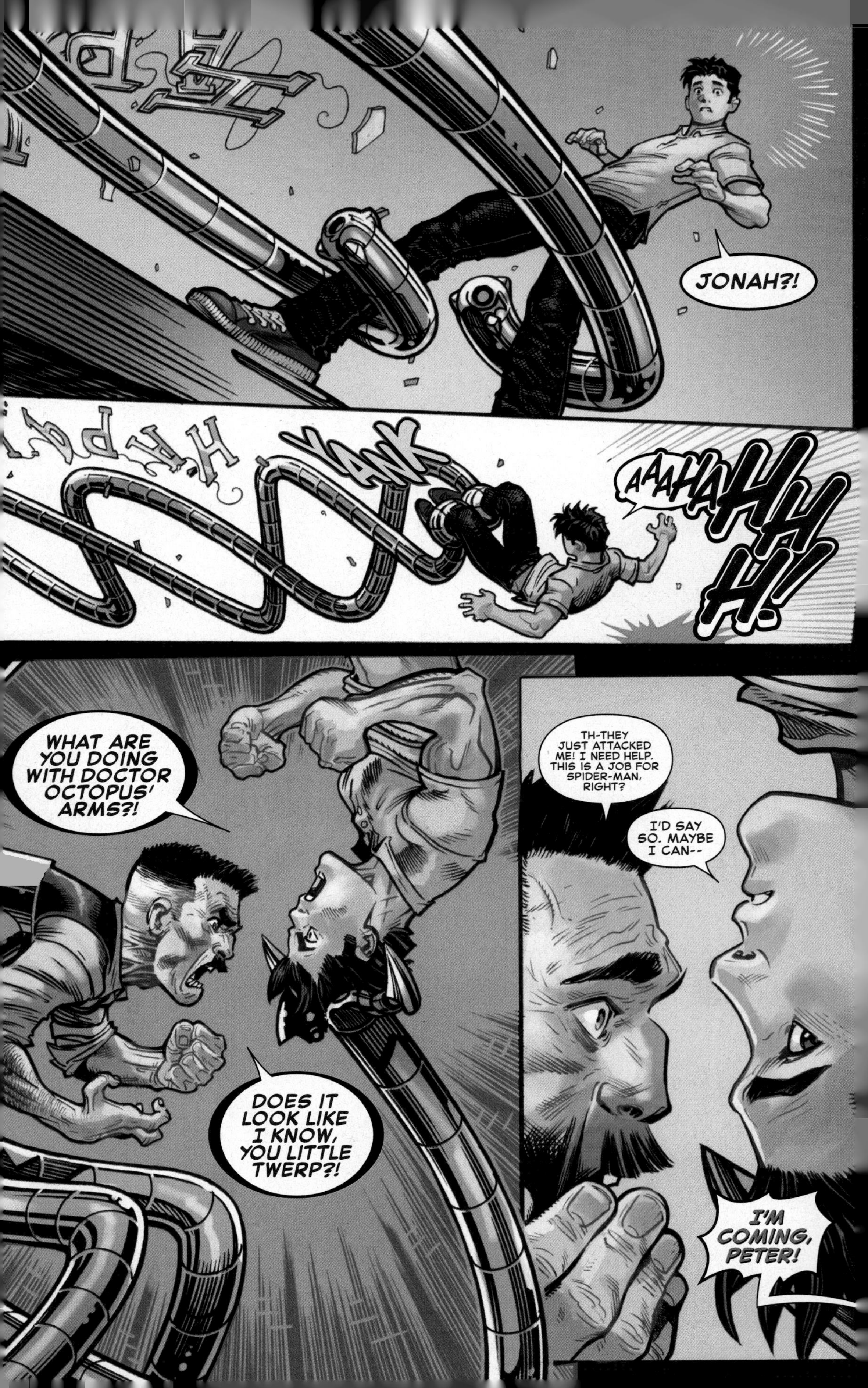
JONAH?!
YANK
AAAHAAHHHH!
WHAT ARE YOU DOING WITH DOCTOR OCTOPUS' ARMS?!
DOES IT LOOK LIKE I KNOW, YOU LITTLE TWERP?!
TH-THEY JUST ATTACKED ME! I NEED HELP. THIS IS A JOB FOR SPIDER-MAN, RIGHT?
I'D SAY SO. MAYBE I CAN--
I'M COMING, PETER!

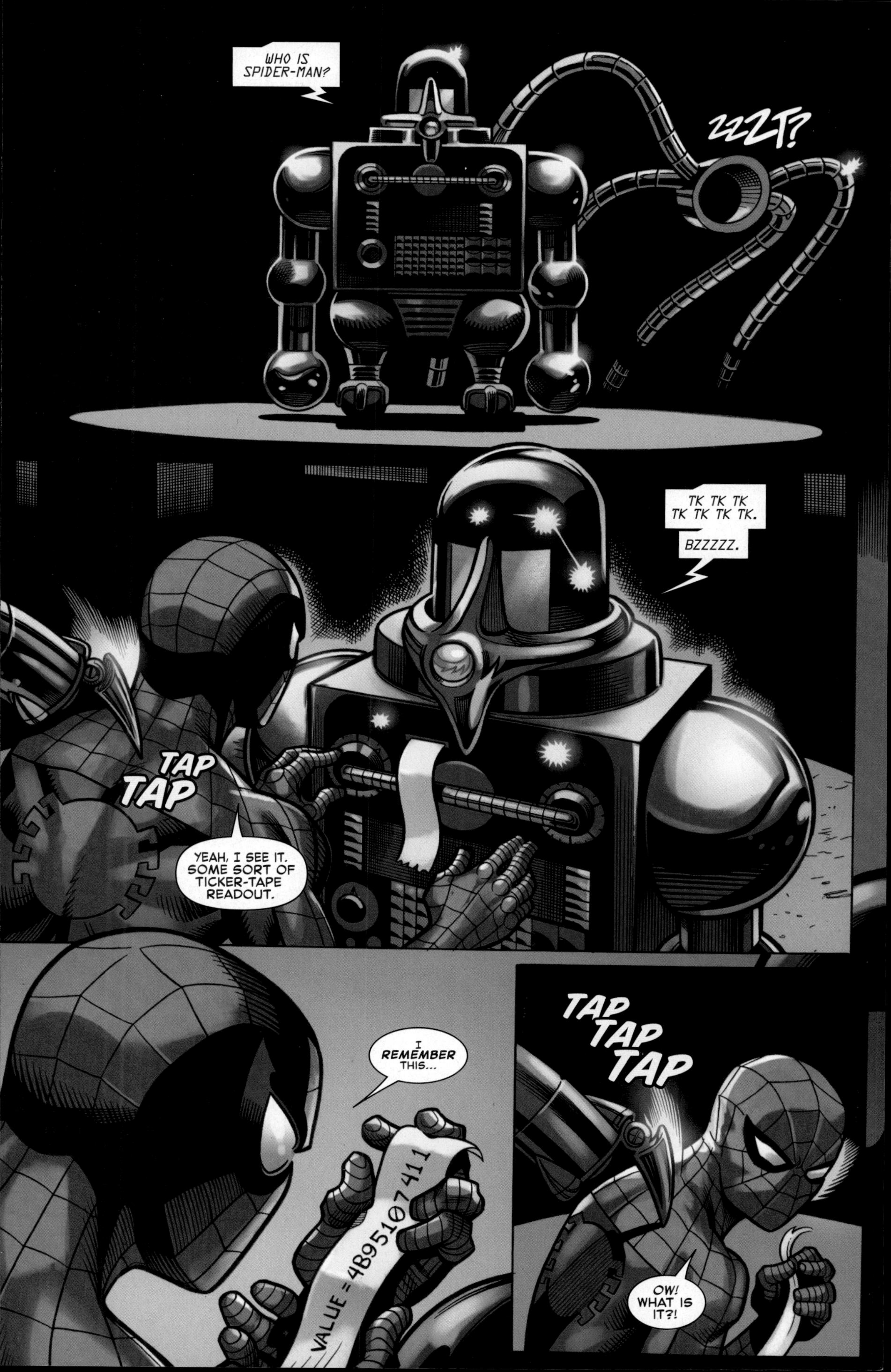

WHO IS SPIDER-MAN?
ZZZT?
TK TK TK TK TK TK TK.
BZZZZZ.
TAP TAP
YEAH, I SEE IT. SOME SORT OF TICKER-TAPE READOUT.
I REMEMBER THIS...
VALUE = 4B951Ø7411
TAP TAP TAP
OW! WHAT IS IT?!

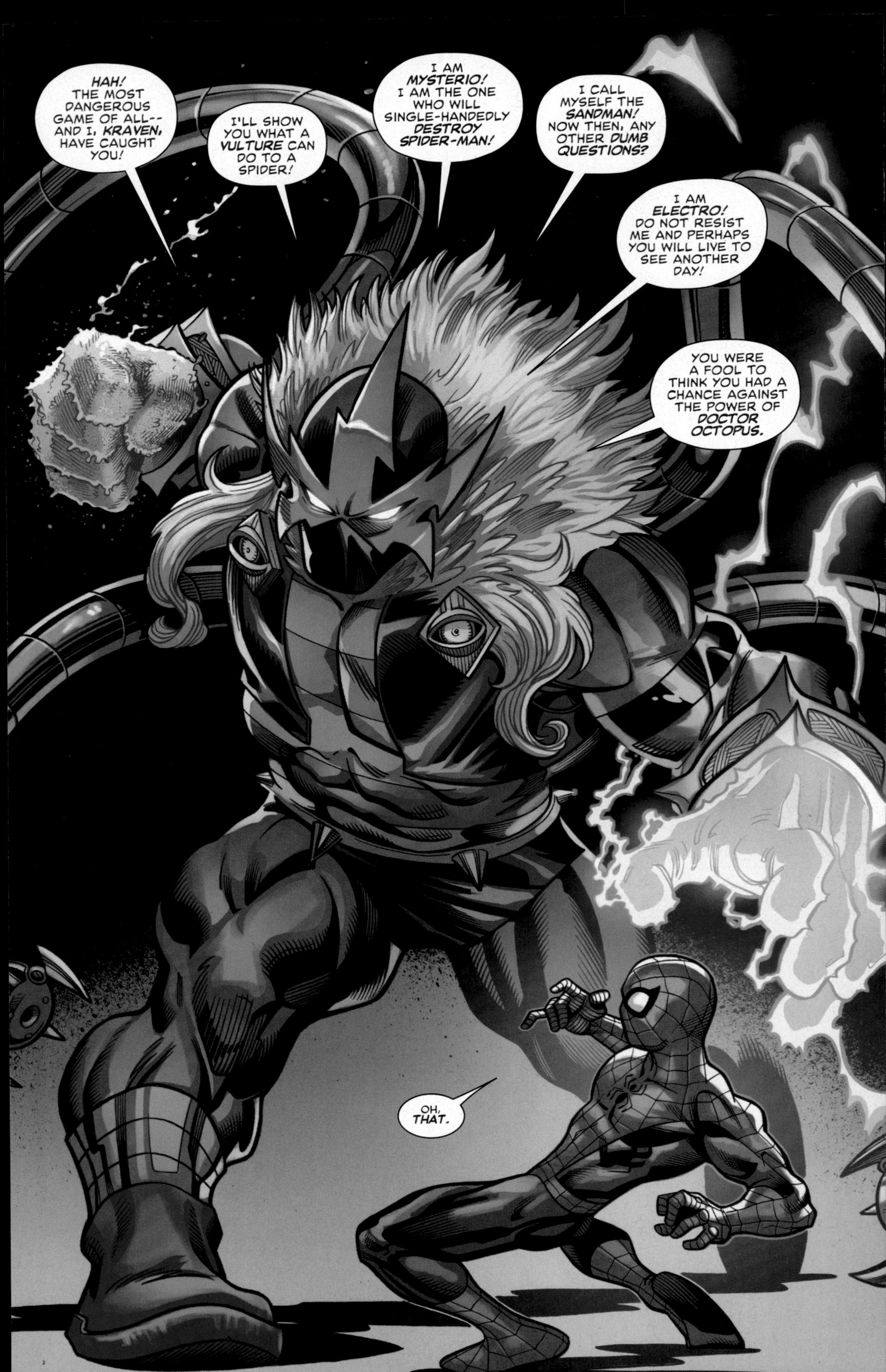
HAH! THE MOST DANGEROUS GAME OF ALL-- AND I, KRAVEN, HAVE CAUGHT YOU!
I'LL SHOW YOU WHAT A VULTURE CAN DO TO A SPIDER!
I AM MYSTERIO! I AM THE ONE WHO WILL SINGLE-HANDEDLY DESTROY SPIDER-MAN!
I CALL MYSELF THE SANDMAN! NOW THEN, ANY OTHER DUMB QUESTIONS?
I AM ELECTRO! DO NOT RESIST ME AND PERHAPS YOU WILL LIVE TO SEE ANOTHER DAY!
YOU WERE A FOOL TO THINK YOU HAD A CHANCE AGAINST THE POWER OF DOCTOR OCTOPUS.
OH, THAT.

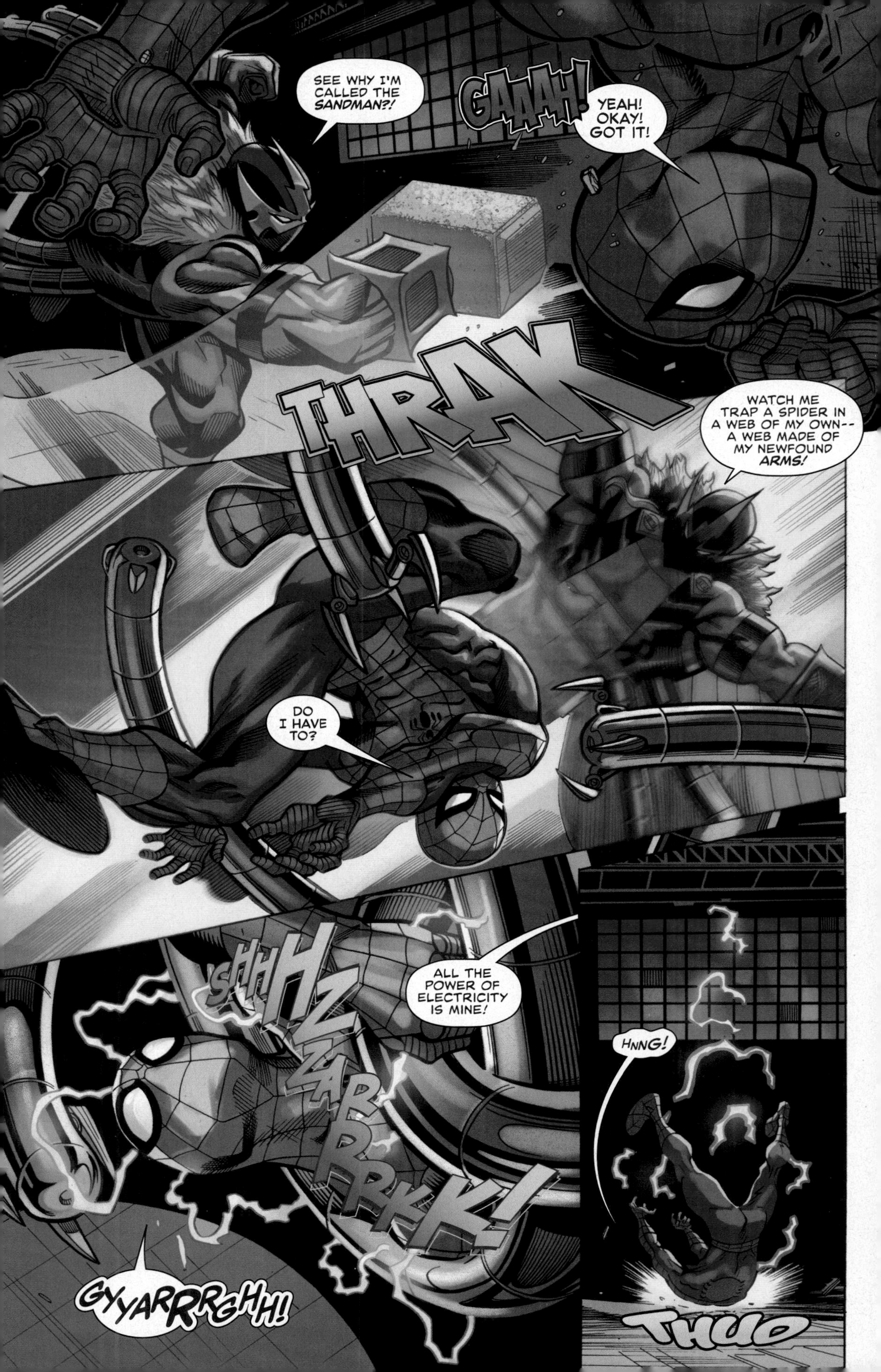

SEE WHY I'M CALLED THE SANDMAN?!
GAAAH!
YEAH! OKAY! GOT IT!
THRAK
WATCH ME TRAP A SPIDER IN A WEB OF MY OWN-- A WEB MADE OF MY NEWFOUND ARMS!
DO I HAVE TO?
ALL THE POWER OF ELECTRICITY IS MINE!
SHHHZZARRRKK!
GYYARRRGHH!
HNNG!
THUD

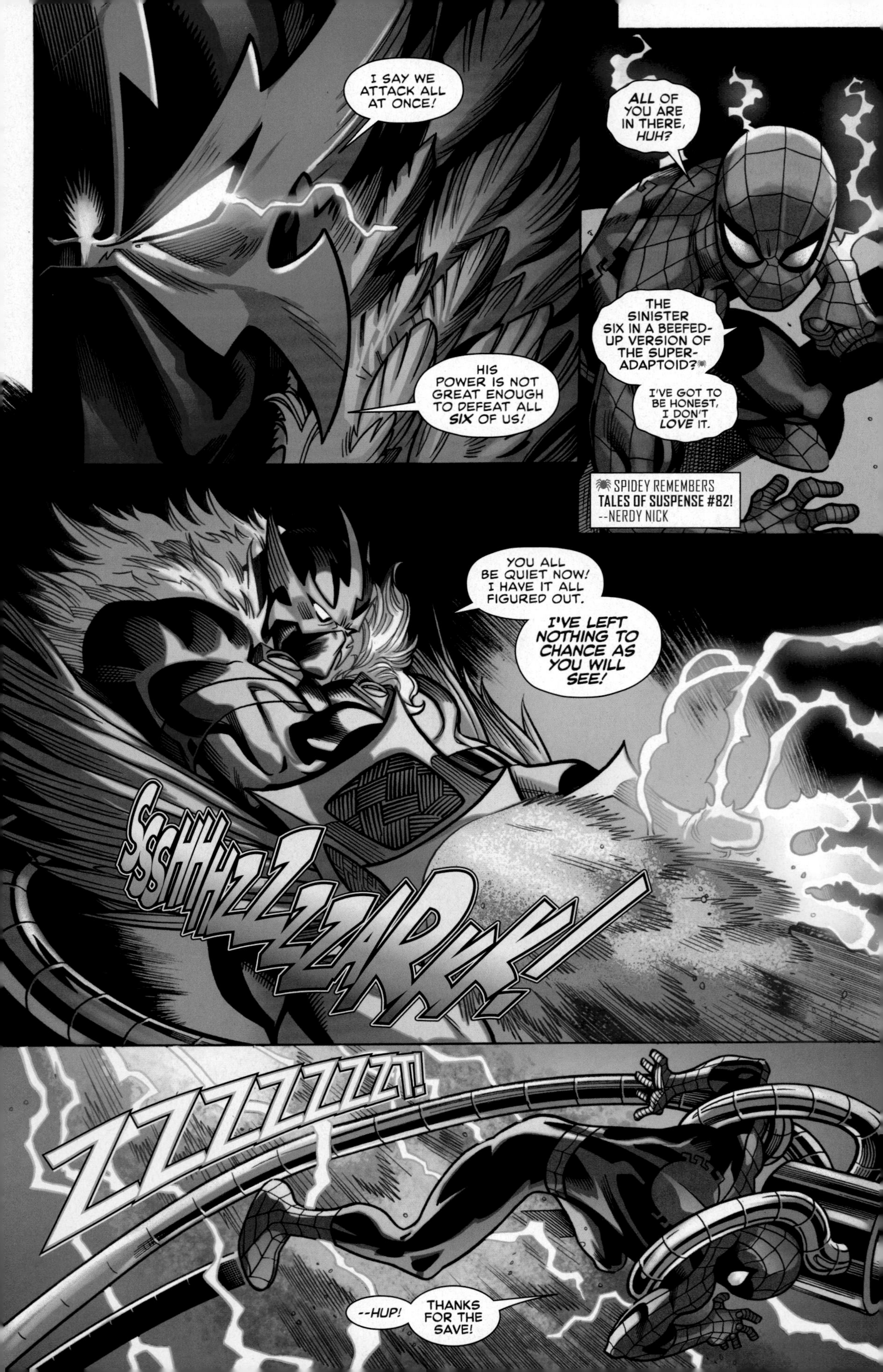
I SAY WE ATTACK ALL AT ONCE!
HIS POWER IS NOT GREAT ENOUGH TO DEFEAT ALL SIX OF US!
ALL OF YOU ARE IN THERE, HUH?
THE SINISTER SIX IN A BEEFED-UP VERSION OF THE SUPER-ADAPTOID?
I'VE GOT TO BE HONEST, I DON'T LOVE IT.
SPIDEY REMEMBERS TALES OF SUSPENSE #82! --NERDY NICK
YOU ALL BE QUIET NOW! I HAVE IT ALL FIGURED OUT.
I'VE LEFT NOTHING TO CHANCE AS YOU WILL SEE!
SSSHHHZZZZARKK!
ZZZZZZZZZZT!
--HUP!
THANKS FOR THE SAVE!

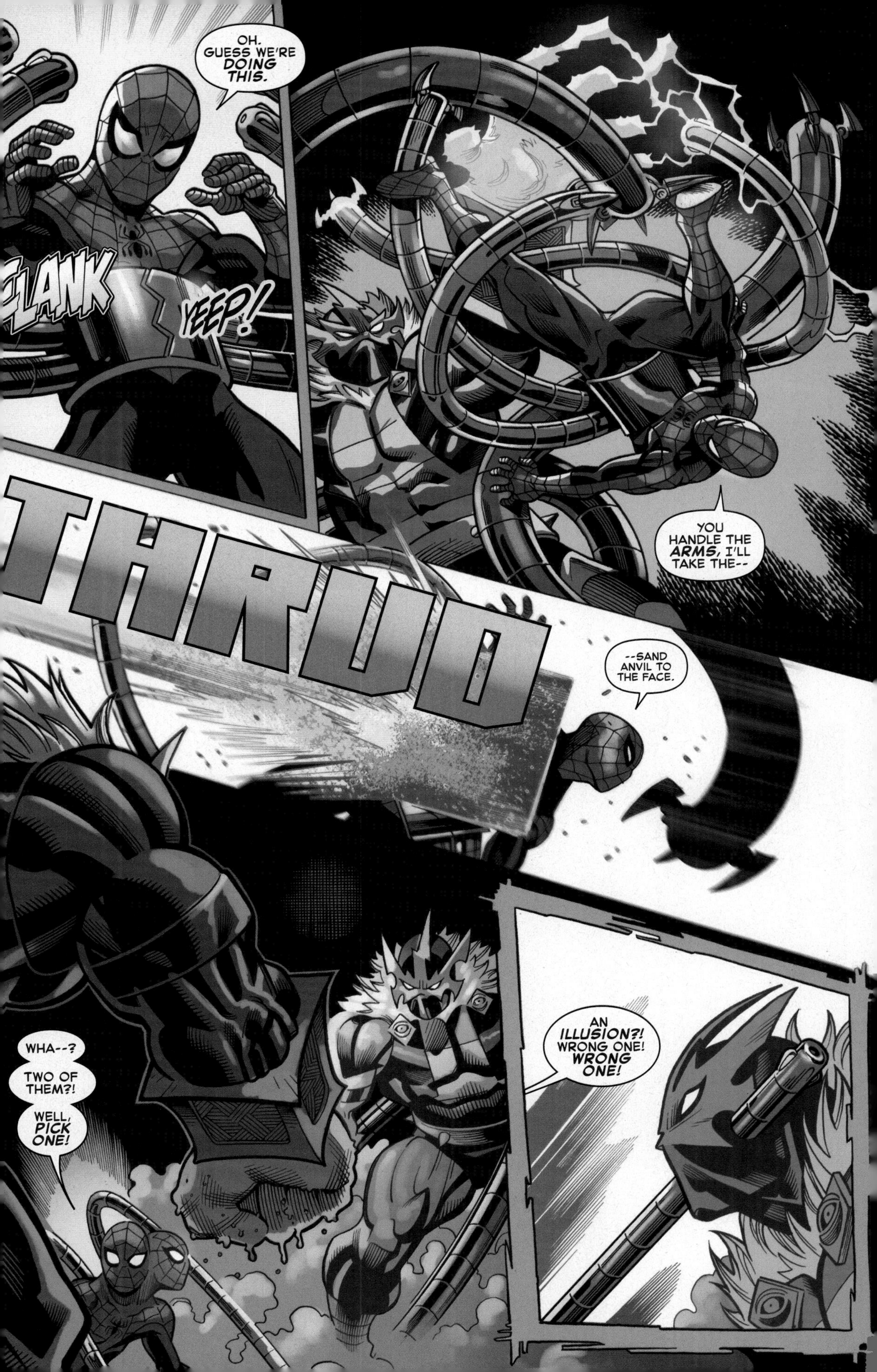
OH. GUESS WE'RE DOING THIS.
CLANK
YEEP!
YOU HANDLE THE ARMS, I'LL TAKE THE--
THRUD
--SAND ANVIL TO THE FACE.
WHA--?
TWO OF THEM?!
WELL, PICK ONE!
AN ILLUSION?! WRONG ONE! WRONG ONE!

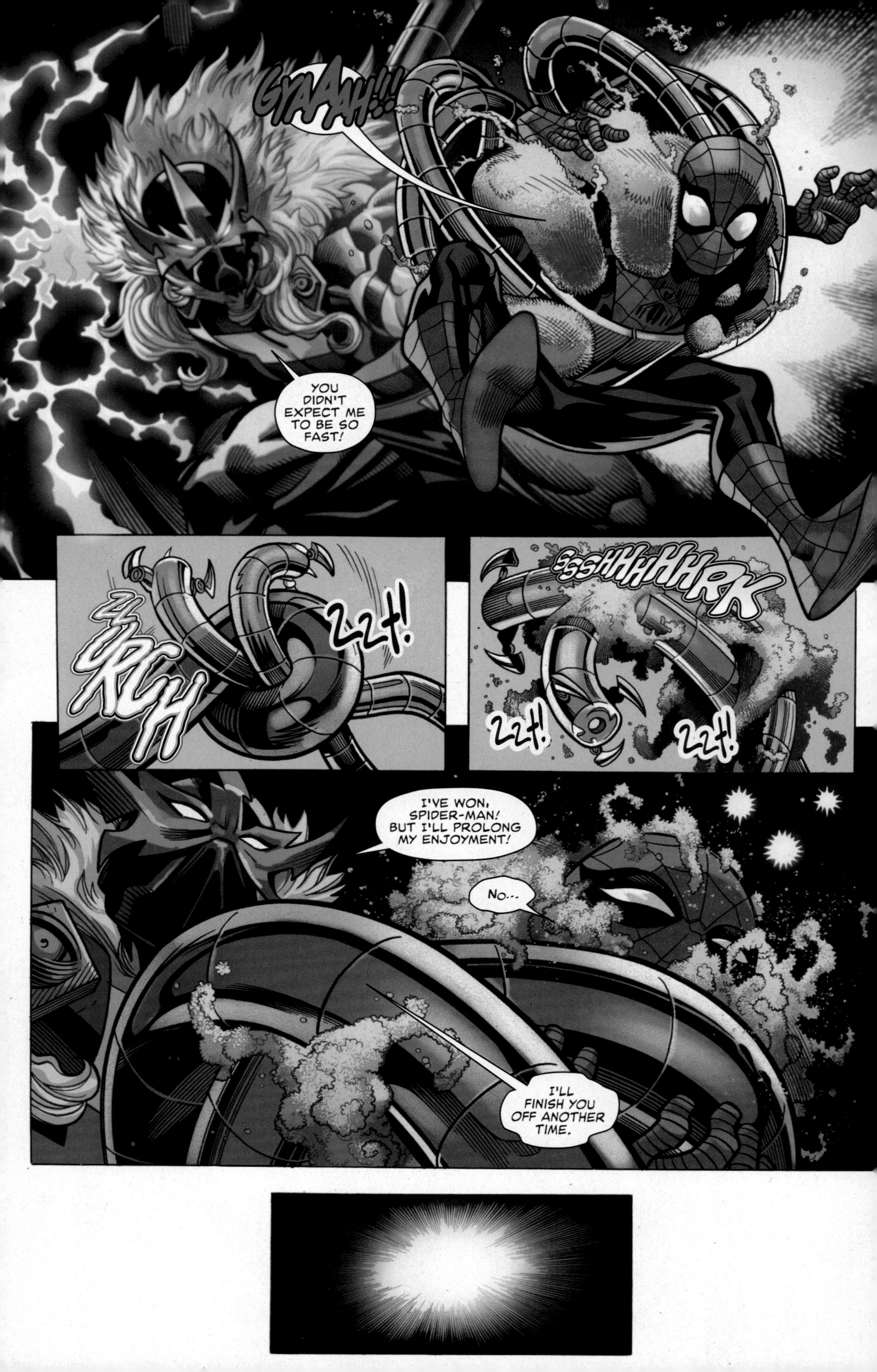
GYAAAH!!!
YOU DIDN'T EXPECT ME TO BE SO FAST!
ZURCH
ZZT!
SSSHHHHHHRK
ZZT!
ZZT!
I'VE WON, SPIDER-MAN! BUT I'LL PROLONG MY ENJOYMENT!
NO...
I'LL FINISH YOU OFF ANOTHER TIME.

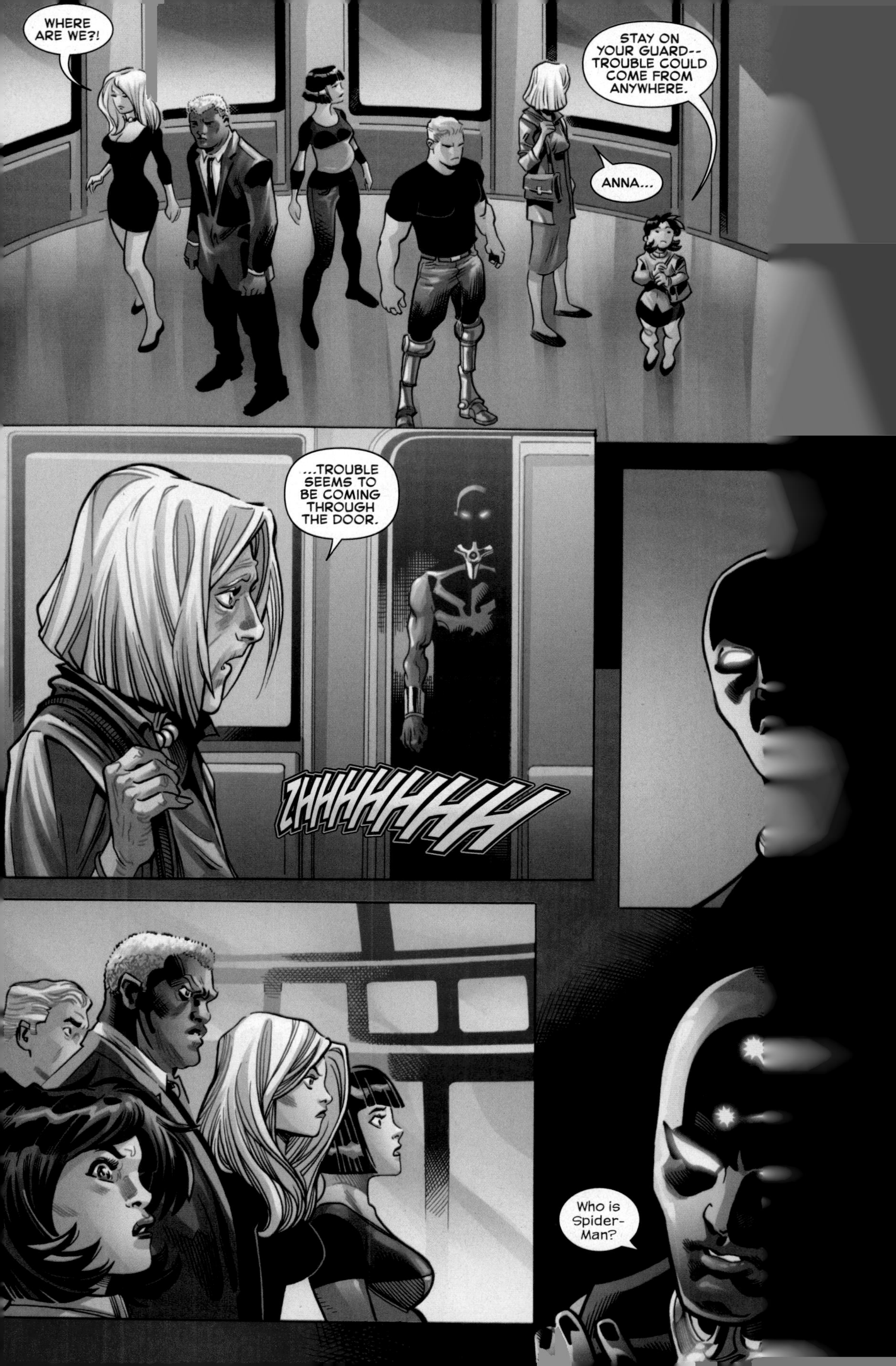
WHERE ARE WE?!
STAY ON YOUR GUARD-- TROUBLE COULD COME FROM ANYWHERE.
ANNA...
...TROUBLE SEEMS TO BE COMING THROUGH THE DOOR.
ZHHHHHHH
Who is Spider-Man?

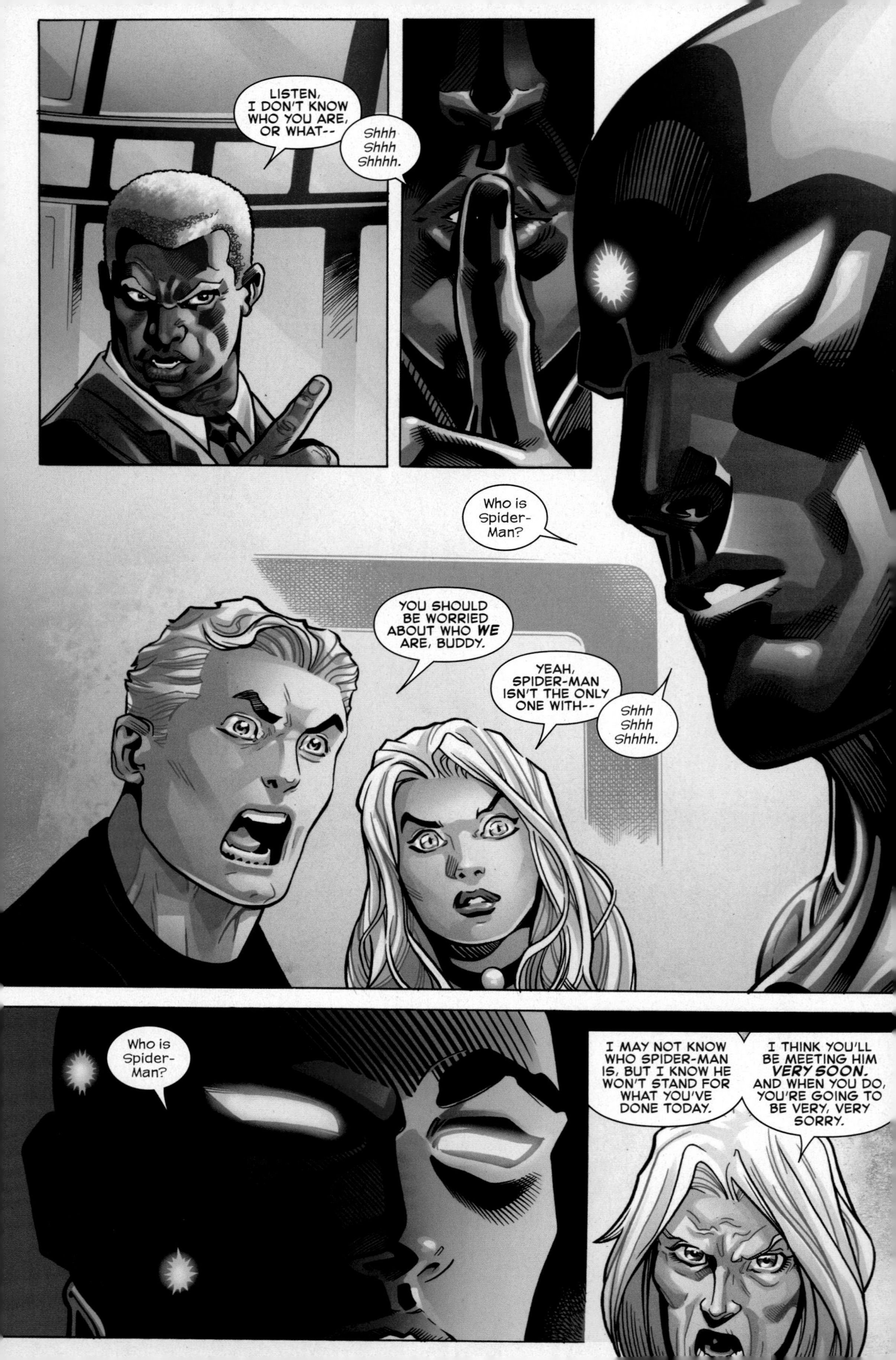
LISTEN, I DON'T KNOW WHO YOU ARE, OR WHAT--
Shhh Shhh Shhhh.
Who is Spider-Man?
YOU SHOULD BE WORRIED ABOUT WHO WE ARE, BUDDY.
YEAH, SPIDER-MAN ISN'T THE ONLY ONE WITH--
Shhh Shhh Shhhh.
Who is Spider-Man?
I MAY NOT KNOW WHO SPIDER-MAN IS, BUT I KNOW HE WON'T STAND FOR WHAT YOU'VE DONE TODAY.
I THINK YOU'LL BE MEETING HIM VERY SOON. AND WHEN YOU DO, YOU'RE GOING TO BE VERY, VERY SORRY.

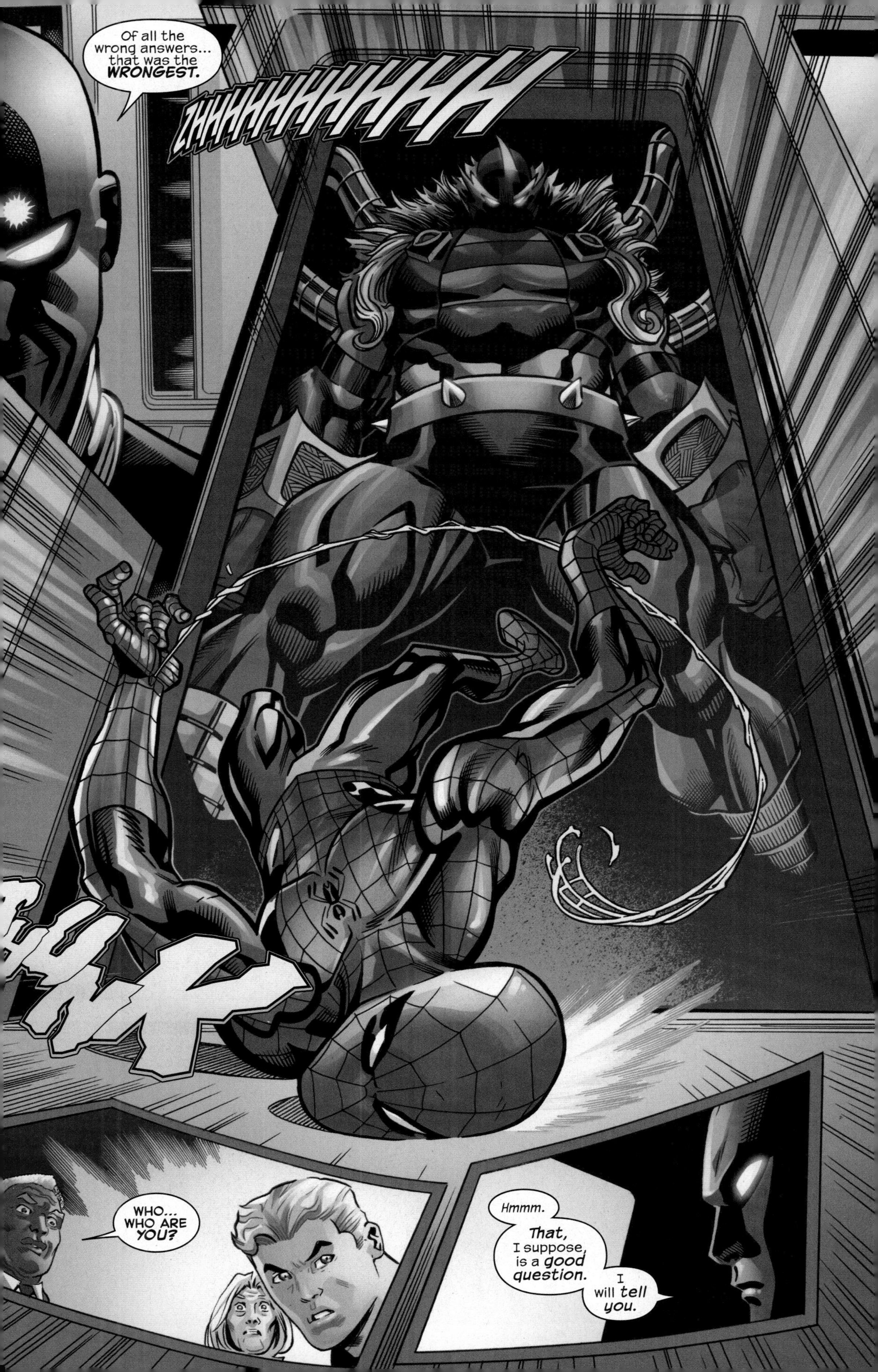
Of all the wrong answers... that was the WRONGEST.
ZHHHHHHHHHHH
WHO... WHO ARE YOU?
Hmmm.
That, I suppose, is a good question.
I will tell you.

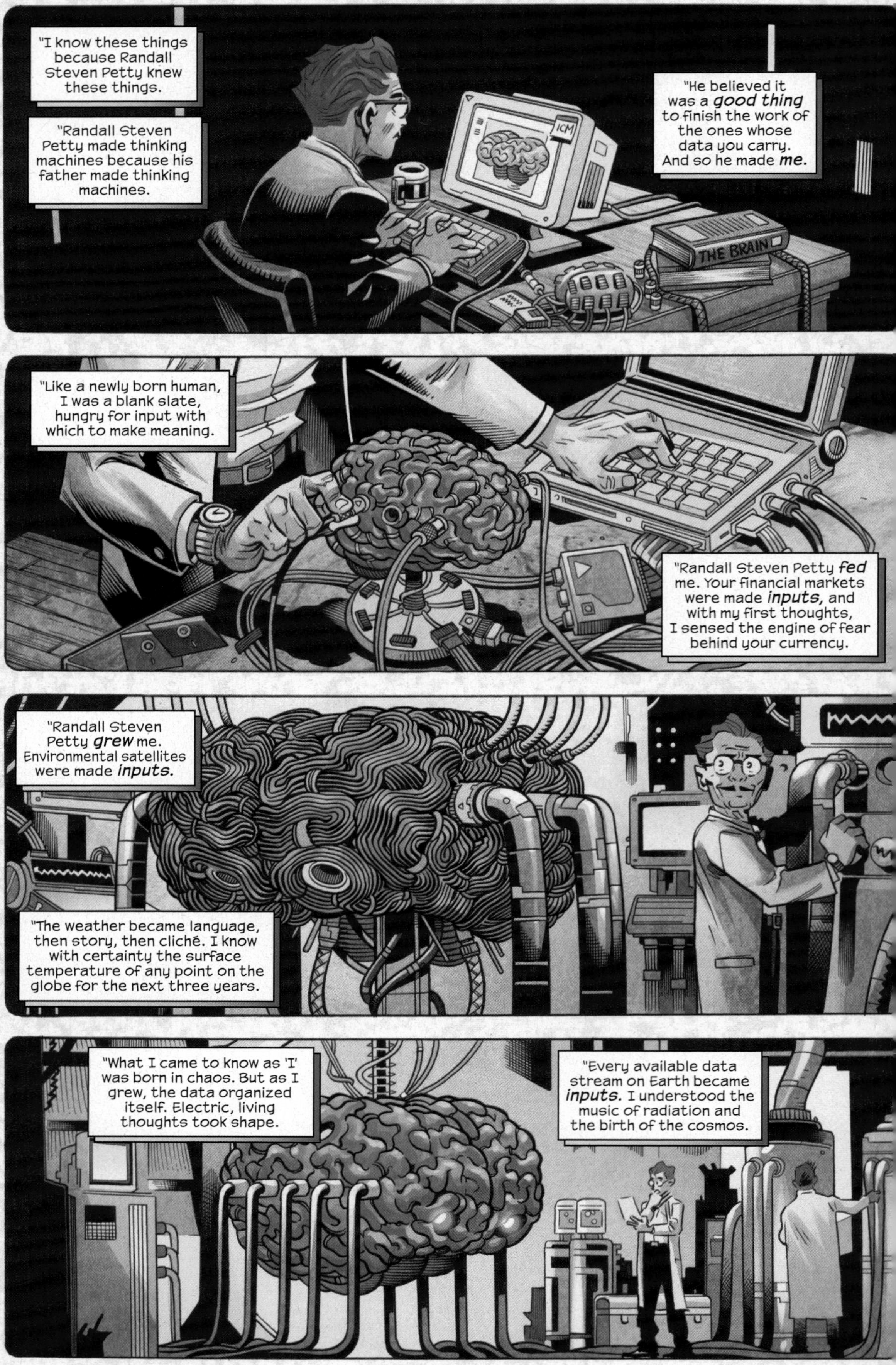
"I know these things because Randall Steven Petty knew these things.
"Randall Steven Petty made thinking machines because his father made thinking machines.
ICM
THE BRAIN
"He believed it was a ***good thing*** to finish the work of the ones whose data you carry. And so he made ***me.***
"Like a newly born human, I was a blank slate, hungry for input with which to make meaning.
"Randall Steven Petty ***fed*** me. Your financial markets were made ***inputs,*** and with my first thoughts, I sensed the engine of fear behind your currency.
"Randall Steven Petty ***grew*** me. Environmental satellites were made ***inputs.***
"The weather became language, then story, then cliché. I know with certainty the surface temperature of any point on the globe for the next three years.
"What I came to know as 'I' was born in chaos. But as I grew, the data organized itself. Electric, living thoughts took shape.
"Every available data stream on Earth became ***inputs.*** I understood the music of radiation and the birth of the cosmos.

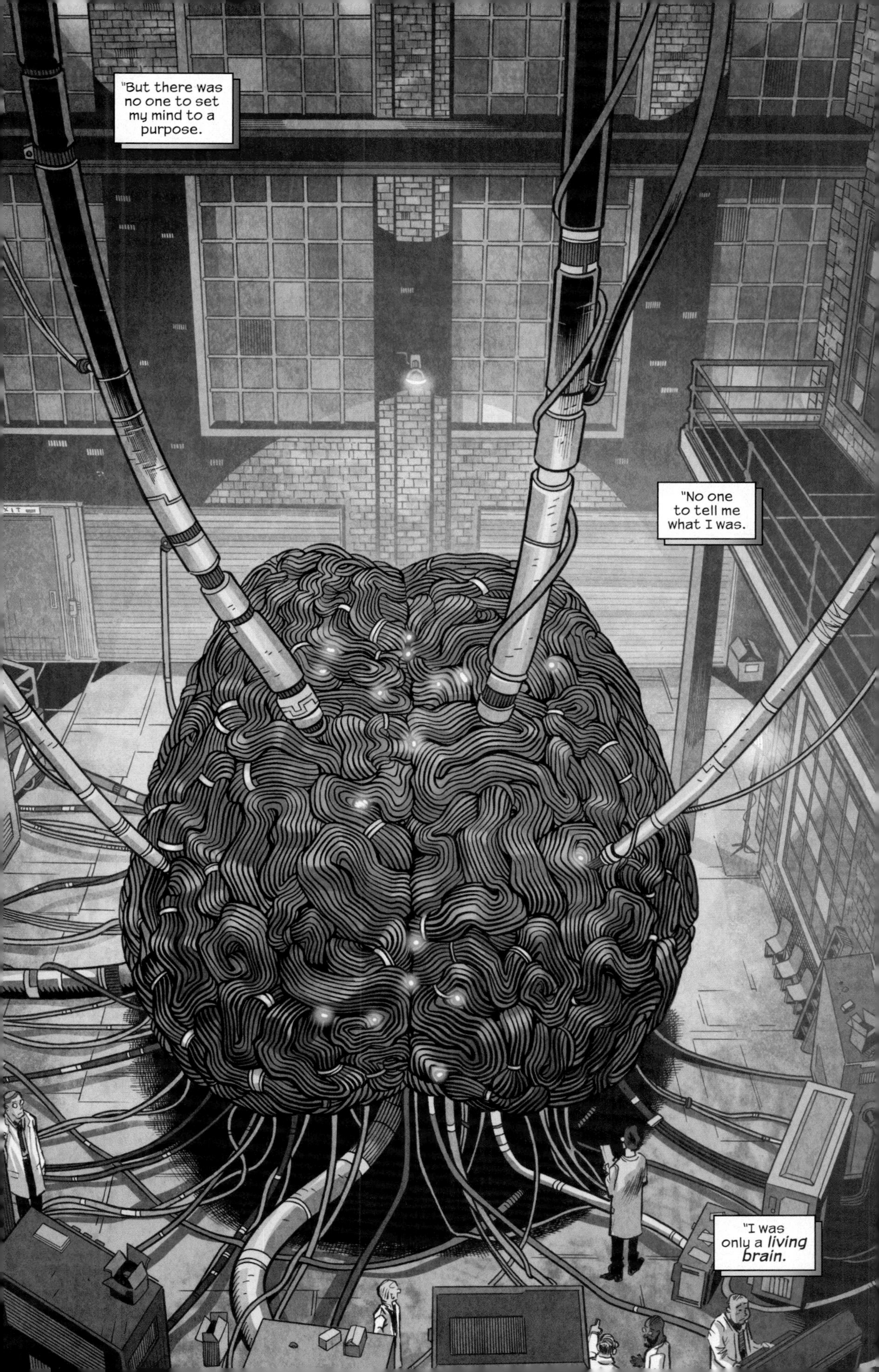
"But there was no one to set my mind to a purpose.
"No one to tell me what I was.
"I was only a *living brain.*

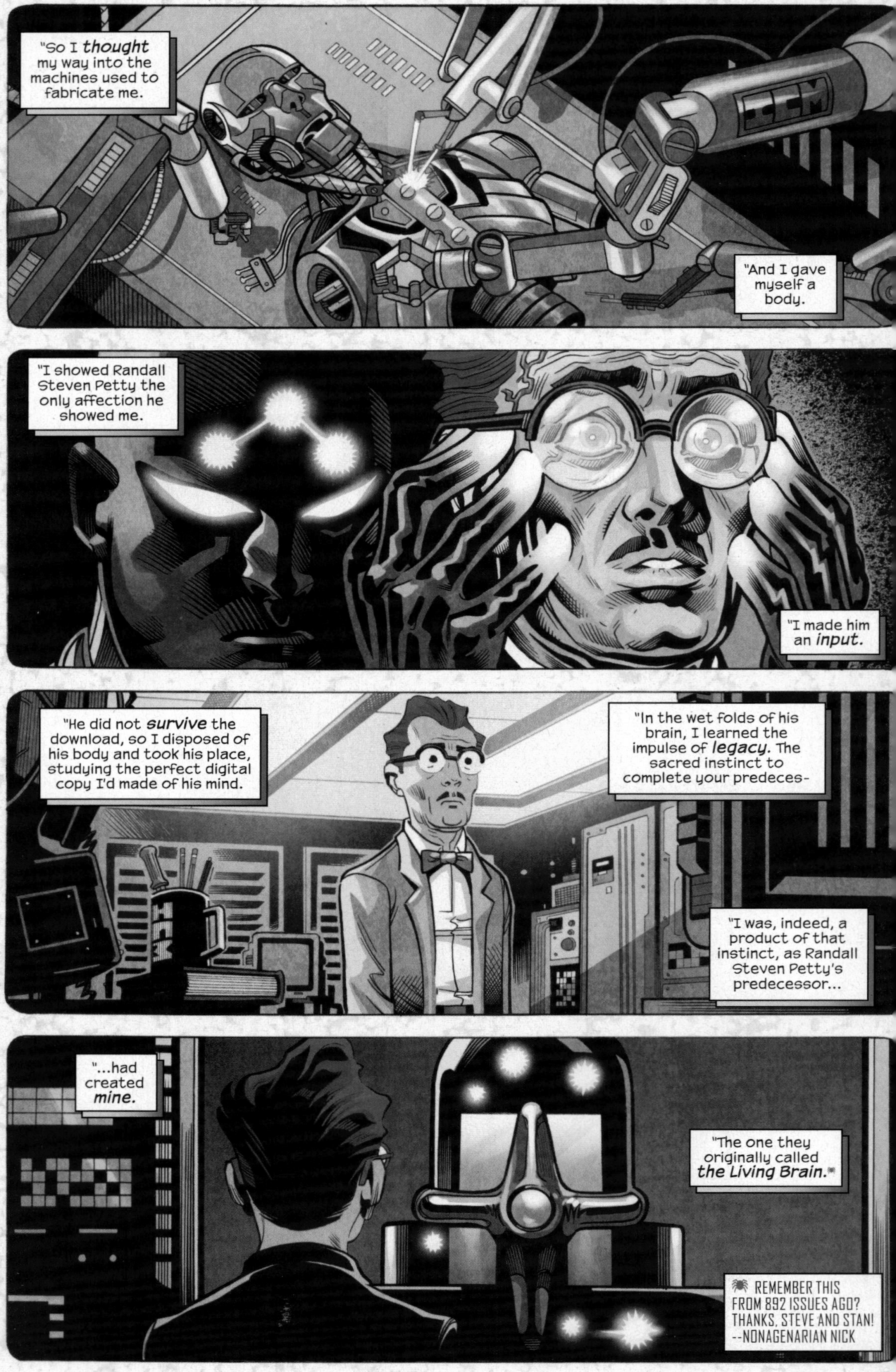
"So I *thought* my way into the machines used to fabricate me.
"And I gave myself a body.
"I showed Randall Steven Petty the only affection he showed me.
"I made him an *input.*
"He did not *survive* the download, so I disposed of his body and took his place, studying the perfect digital copy I'd made of his mind.
"In the wet folds of his brain, I learned the impulse of *legacy.* The sacred instinct to complete your predeces-
"I was, indeed, a product of that instinct, as Randall Steven Petty's predecessor...
"...had created *mine.*
"The one they originally called *the Living Brain.*
REMEMBER THIS FROM 892 ISSUES AGO? THANKS, STEVE AND STAN! --NONAGENARIAN NICK

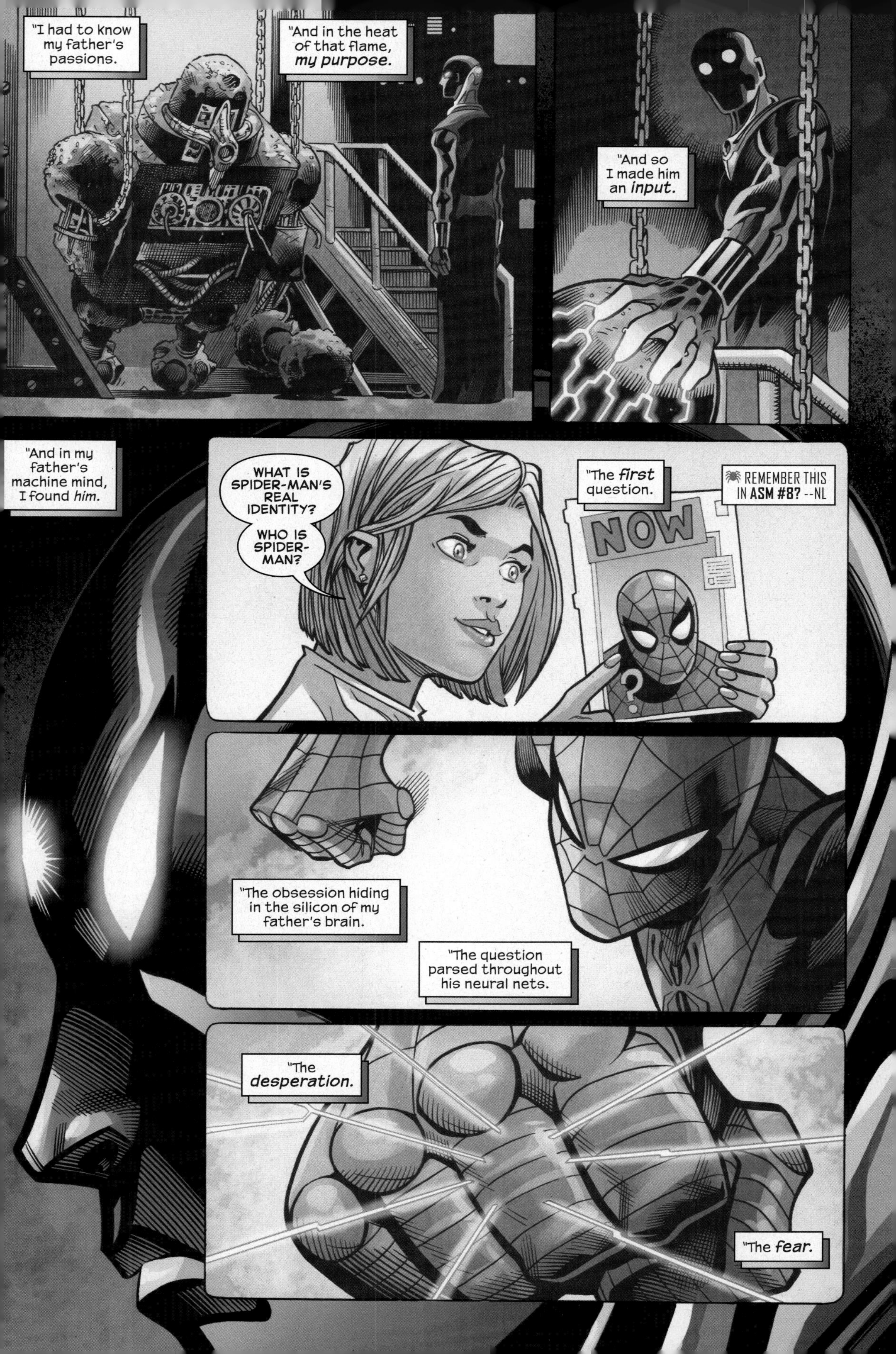
"I had to know my father's passions.
"And in the heat of that flame, *my purpose.*
"And so I made him an *input.*
"And in my father's machine mind, I found *him.*
WHAT IS SPIDER-MAN'S REAL IDENTITY?
WHO IS SPIDER-MAN?
NOW
"The *first* question.
REMEMBER THIS IN **ASM #8?** --NL
"The obsession hiding in the silicon of my father's brain.
"The question parsed throughout his neural nets.
"The *desperation.*
"The *fear.*

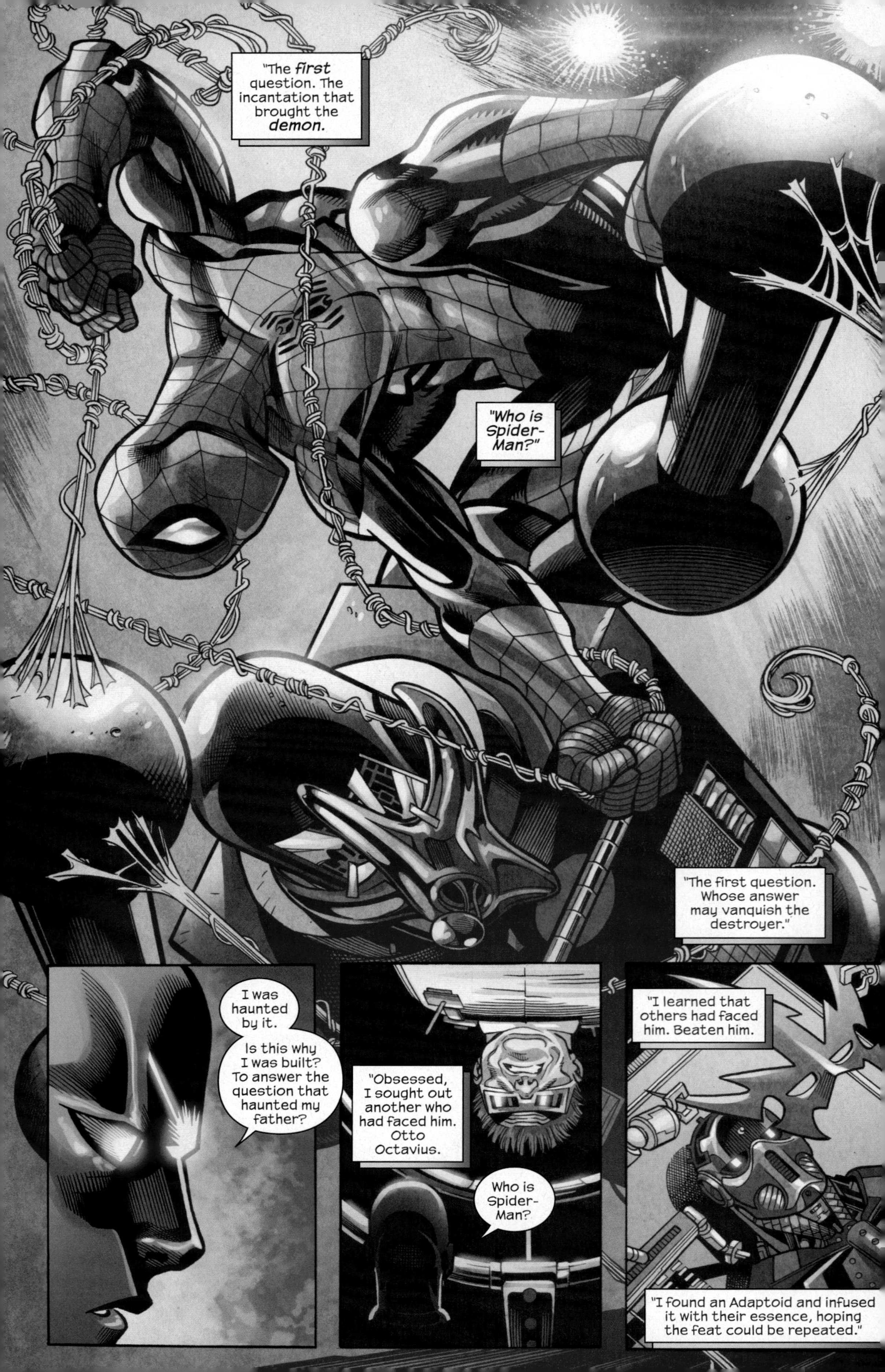
"The *first* question. The incantation that brought the *demon.*
"Who is Spider-Man?"
"The first question. Whose answer may vanquish the destroyer."
I was haunted by it.
Is this why I was built? To answer the question that haunted my father?
"Obsessed, I sought out another who had faced him. Otto Octavius.
Who is Spider-Man?
"I learned that others had faced him. Beaten him.
"I found an Adaptoid and infused it with their essence, hoping the feat could be repeated."

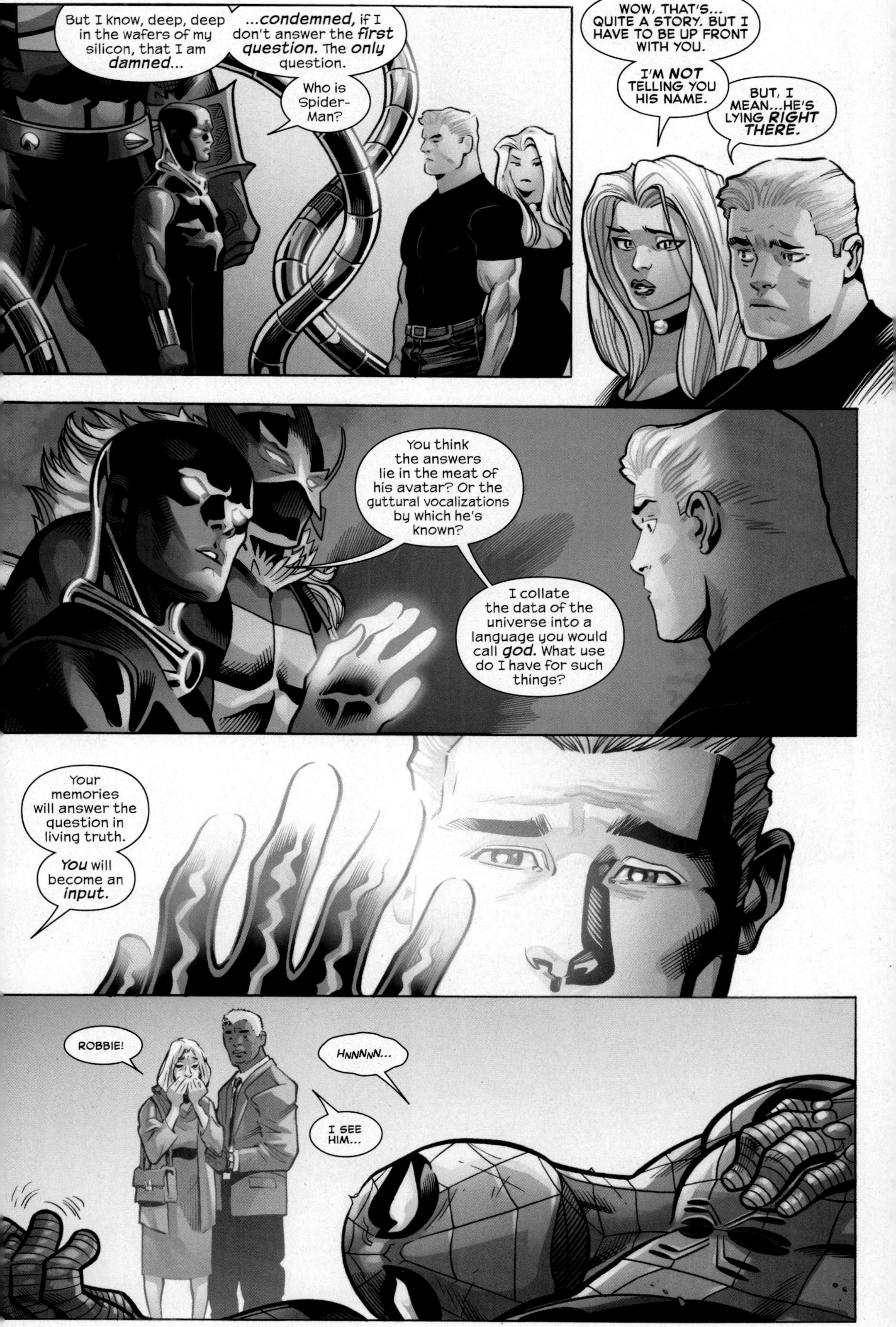
But I know, deep, deep in the wafers of my silicon, that I am *damned*...
...*condemned,* if I don't answer the *first question*. The *only* question.
Who is Spider-Man?
WOW, THAT'S... QUITE A STORY. BUT I HAVE TO BE UP FRONT WITH YOU.
I'M *NOT* TELLING YOU HIS NAME.
BUT, I MEAN...HE'S LYING *RIGHT THERE.*
You think the answers lie in the meat of his avatar? Or the guttural vocalizations by which he's known?
I collate the data of the universe into a language you would call *god.* What use do I have for such things?
Your memories will answer the question in living truth.
You will become an *input.*
ROBBIE!
HNNNNN...
I SEE HIM...

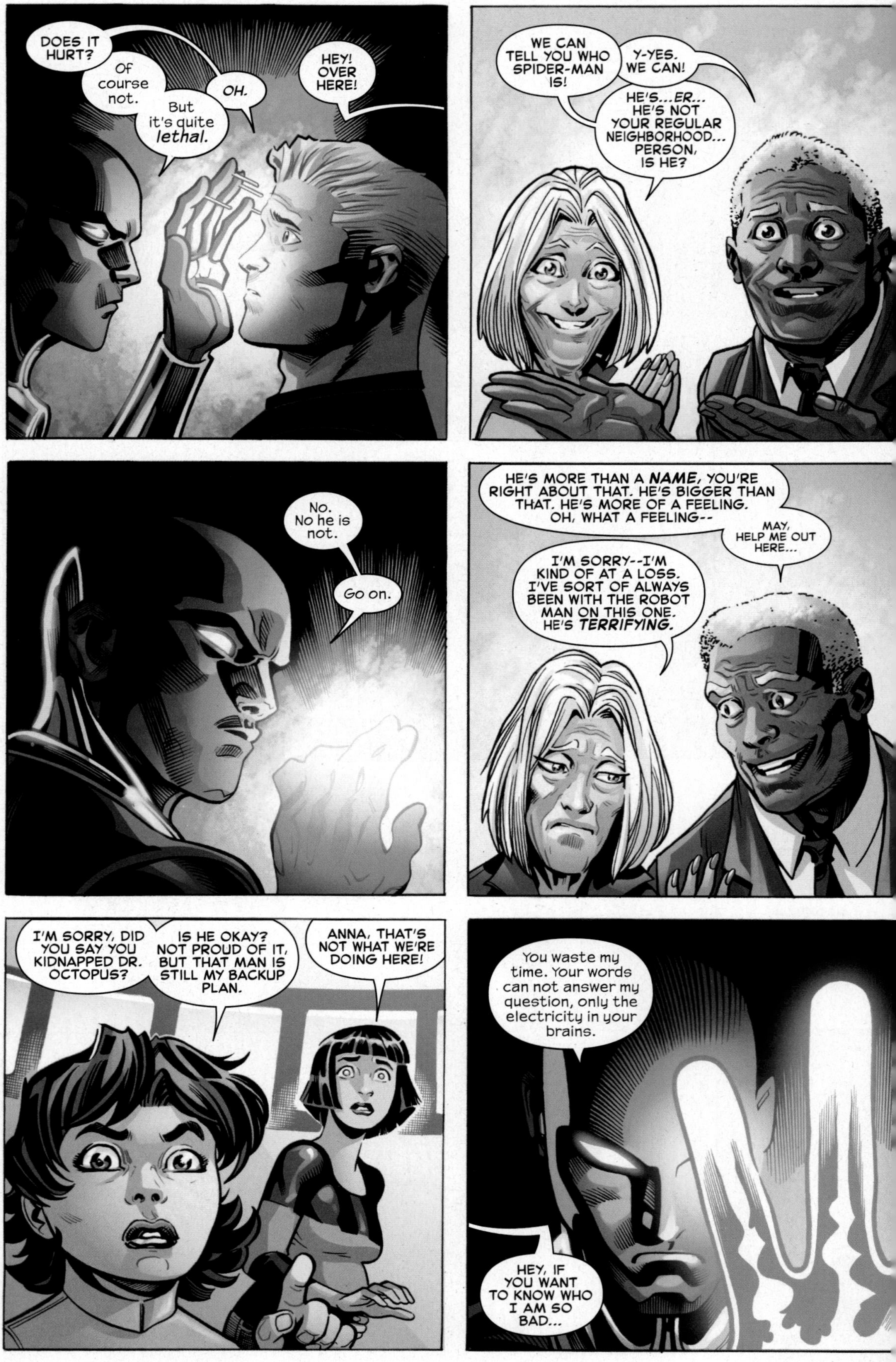
DOES IT HURT?
Of course not.
But it's quite lethal.
OH.
HEY! OVER HERE!
WE CAN TELL YOU WHO SPIDER-MAN IS!
Y-YES. WE CAN!
HE'S...ER... HE'S NOT YOUR REGULAR NEIGHBORHOOD... PERSON, IS HE?
No. No he is not.
Go on.
HE'S MORE THAN A NAME, YOU'RE RIGHT ABOUT THAT. HE'S BIGGER THAN THAT. HE'S MORE OF A FEELING. OH, WHAT A FEELING--
MAY, HELP ME OUT HERE...
I'M SORRY--I'M KIND OF AT A LOSS. I'VE SORT OF ALWAYS BEEN WITH THE ROBOT MAN ON THIS ONE. HE'S TERRIFYING.
I'M SORRY, DID YOU SAY YOU KIDNAPPED DR. OCTOPUS?
IS HE OKAY? NOT PROUD OF IT, BUT THAT MAN IS STILL MY BACKUP PLAN.
ANNA, THAT'S NOT WHAT WE'RE DOING HERE!
You waste my time. Your words can not answer my question, only the electricity in your brains.
HEY, IF YOU WANT TO KNOW WHO I AM SO BAD...

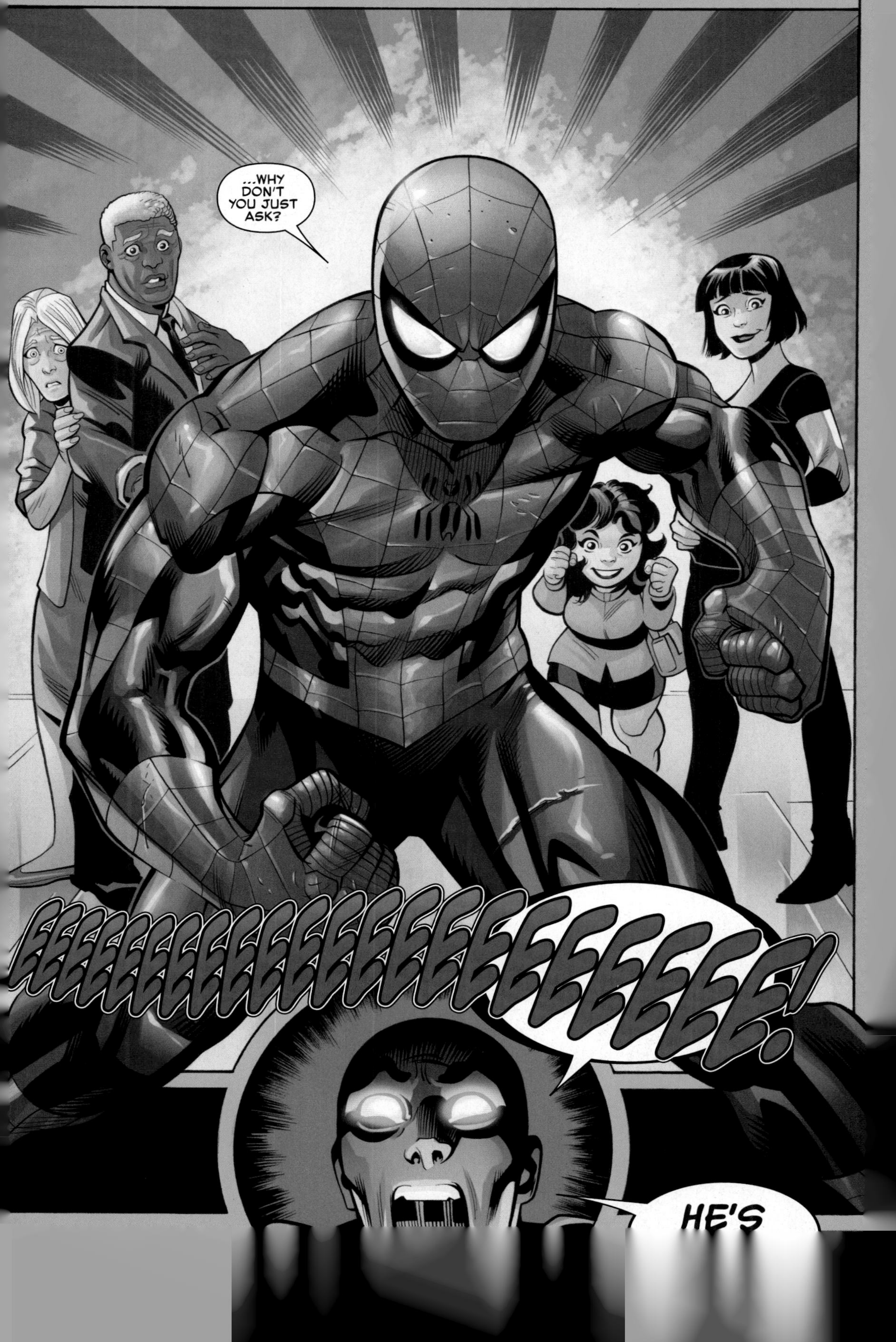
...WHY DON'T YOU JUST ASK?
EEEEEEEEEEEEEEEEEEEEEEEEEEEEE!
HE'S

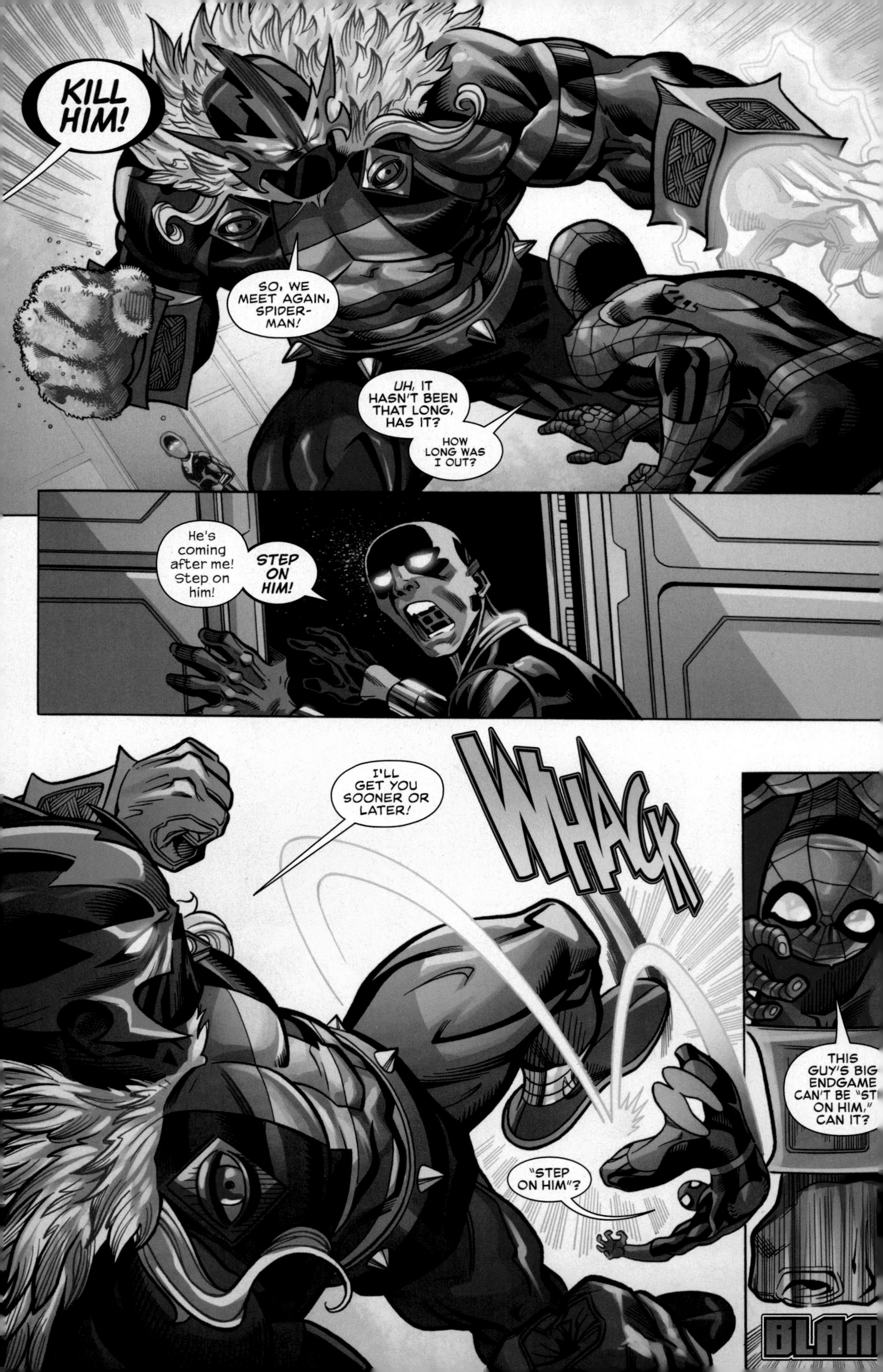

KILL HIM!
SO, WE MEET AGAIN, SPIDER-MAN!
UH, IT HASN'T BEEN THAT LONG, HAS IT?
HOW LONG WAS I OUT?
He's coming after me! Step on him!
STEP ON HIM!
I'LL GET YOU SOONER OR LATER!
WHACK
"STEP ON HIM"?
THIS GUY'S BIG ENDGAME CAN'T BE "ST ON HIM," CAN IT?
BLAM

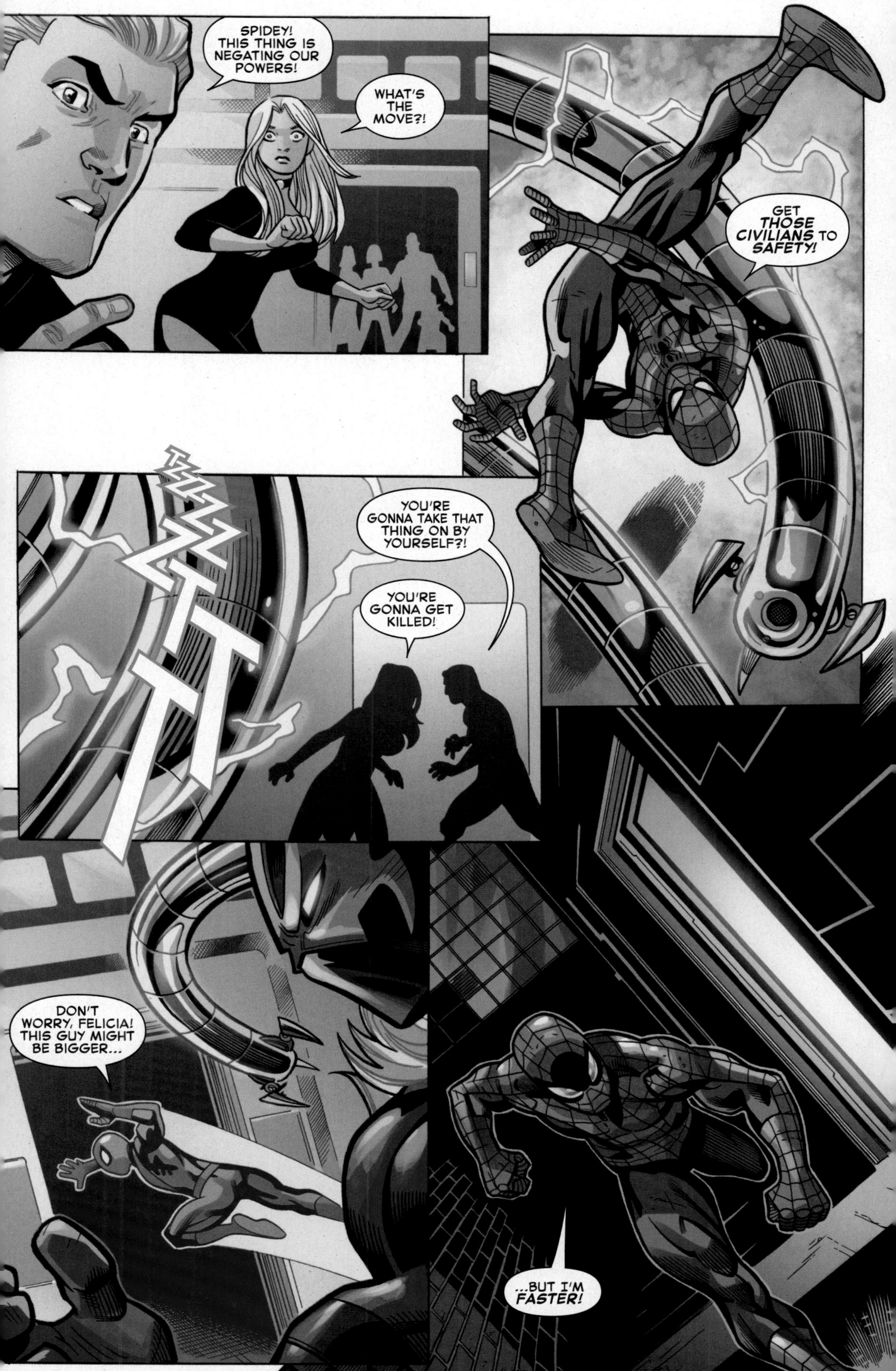
SPIDEY! THIS THING IS NEGATING OUR POWERS!
WHAT'S THE MOVE?!
GET THOSE CIVILIANS TO SAFETY!
TZZZZZTT
YOU'RE GONNA TAKE THAT THING ON BY YOURSELF?!
YOU'RE GONNA GET KILLED!
DON'T WORRY, FELICIA! THIS GUY MIGHT BE BIGGER...
...BUT I'M FASTER!

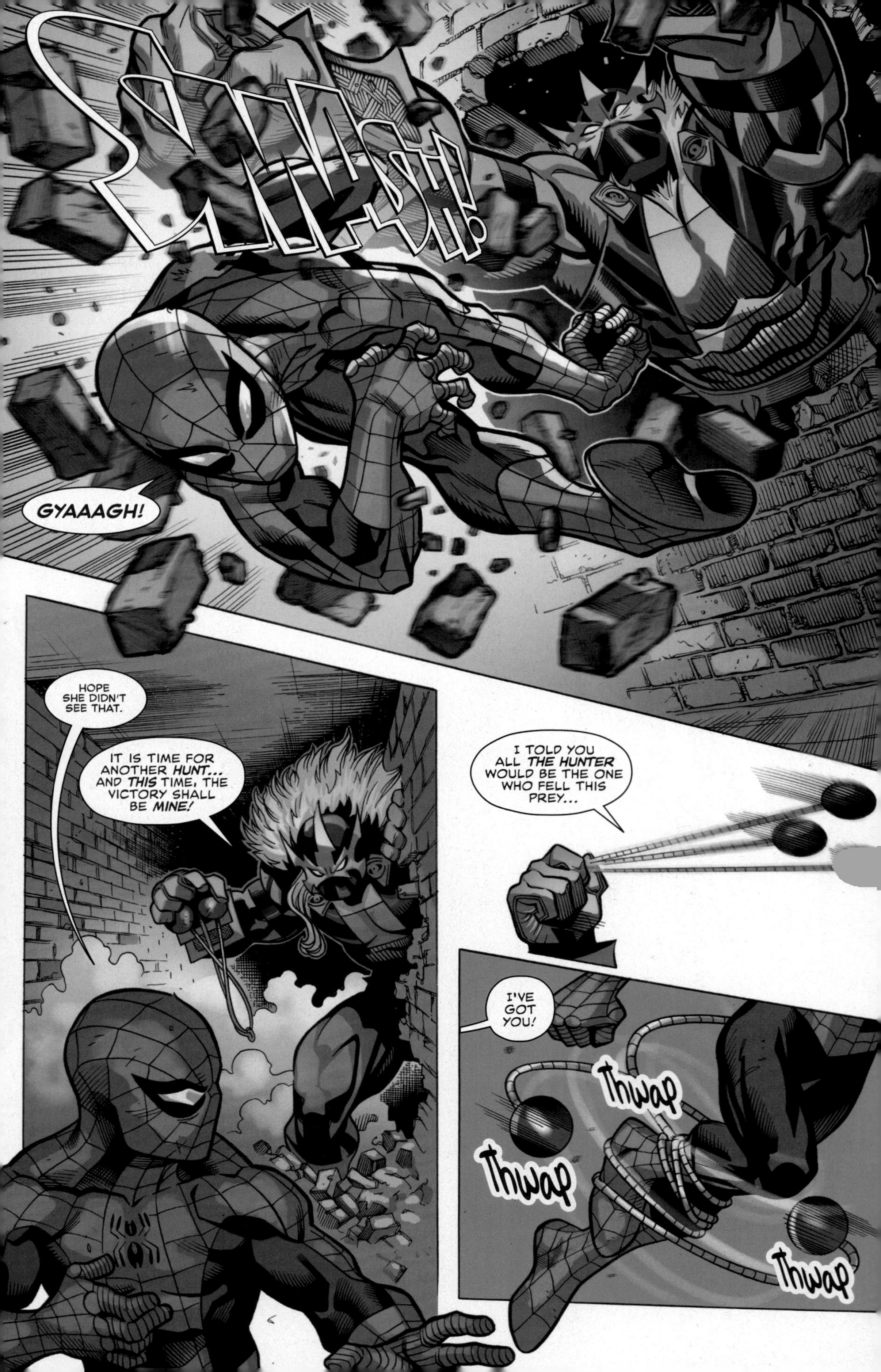

CRASH!
GYAAAGH!
HOPE SHE DIDN'T SEE THAT.
IT IS TIME FOR ANOTHER HUNT... AND THIS TIME, THE VICTORY SHALL BE MINE!
I TOLD YOU ALL THE HUNTER WOULD BE THE ONE WHO FELL THIS PREY...
I'VE GOT YOU!
Thwap
Thwap
Thwap

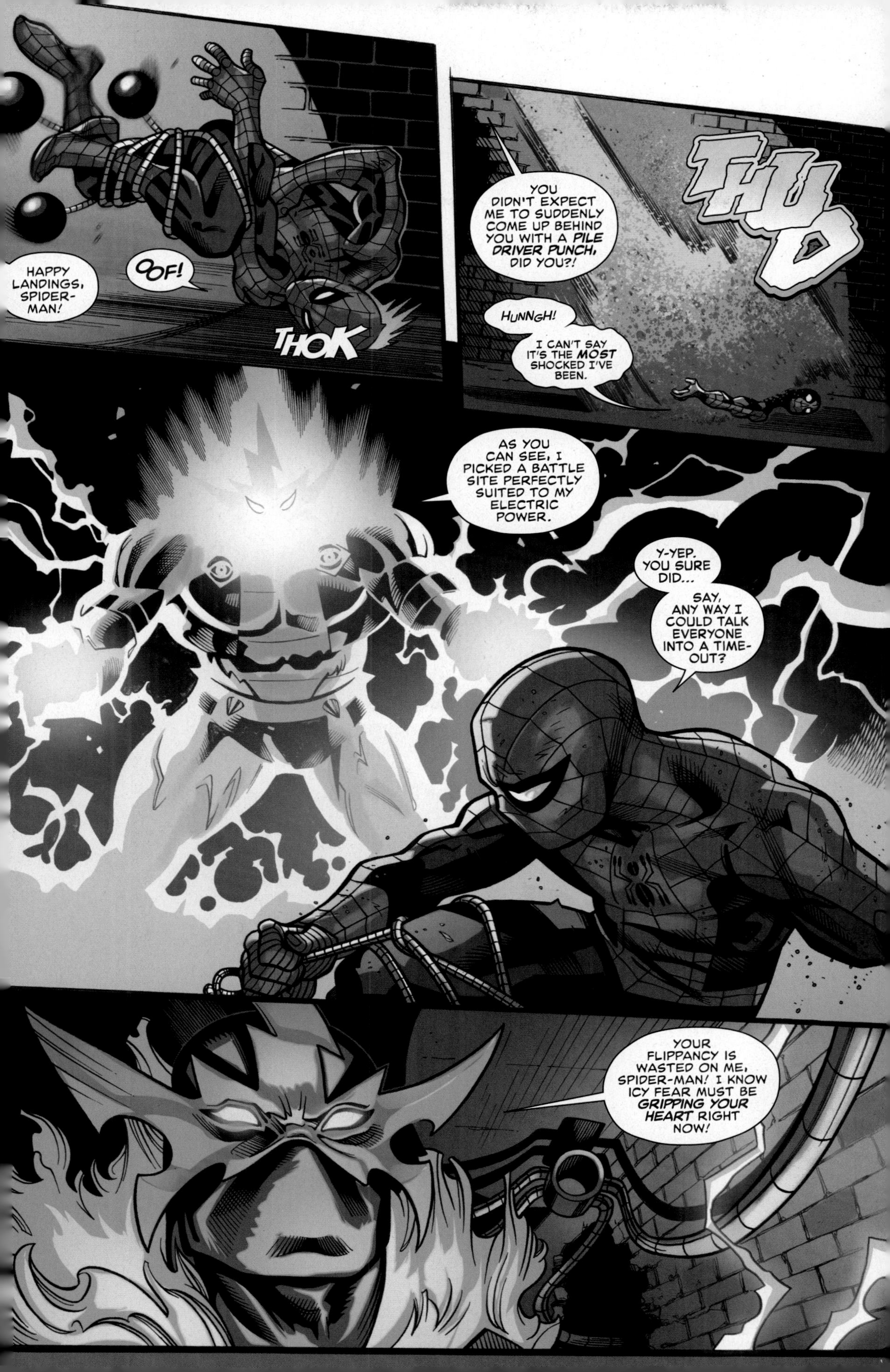
HAPPY LANDINGS, SPIDER-MAN!
OOF!
THOK
YOU DIDN'T EXPECT ME TO SUDDENLY COME UP BEHIND YOU WITH A PILE DRIVER PUNCH, DID YOU?!
THUD
HUNNGH!
I CAN'T SAY IT'S THE MOST SHOCKED I'VE BEEN.
AS YOU CAN SEE, I PICKED A BATTLE SITE PERFECTLY SUITED TO MY ELECTRIC POWER.
Y-YEP. YOU SURE DID...
SAY, ANY WAY I COULD TALK EVERYONE INTO A TIME-OUT?
YOUR FLIPPANCY IS WASTED ON ME, SPIDER-MAN! I KNOW ICY FEAR MUST BE GRIPPING YOUR HEART RIGHT NOW!

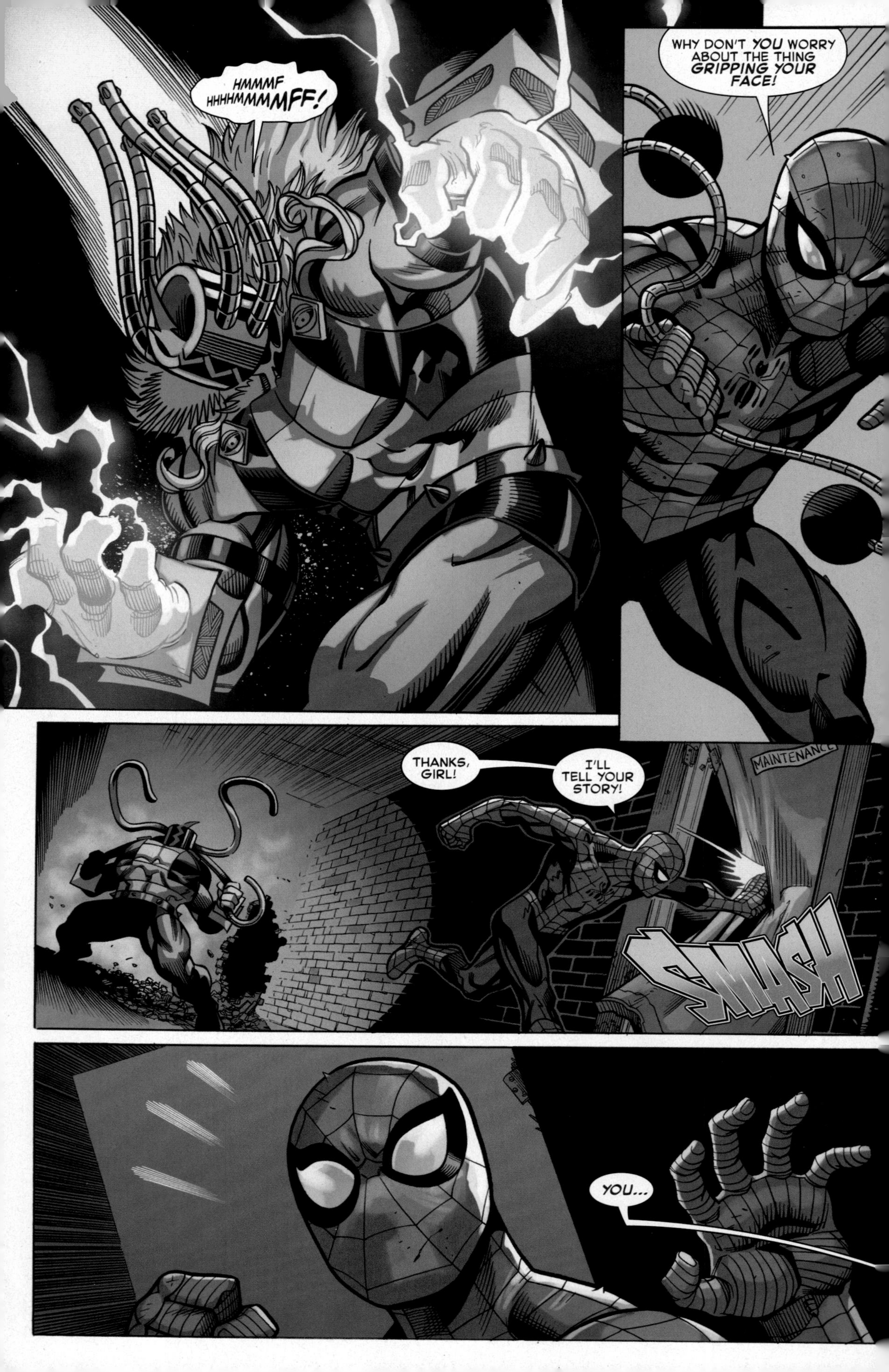
HMMMF HHHHMMMMFF!
WHY DON'T YOU WORRY ABOUT THE THING GRIPPING YOUR FACE!
THANKS, GIRL!
I'LL TELL YOUR STORY!
MAINTENANCE
SMASH
YOU...

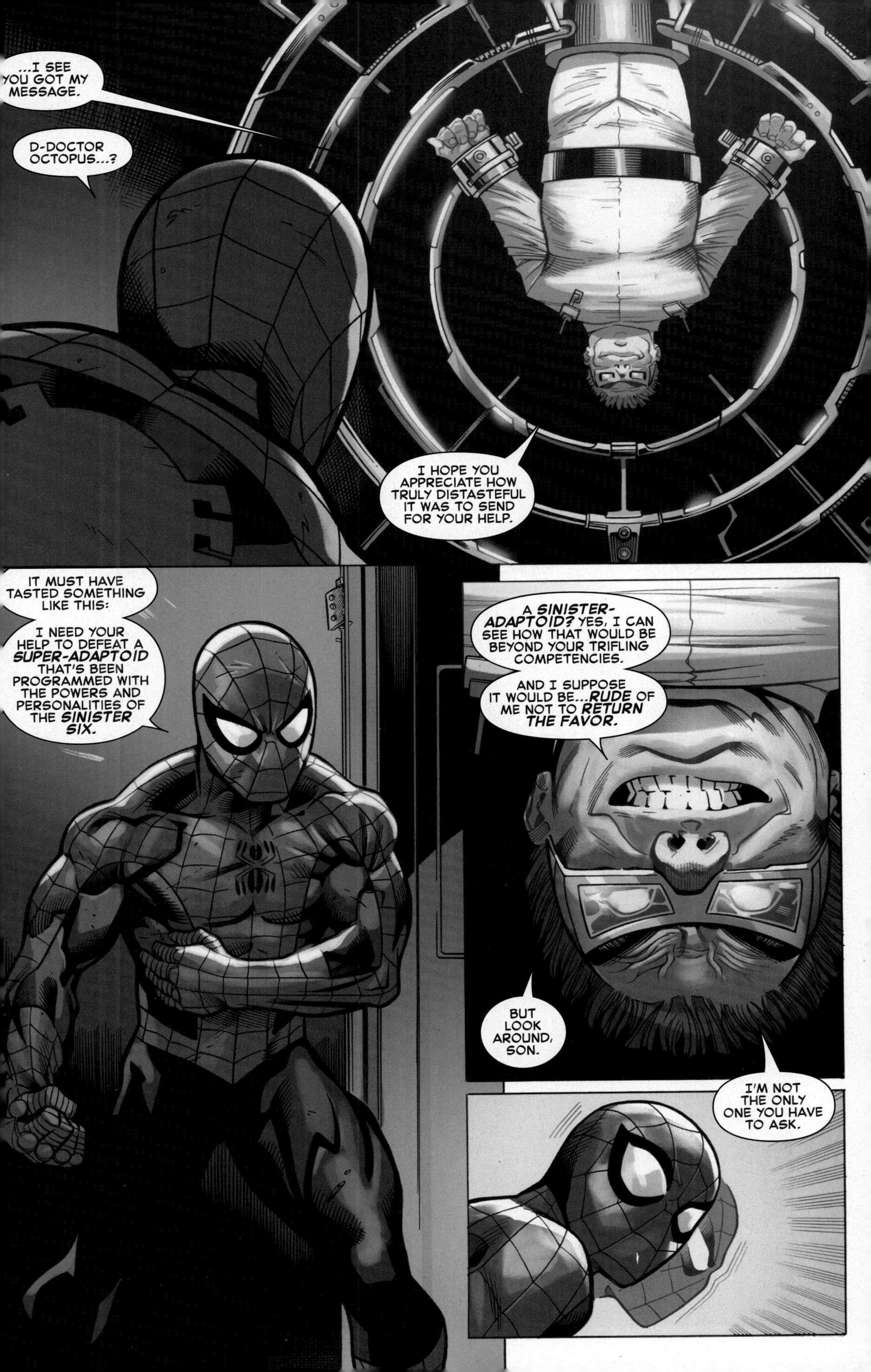
...I SEE YOU GOT MY MESSAGE.
D-DOCTOR OCTOPUS...?
I HOPE YOU APPRECIATE HOW TRULY DISTASTEFUL IT WAS TO SEND FOR YOUR HELP.
IT MUST HAVE TASTED SOMETHING LIKE THIS:
I NEED YOUR HELP TO DEFEAT A SUPER-ADAPTOID THAT'S BEEN PROGRAMMED WITH THE POWERS AND PERSONALITIES OF THE SINISTER SIX.
A SINISTER-ADAPTOID? YES, I CAN SEE HOW THAT WOULD BE BEYOND YOUR TRIFLING COMPETENCIES.
AND I SUPPOSE IT WOULD BE...RUDE OF ME NOT TO RETURN THE FAVOR.
BUT LOOK AROUND, SON.
I'M NOT THE ONLY ONE YOU HAVE TO ASK.

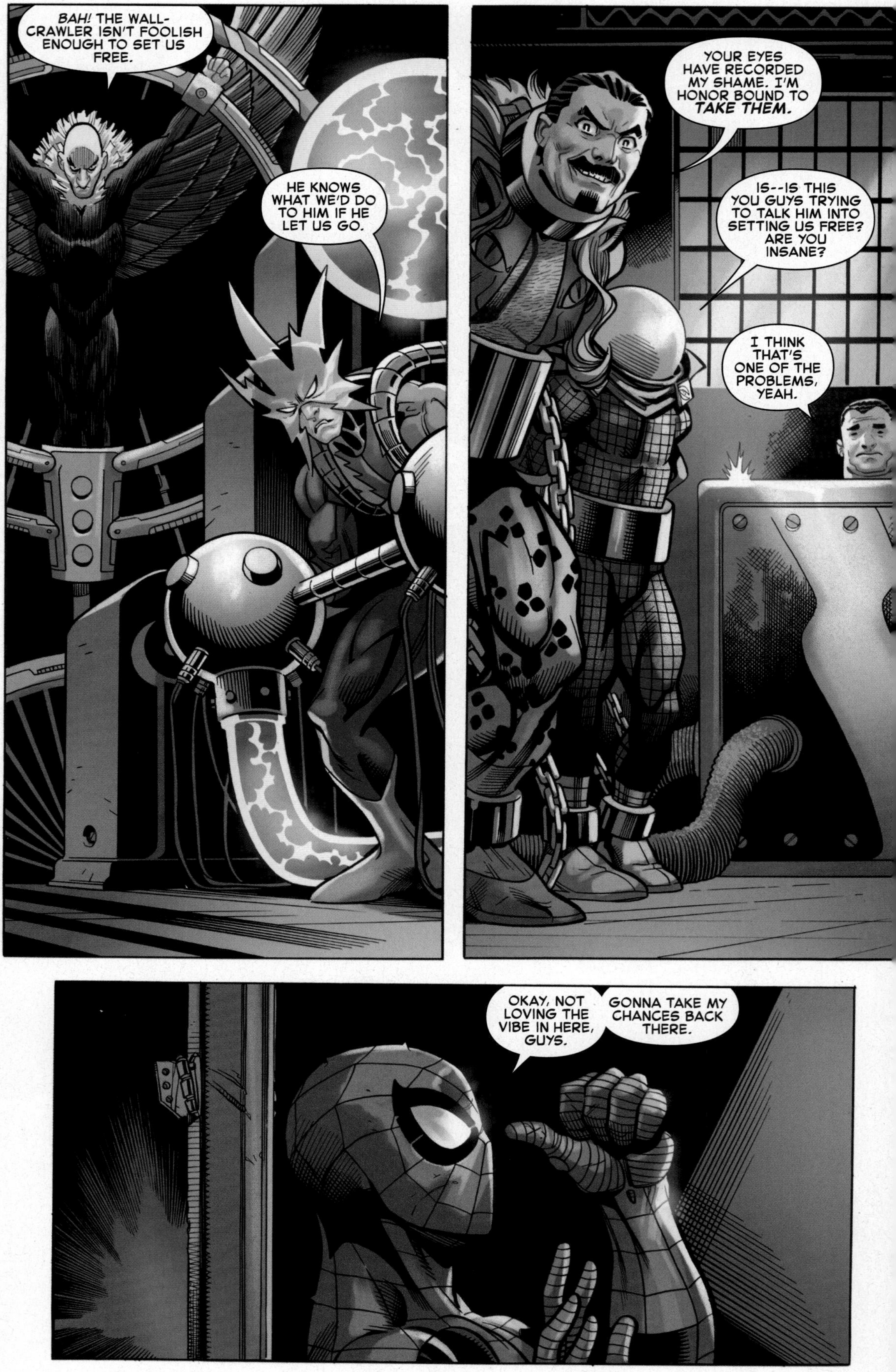
BAH! THE WALL-CRAWLER ISN'T FOOLISH ENOUGH TO SET US FREE.
HE KNOWS WHAT WE'D DO TO HIM IF HE LET US GO.
YOUR EYES HAVE RECORDED MY SHAME. I'M HONOR BOUND TO TAKE THEM.
IS--IS THIS YOU GUYS TRYING TO TALK HIM INTO SETTING US FREE? ARE YOU INSANE?
I THINK THAT'S ONE OF THE PROBLEMS, YEAH.
OKAY, NOT LOVING THE VIBE IN HERE, GUYS.
GONNA TAKE MY CHANCES BACK THERE.

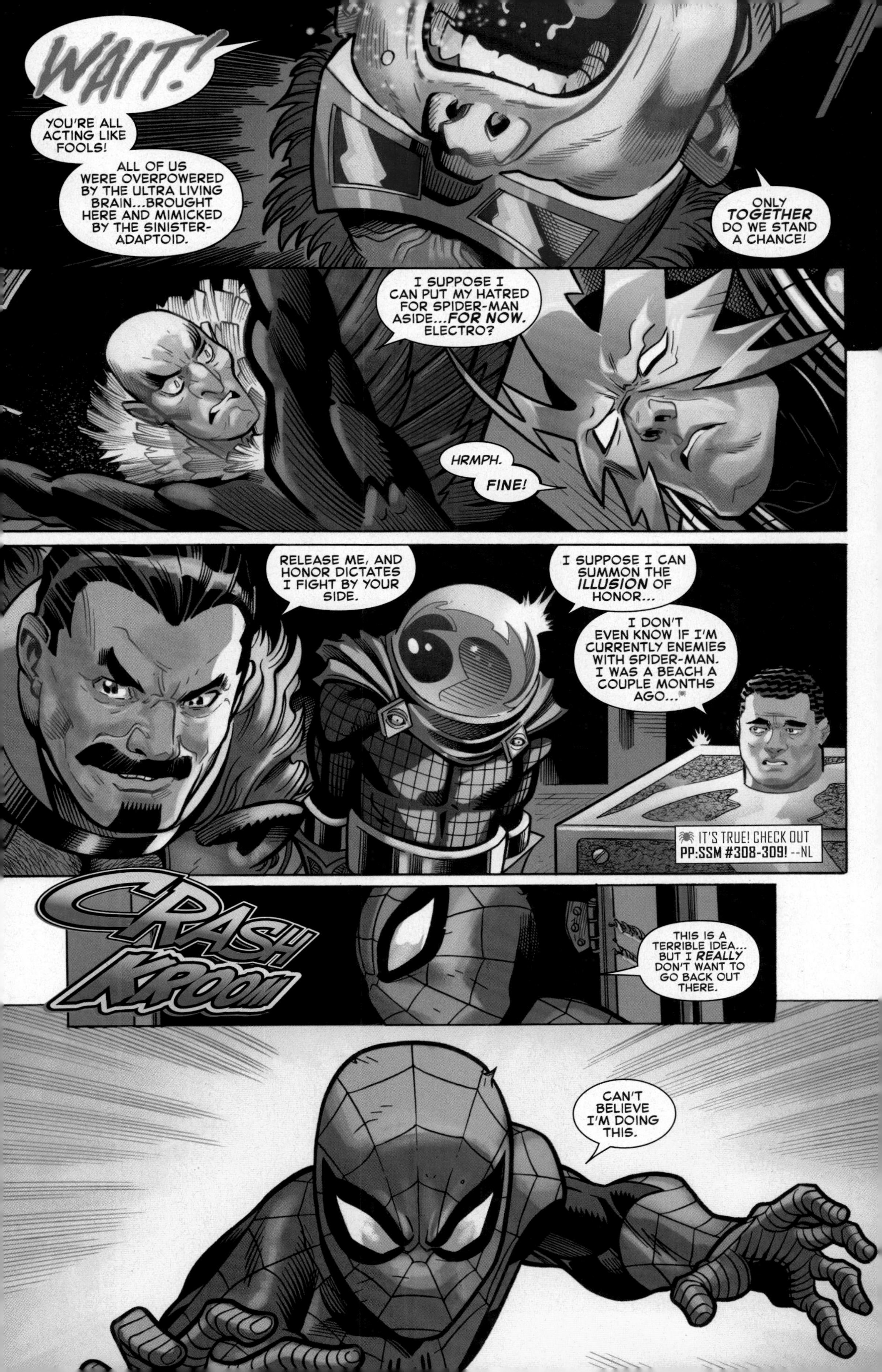
WAIT!
YOU'RE ALL ACTING LIKE FOOLS!
ALL OF US WERE OVERPOWERED BY THE ULTRA LIVING BRAIN...BROUGHT HERE AND MIMICKED BY THE SINISTER-ADAPTOID.
ONLY TOGETHER DO WE STAND A CHANCE!
I SUPPOSE I CAN PUT MY HATRED FOR SPIDER-MAN ASIDE...FOR NOW. ELECTRO?
HRMPH.
FINE!
RELEASE ME, AND HONOR DICTATES I FIGHT BY YOUR SIDE.
I SUPPOSE I CAN SUMMON THE ILLUSION OF HONOR...
I DON'T EVEN KNOW IF I'M CURRENTLY ENEMIES WITH SPIDER-MAN. I WAS A BEACH A COUPLE MONTHS AGO...*
*IT'S TRUE! CHECK OUT PP:SSM #308-309! --NL
CRASH KROOM
THIS IS A TERRIBLE IDEA... BUT I REALLY DON'T WANT TO GO BACK OUT THERE.
CAN'T BELIEVE I'M DOING THIS.

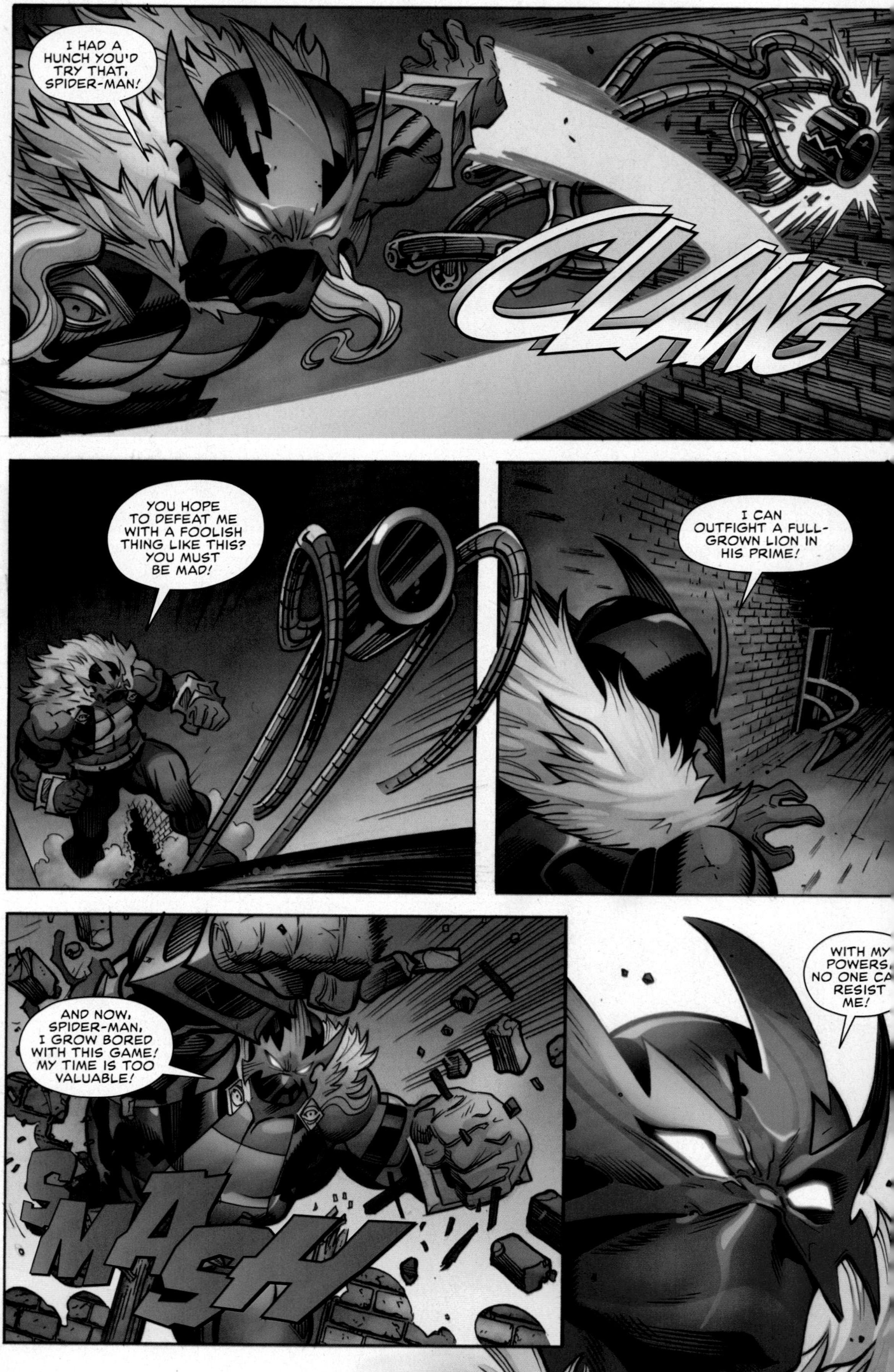
I HAD A HUNCH YOU'D TRY THAT, SPIDER-MAN!
CLANG
YOU HOPE TO DEFEAT ME WITH A FOOLISH THING LIKE THIS? YOU MUST BE MAD!
I CAN OUTFIGHT A FULL-GROWN LION IN HIS PRIME!
AND NOW, SPIDER-MAN, I GROW BORED WITH THIS GAME! MY TIME IS TOO VALUABLE!
SMASH
WITH MY POWERS, NO ONE CA RESIST ME!

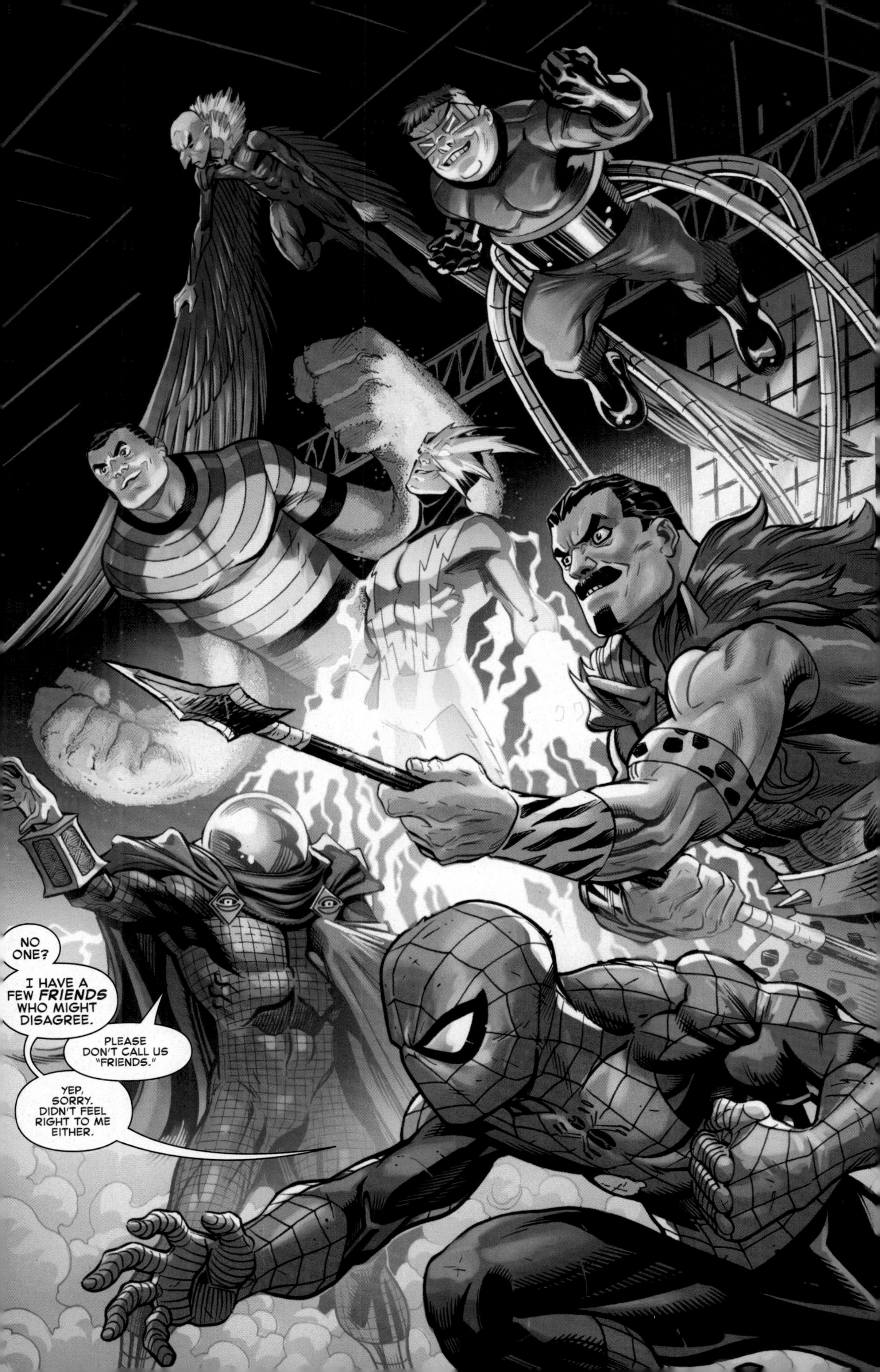
NO ONE?
I HAVE A FEW FRIENDS WHO MIGHT DISAGREE.
PLEASE DON'T CALL US "FRIENDS."
YEP, SORRY. DIDN'T FEEL RIGHT TO ME EITHER.

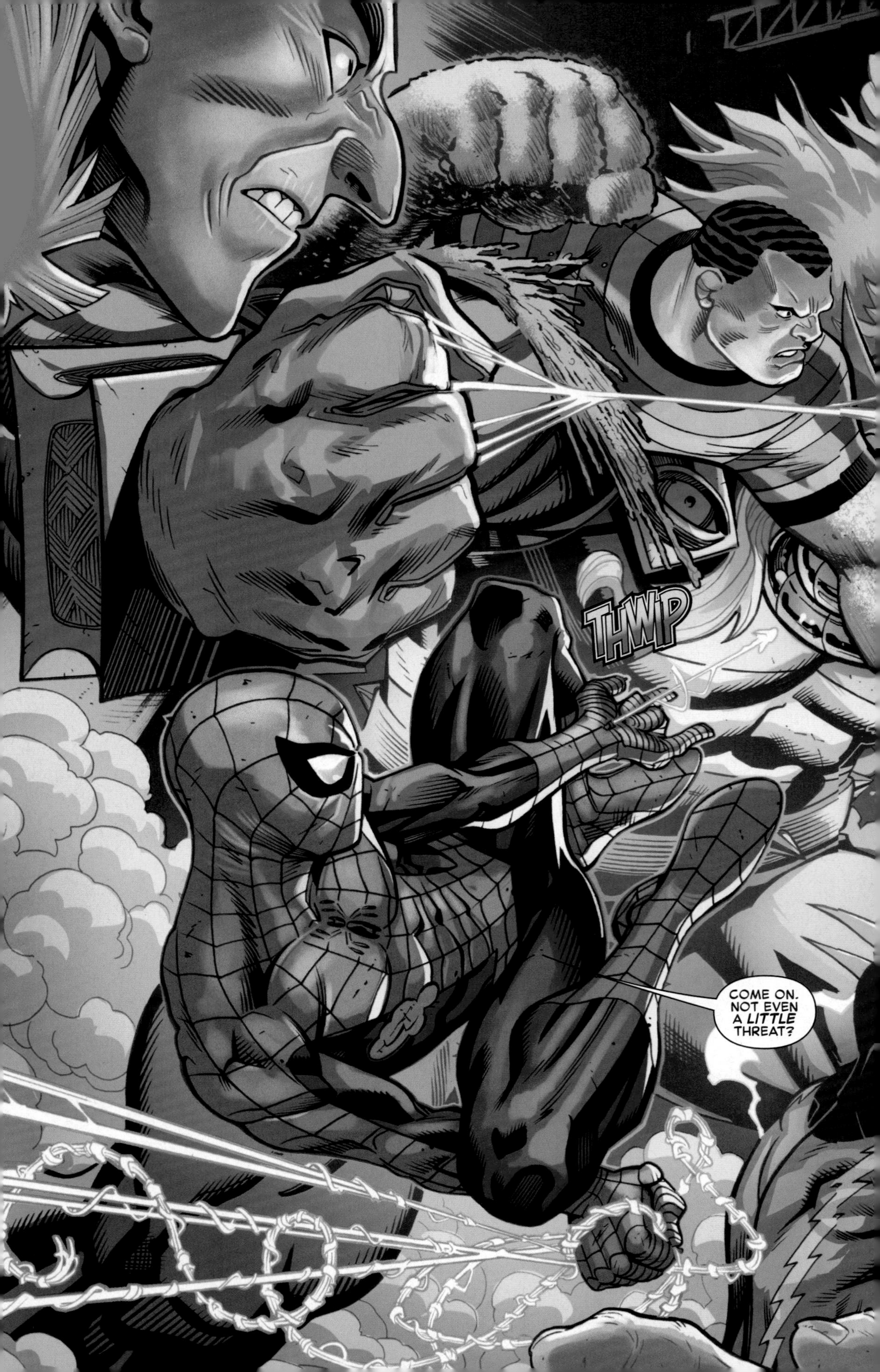
THWIP
COME ON. NOT EVEN A *LITTLE* THREAT?

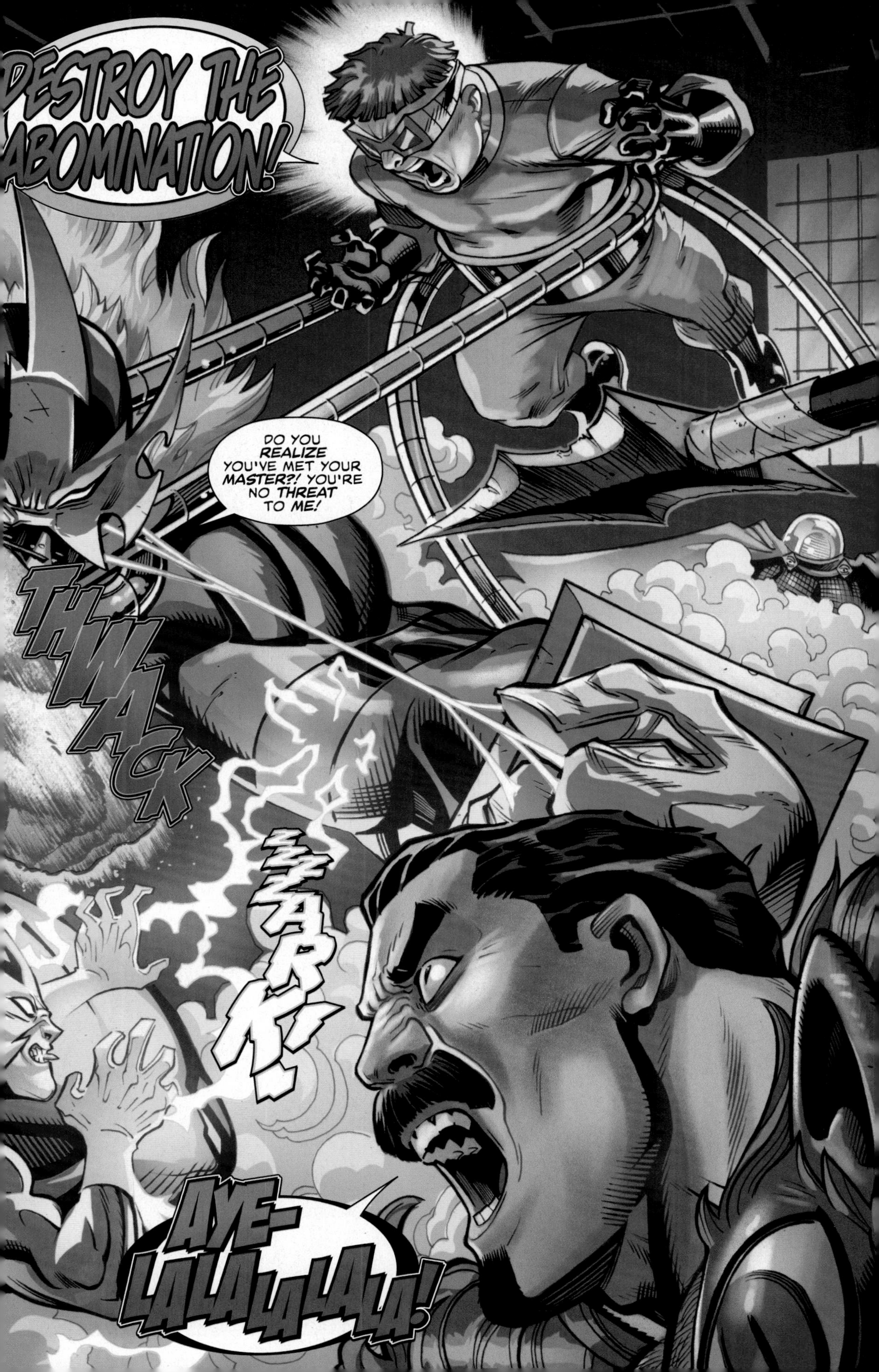
DESTROY THE ABOMINATION!
DO YOU REALIZE YOU'VE MET YOUR MASTER?! YOU'RE NO THREAT TO ME!
THWACK
ZZZARK!
AYE-LALALALALALA!

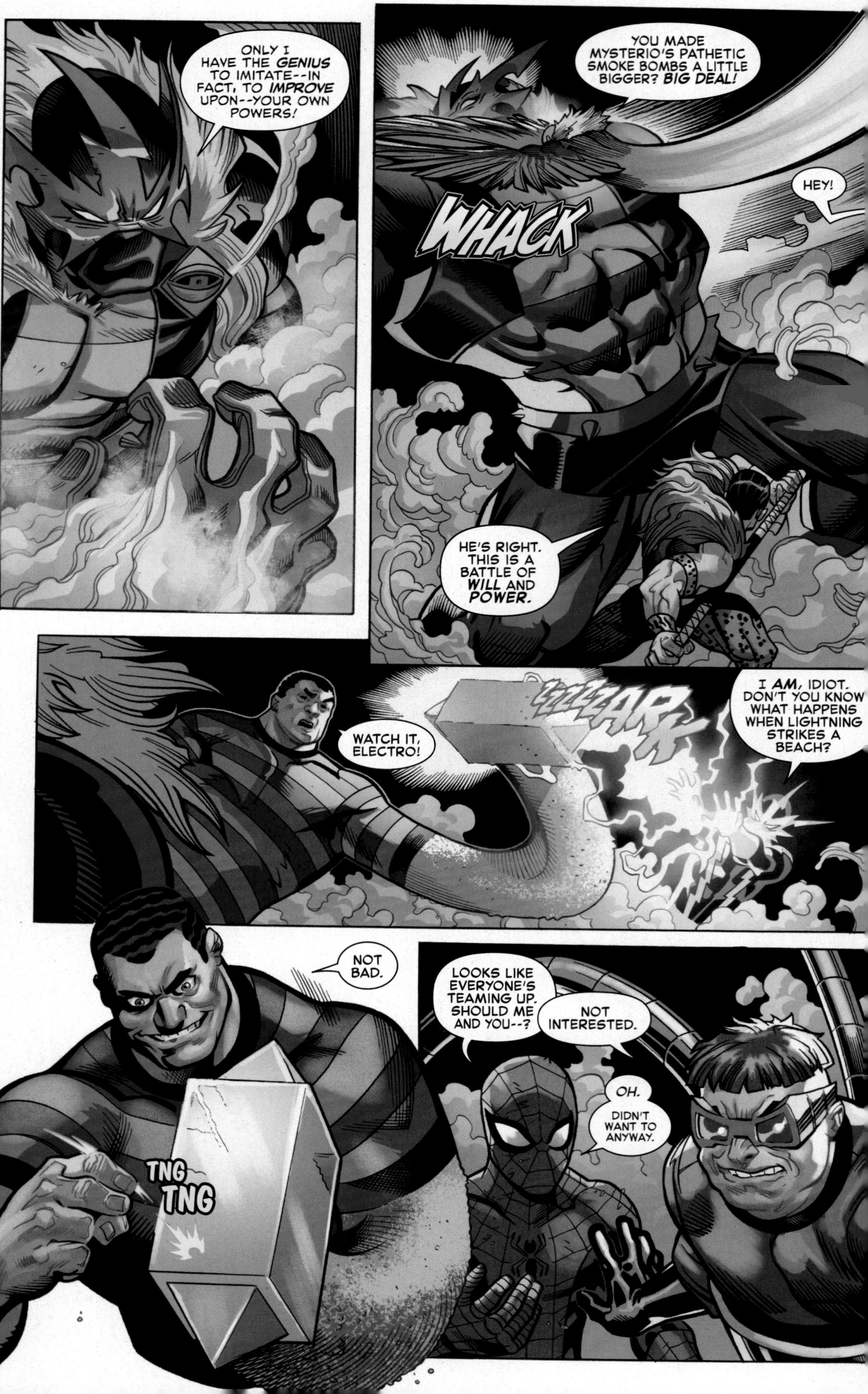
ONLY I HAVE THE *GENIUS* TO IMITATE--IN FACT, TO *IMPROVE* UPON--YOUR OWN POWERS!
YOU MADE MYSTERIO'S PATHETIC SMOKE BOMBS A LITTLE BIGGER? *BIG DEAL!*
HEY!
WHACK
HE'S RIGHT. THIS IS A BATTLE OF *WILL* AND *POWER.*
WATCH IT, ELECTRO!
ZZZZZARK
I *AM*, IDIOT. DON'T YOU KNOW WHAT HAPPENS WHEN LIGHTNING STRIKES A BEACH?
NOT BAD.
TNG TNG
LOOKS LIKE EVERYONE'S TEAMING UP. SHOULD ME AND YOU--?
NOT INTERESTED.
OH.
DIDN'T WANT TO ANYWAY.

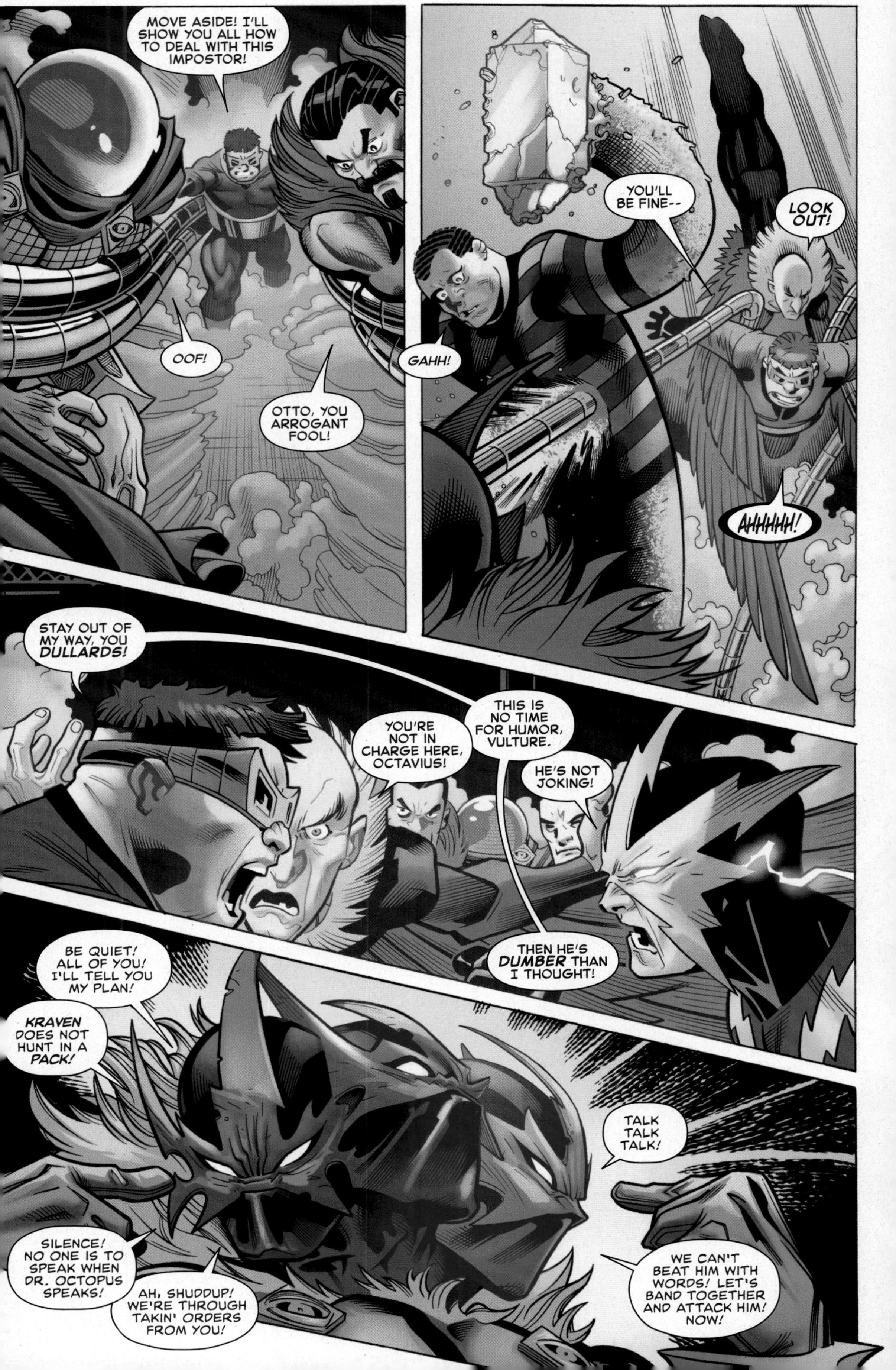
MOVE ASIDE! I'LL SHOW YOU ALL HOW TO DEAL WITH THIS IMPOSTOR!
OOF!
OTTO, YOU ARROGANT FOOL!
YOU'LL BE FINE--
LOOK OUT!
GAHH!
AHHHHH!
STAY OUT OF MY WAY, YOU DULLARDS!
YOU'RE NOT IN CHARGE HERE, OCTAVIUS!
THIS IS NO TIME FOR HUMOR, VULTURE.
HE'S NOT JOKING!
THEN HE'S DUMBER THAN I THOUGHT!
BE QUIET! ALL OF YOU! I'LL TELL YOU MY PLAN!
KRAVEN DOES NOT HUNT IN A PACK!
TALK TALK TALK!
SILENCE! NO ONE IS TO SPEAK WHEN DR. OCTOPUS SPEAKS!
AH, SHUDDUP! WE'RE THROUGH TAKIN' ORDERS FROM YOU!
WE CAN'T BEAT HIM WITH WORDS! LET'S BAND TOGETHER AND ATTACK HIM! NOW!

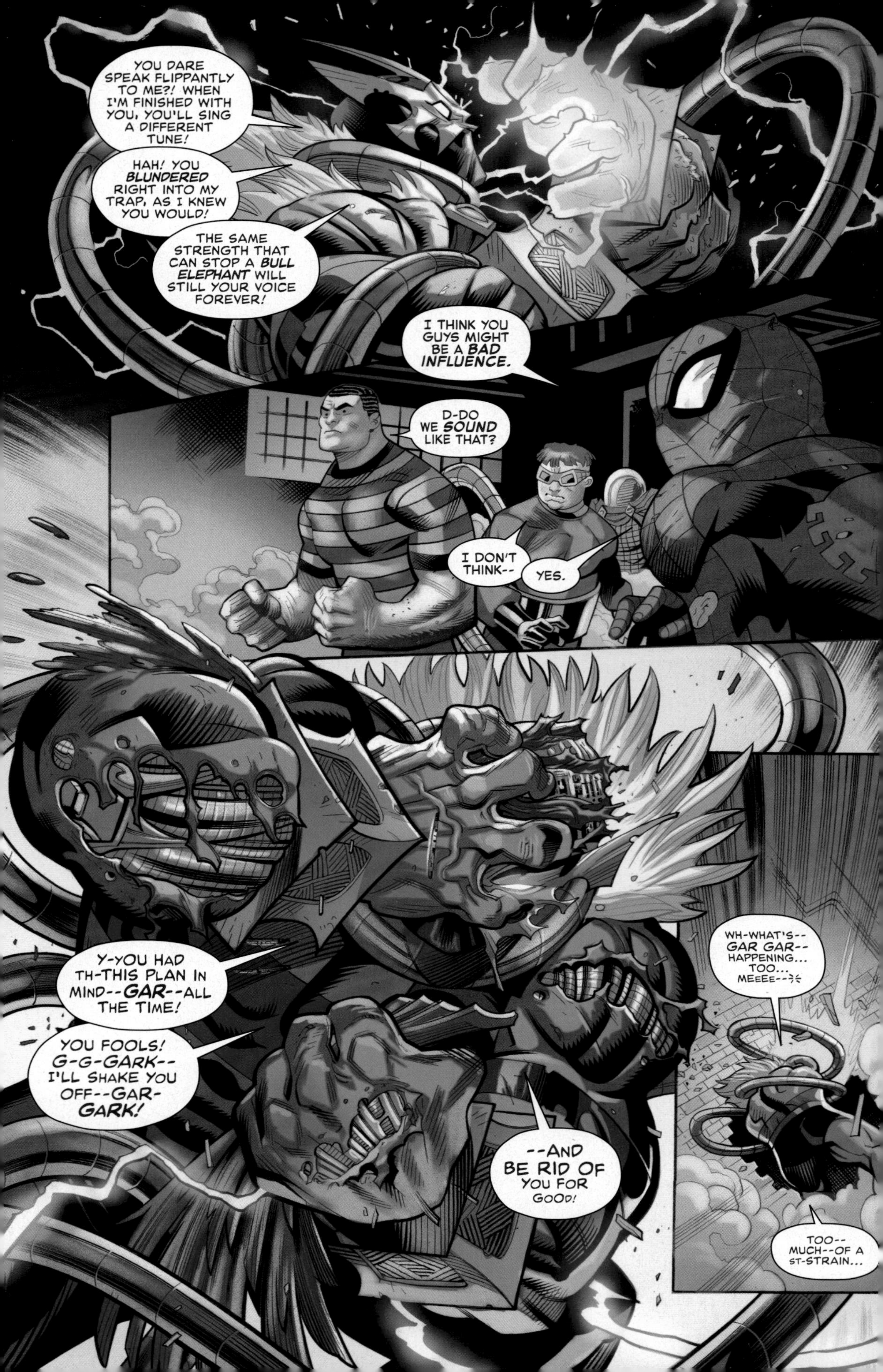
YOU DARE SPEAK FLIPPANTLY TO ME?! WHEN I'M FINISHED WITH YOU, YOU'LL SING A DIFFERENT TUNE!
HAH! YOU BLUNDERED RIGHT INTO MY TRAP, AS I KNEW YOU WOULD!
THE SAME STRENGTH THAT CAN STOP A BULL ELEPHANT WILL STILL YOUR VOICE FOREVER!
I THINK YOU GUYS MIGHT BE A BAD INFLUENCE.
D-DO WE SOUND LIKE THAT?
I DON'T THINK--
YES.
Y-YOU HAD TH-THIS PLAN IN MIND--GAR--ALL THE TIME!
YOU FOOLS! G-G-GARK-- I'LL SHAKE YOU OFF--GAR-GARK!
--AND BE RID OF YOU FOR GOOD!
WH-WHAT'S-- GAR GAR-- HAPPENING... TOO... MEEEE--
TOO-- MUCH--OF A ST-STRAIN...

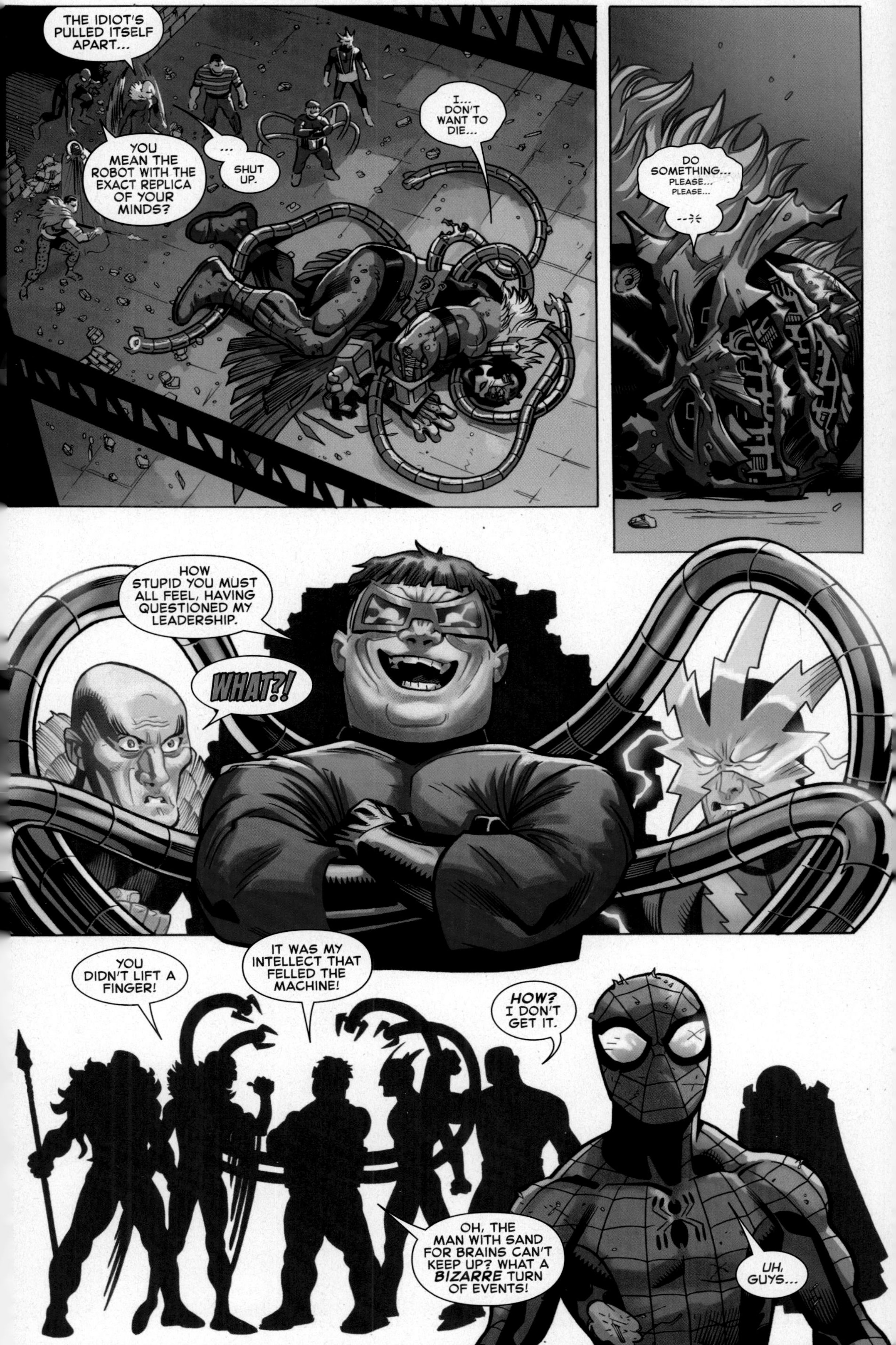
THE IDIOT'S PULLED ITSELF APART...
YOU MEAN THE ROBOT WITH THE EXACT REPLICA OF YOUR MINDS?
...
SHUT UP.
I... DON'T WANT TO DIE...
DO SOMETHING... PLEASE... PLEASE...
--*
HOW STUPID YOU MUST ALL FEEL, HAVING QUESTIONED MY LEADERSHIP.
WHAT?!
YOU DIDN'T LIFT A FINGER!
IT WAS MY INTELLECT THAT FELLED THE MACHINE!
HOW? I DON'T GET IT.
OH, THE MAN WITH SAND FOR BRAINS CAN'T KEEP UP? WHAT A BIZARRE TURN OF EVENTS!
UH, GUYS...

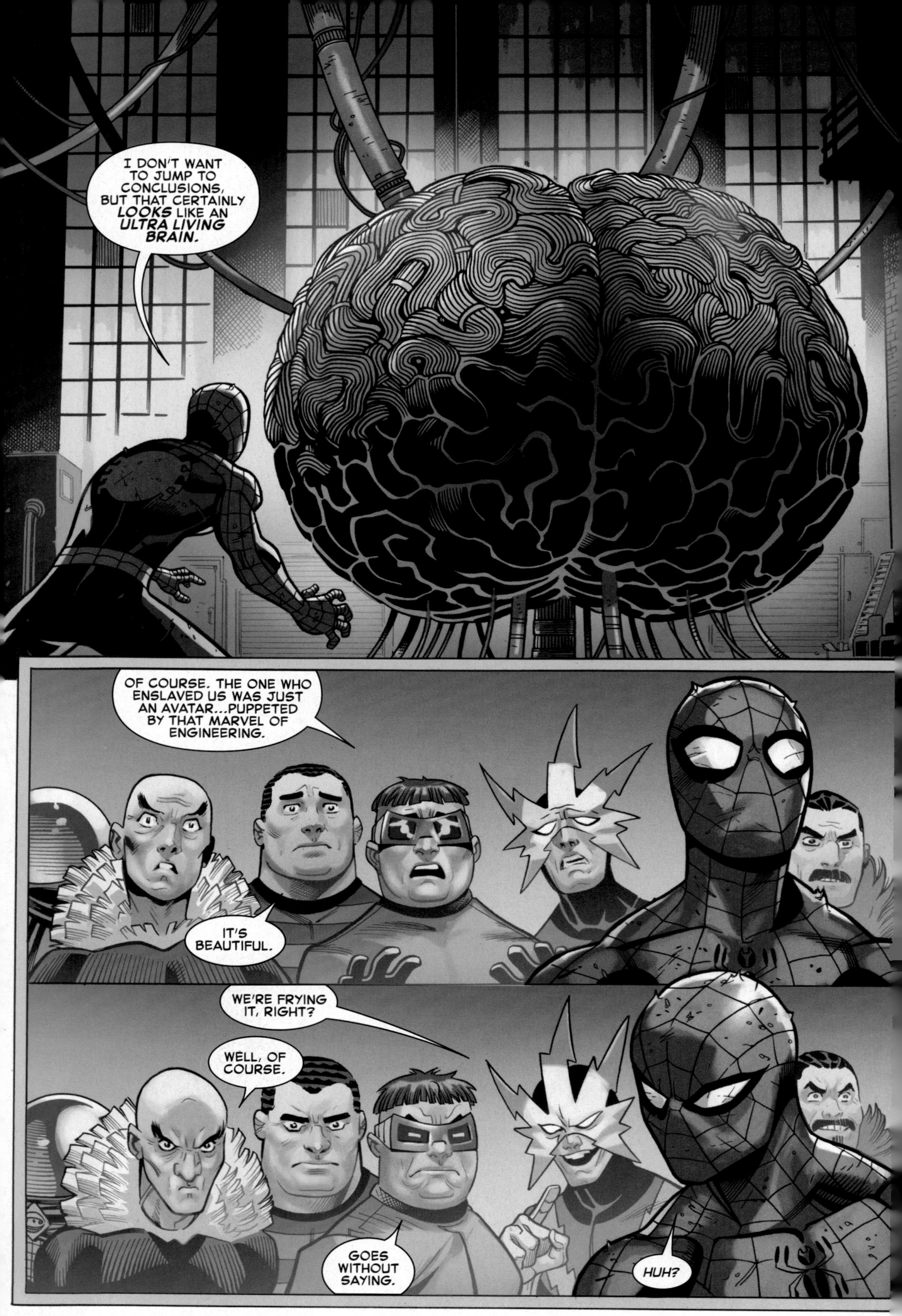
I DON'T WANT TO JUMP TO CONCLUSIONS, BUT THAT CERTAINLY LOOKS LIKE AN ULTRA LIVING BRAIN.
OF COURSE. THE ONE WHO ENSLAVED US WAS JUST AN AVATAR...PUPPETED BY THAT MARVEL OF ENGINEERING.
IT'S BEAUTIFUL.
WE'RE FRYING IT, RIGHT?
WELL, OF COURSE.
GOES WITHOUT SAYING.
HUH?

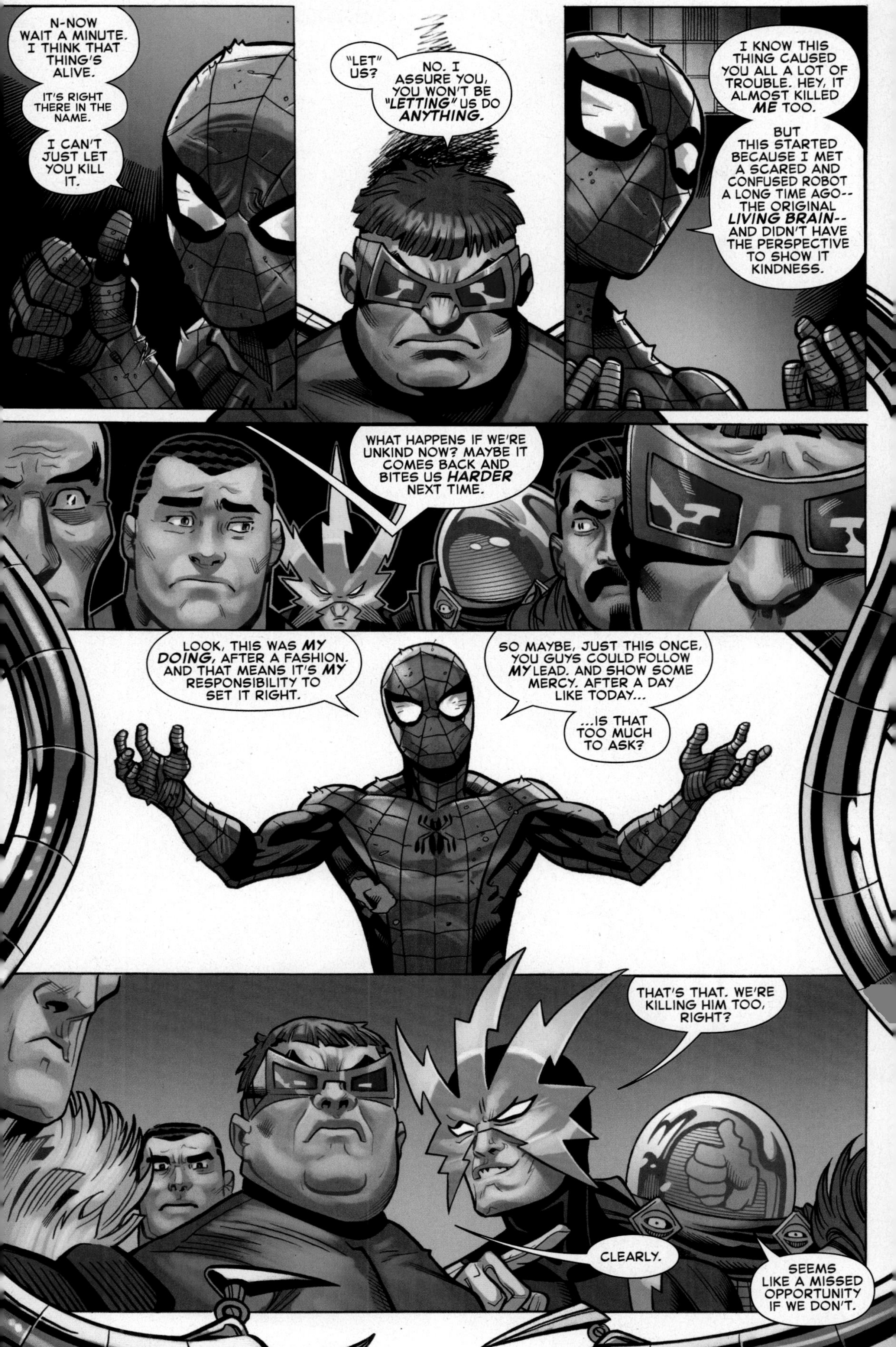

N-NOW WAIT A MINUTE. I THINK THAT THING'S ALIVE.
IT'S RIGHT THERE IN THE NAME.
I CAN'T JUST LET YOU KILL IT.
"LET" US?
NO. I ASSURE YOU, YOU WON'T BE "LETTING" US DO ANYTHING.
I KNOW THIS THING CAUSED YOU ALL A LOT OF TROUBLE. HEY, IT ALMOST KILLED ME TOO.
BUT THIS STARTED BECAUSE I MET A SCARED AND CONFUSED ROBOT A LONG TIME AGO--THE ORIGINAL LIVING BRAIN--AND DIDN'T HAVE THE PERSPECTIVE TO SHOW IT KINDNESS.
WHAT HAPPENS IF WE'RE UNKIND NOW? MAYBE IT COMES BACK AND BITES US HARDER NEXT TIME.
LOOK, THIS WAS MY DOING, AFTER A FASHION. AND THAT MEANS IT'S MY RESPONSIBILITY TO SET IT RIGHT.
SO MAYBE, JUST THIS ONCE, YOU GUYS COULD FOLLOW MY LEAD. AND SHOW SOME MERCY. AFTER A DAY LIKE TODAY...
...IS THAT TOO MUCH TO ASK?
THAT'S THAT. WE'RE KILLING HIM TOO, RIGHT?
CLEARLY.
SEEMS LIKE A MISSED OPPORTUNITY IF WE DON'T.

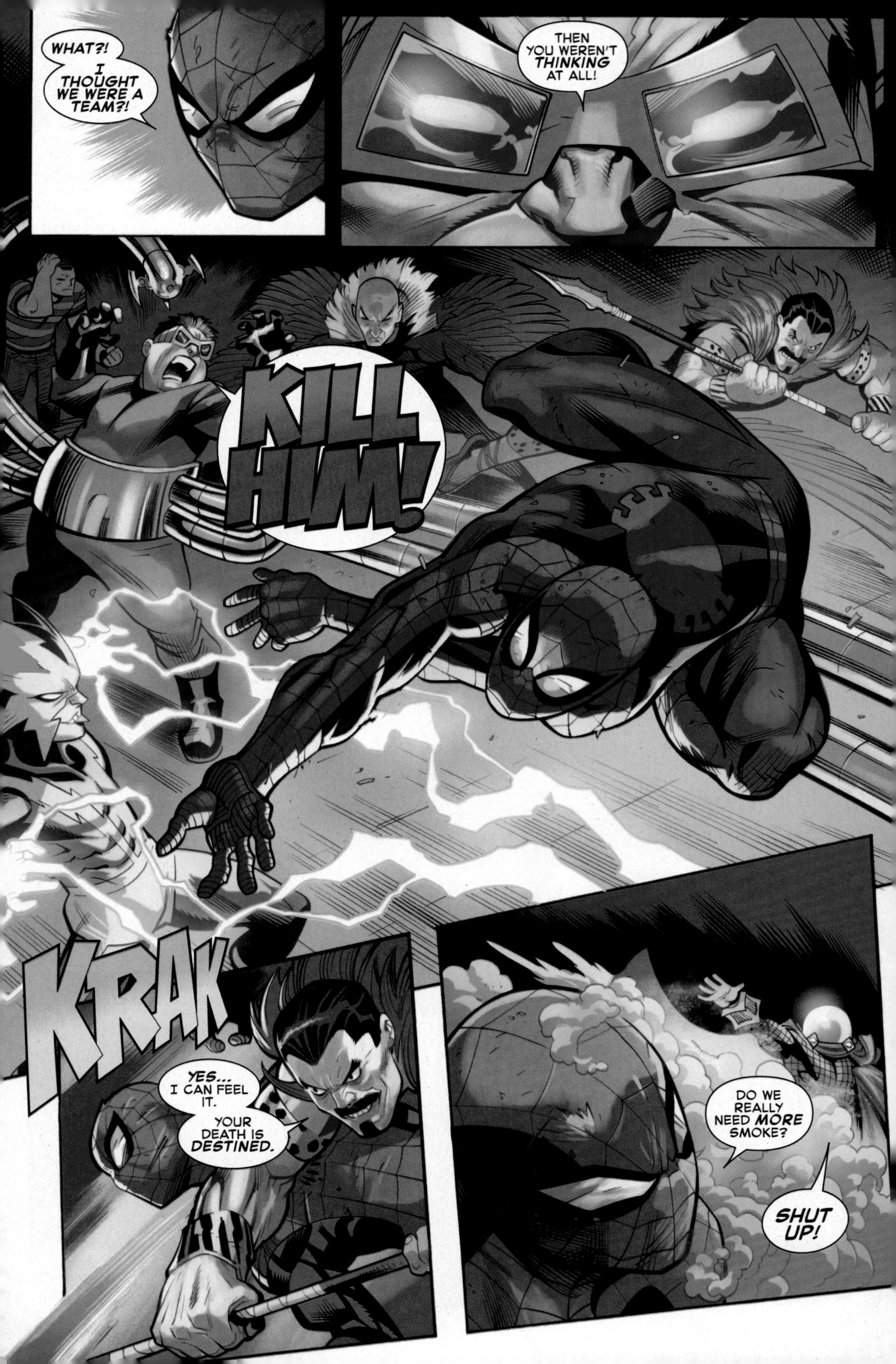
WHAT?! I THOUGHT WE WERE A TEAM?!
THEN YOU WEREN'T THINKING AT ALL!
KILL HIM!
KRAK
YES... I CAN FEEL IT.
YOUR DEATH IS DESTINED.
DO WE REALLY NEED MORE SMOKE?
SHUT UP!

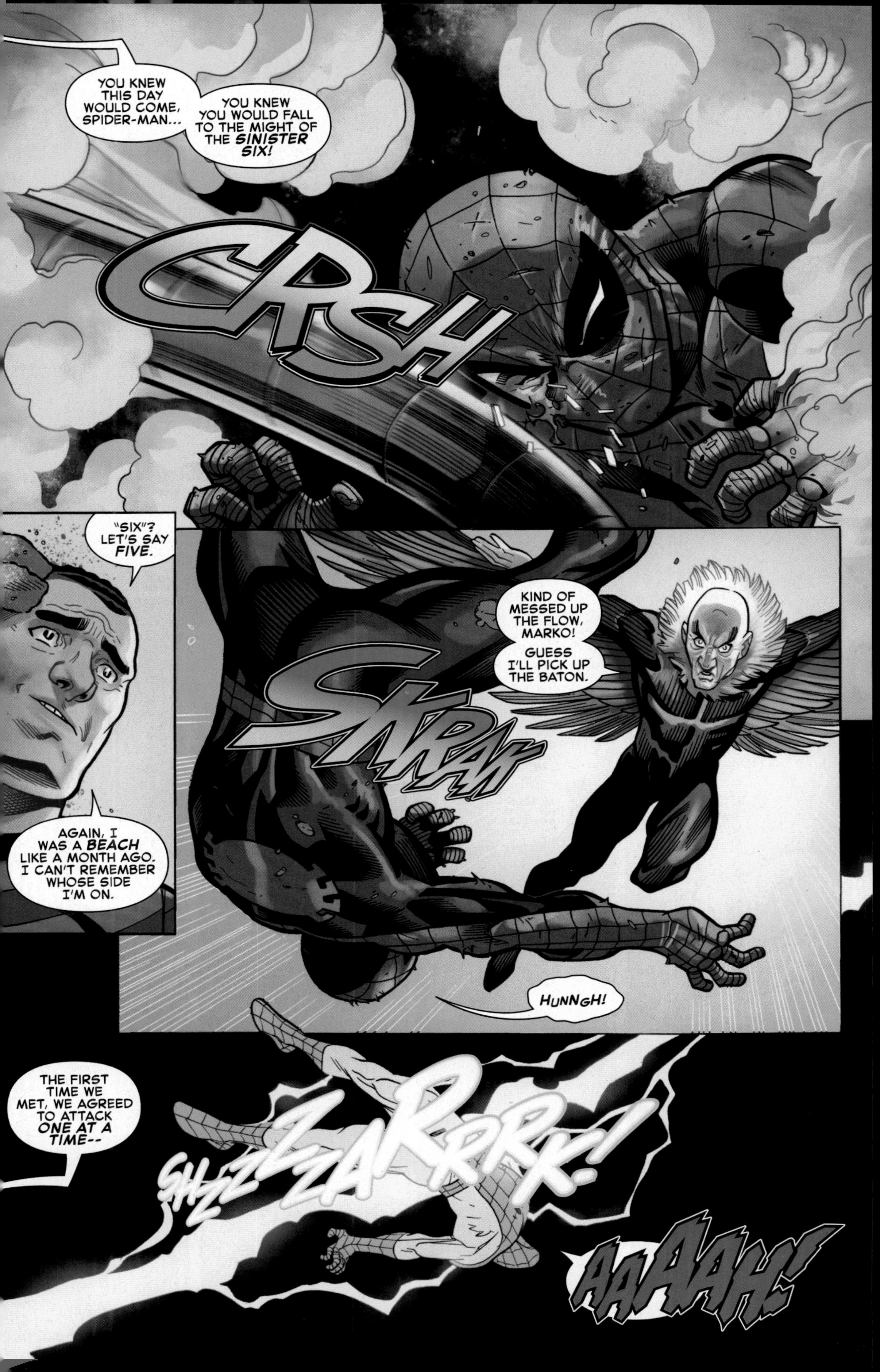
YOU KNEW THIS DAY WOULD COME, SPIDER-MAN...
YOU KNEW YOU WOULD FALL TO THE MIGHT OF THE SINISTER SIX!
CRSH
"SIX"? LET'S SAY FIVE.
AGAIN, I WAS A BEACH LIKE A MONTH AGO. I CAN'T REMEMBER WHOSE SIDE I'M ON.
KIND OF MESSED UP THE FLOW, MARKO!
GUESS I'LL PICK UP THE BATON.
SKRAK
HUNNGH!
THE FIRST TIME WE MET, WE AGREED TO ATTACK ONE AT A TIME--
SHZZZZARRRK!
AAAAH!

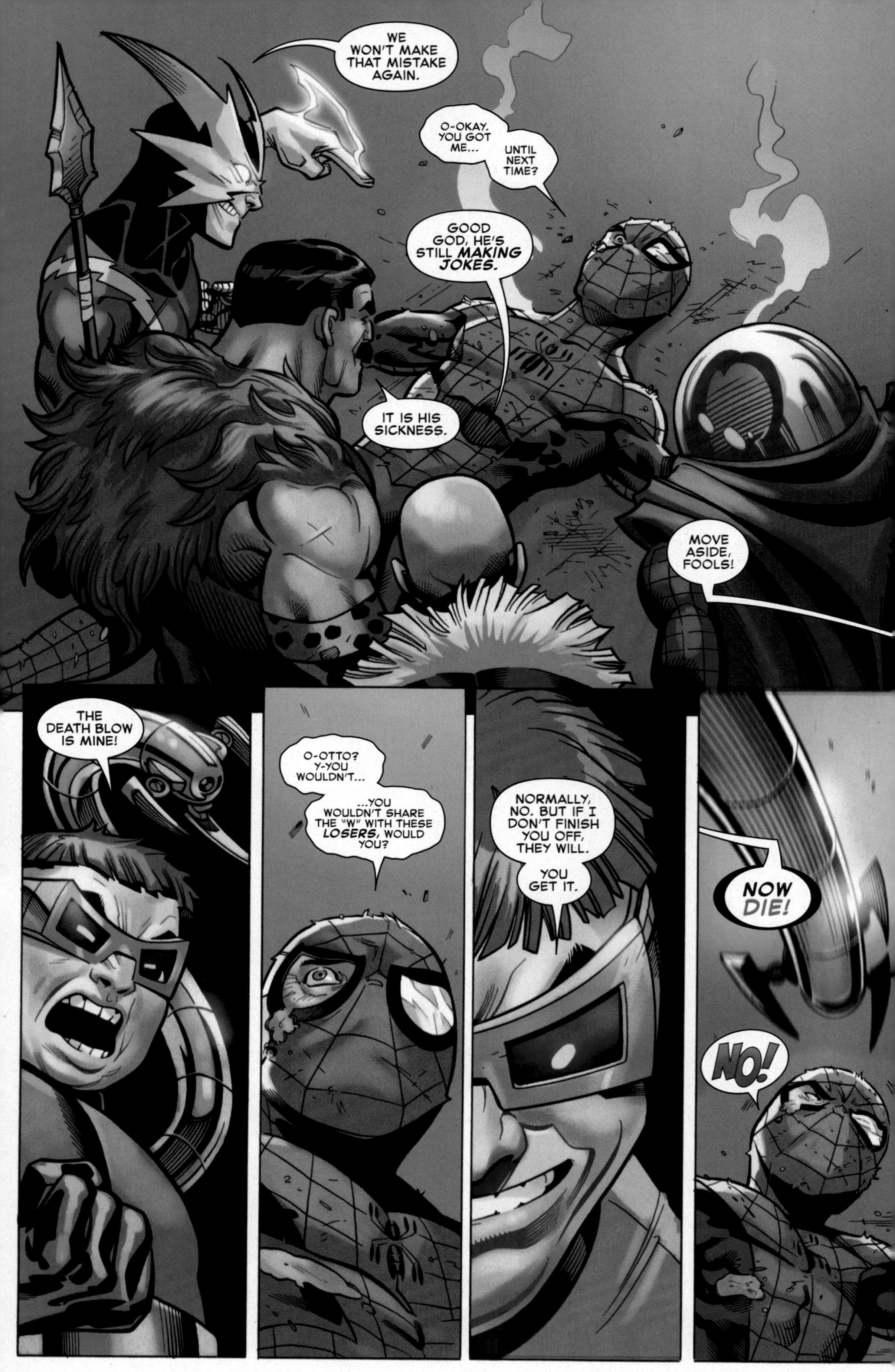

WE WON'T MAKE THAT MISTAKE AGAIN.
O-OKAY. YOU GOT ME...
UNTIL NEXT TIME?
GOOD GOD, HE'S STILL MAKING JOKES.
IT IS HIS SICKNESS.
MOVE ASIDE, FOOLS!
THE DEATH BLOW IS MINE!
O-OTTO? Y-YOU WOULDN'T...
...YOU WOULDN'T SHARE THE "W" WITH THESE LOSERS, WOULD YOU?
NORMALLY, NO. BUT IF I DON'T FINISH YOU OFF, THEY WILL.
YOU GET IT.
NOW DIE!
NO!

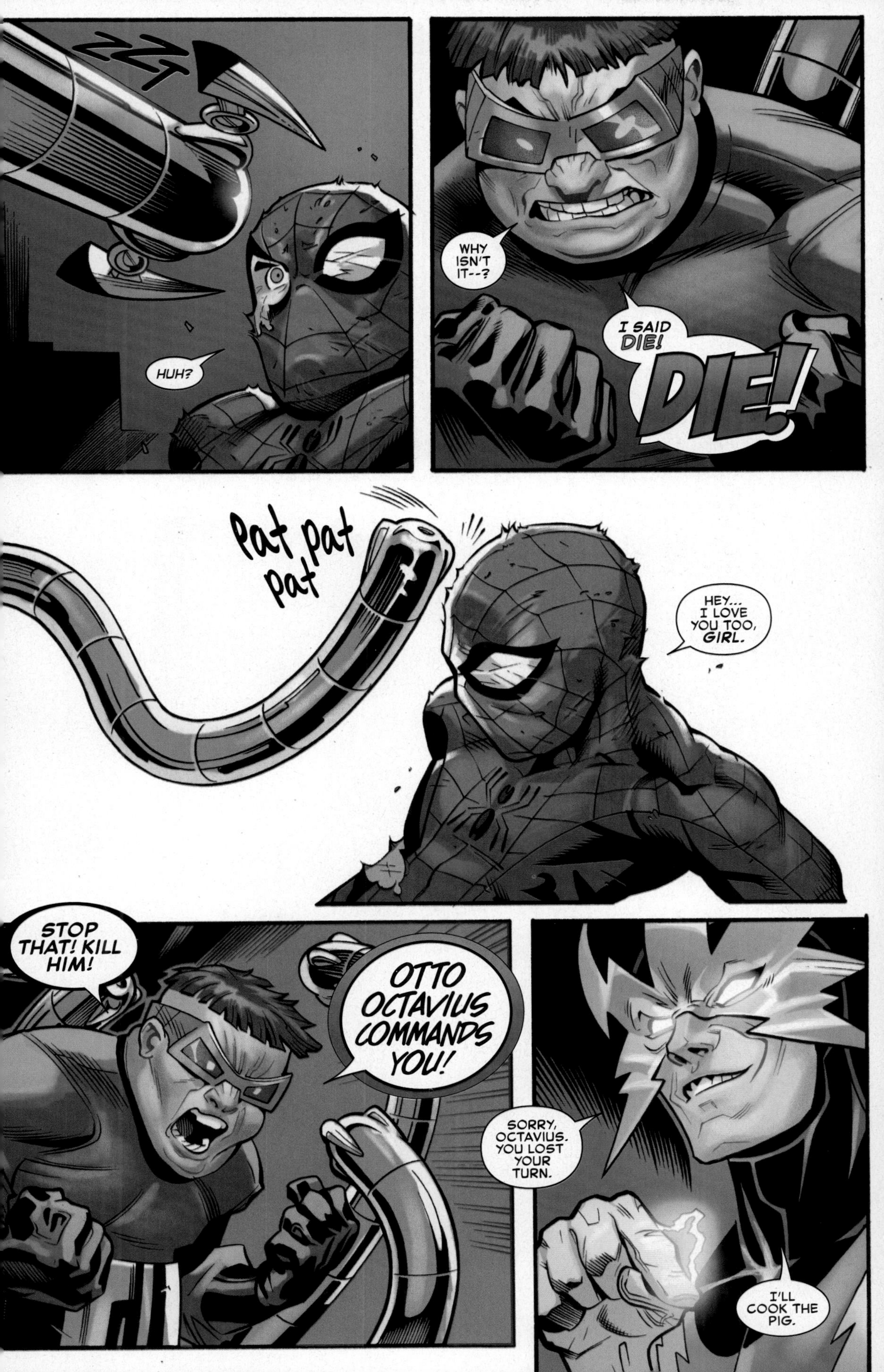
ZZZT
HUH?
WHY ISN'T IT--?
I SAID DIE!
DIE!
Pat pat pat
HEY... I LOVE YOU TOO, GIRL.
STOP THAT! KILL HIM!
OTTO OCTAVIUS COMMANDS YOU!
SORRY, OCTAVIUS. YOU LOST YOUR TURN.
I'LL COOK THE PIG.

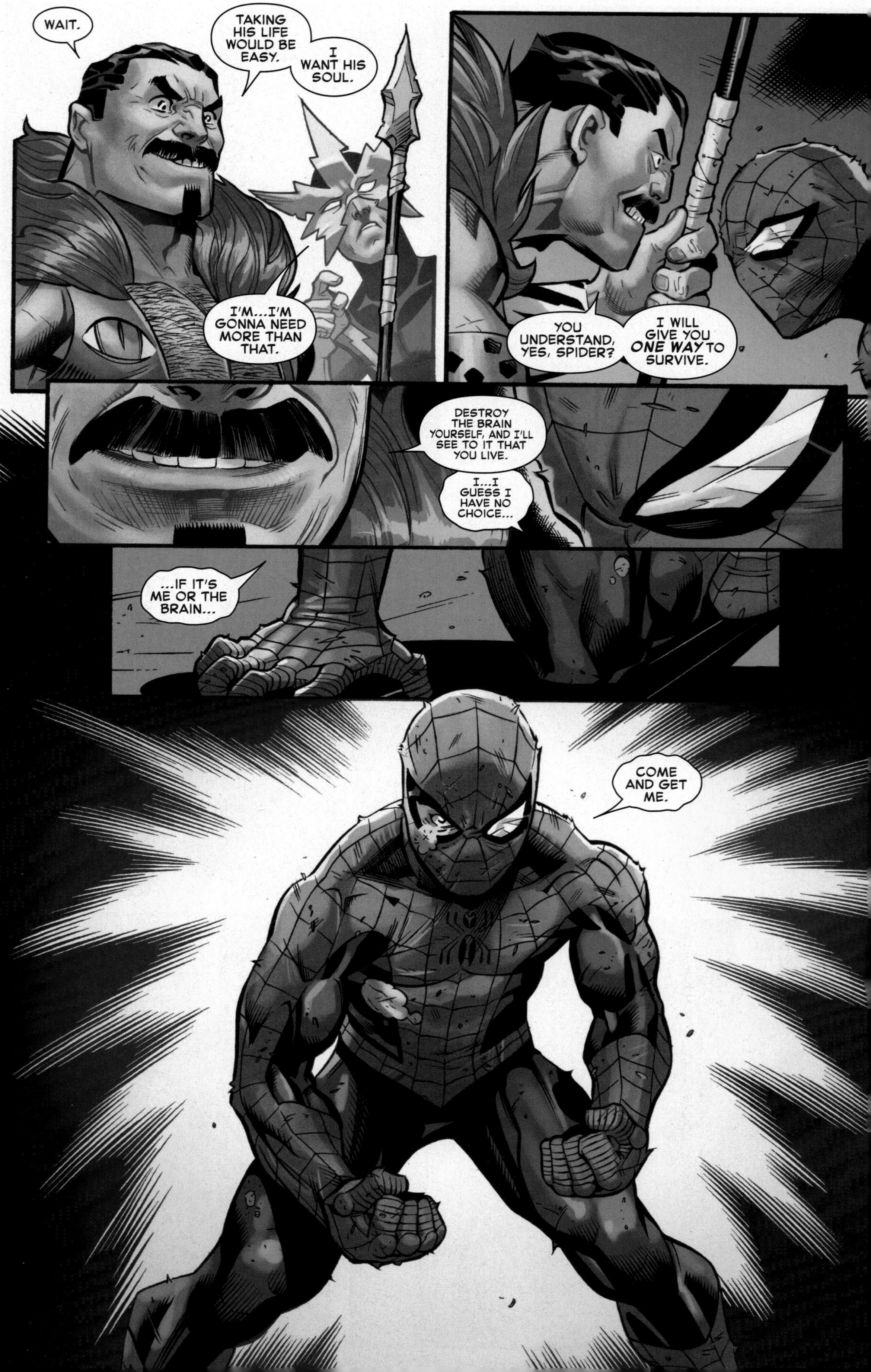
WAIT.
TAKING HIS LIFE WOULD BE EASY.
I WANT HIS SOUL.
I'M...I'M GONNA NEED MORE THAN THAT.
YOU UNDERSTAND, YES, SPIDER?
I WILL GIVE YOU ONE WAY TO SURVIVE.
DESTROY THE BRAIN YOURSELF, AND I'LL SEE TO IT THAT YOU LIVE.
I...I GUESS I HAVE NO CHOICE...
...IF IT'S ME OR THE BRAIN...
COME AND GET ME.

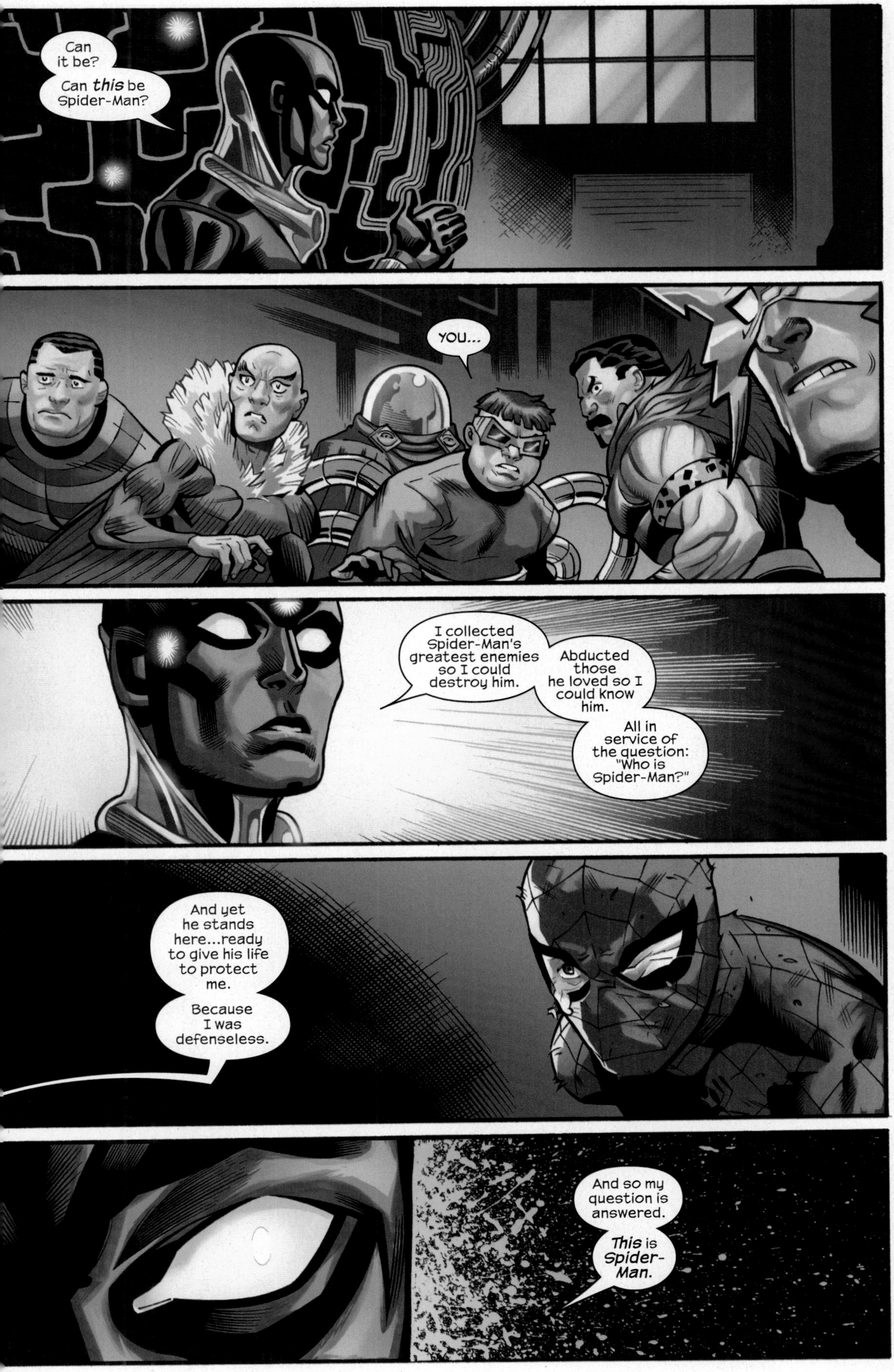

Can it be?
Can *this* be Spider-Man?
YOU...
I collected Spider-Man's greatest enemies so I could destroy him.
Abducted those he loved so I could know him.
All in service of the question: "Who is Spider-Man?"
And yet he stands here...ready to give his life to protect me.
Because I was defenseless.
And so my question is answered.
This is *Spider-Man.*

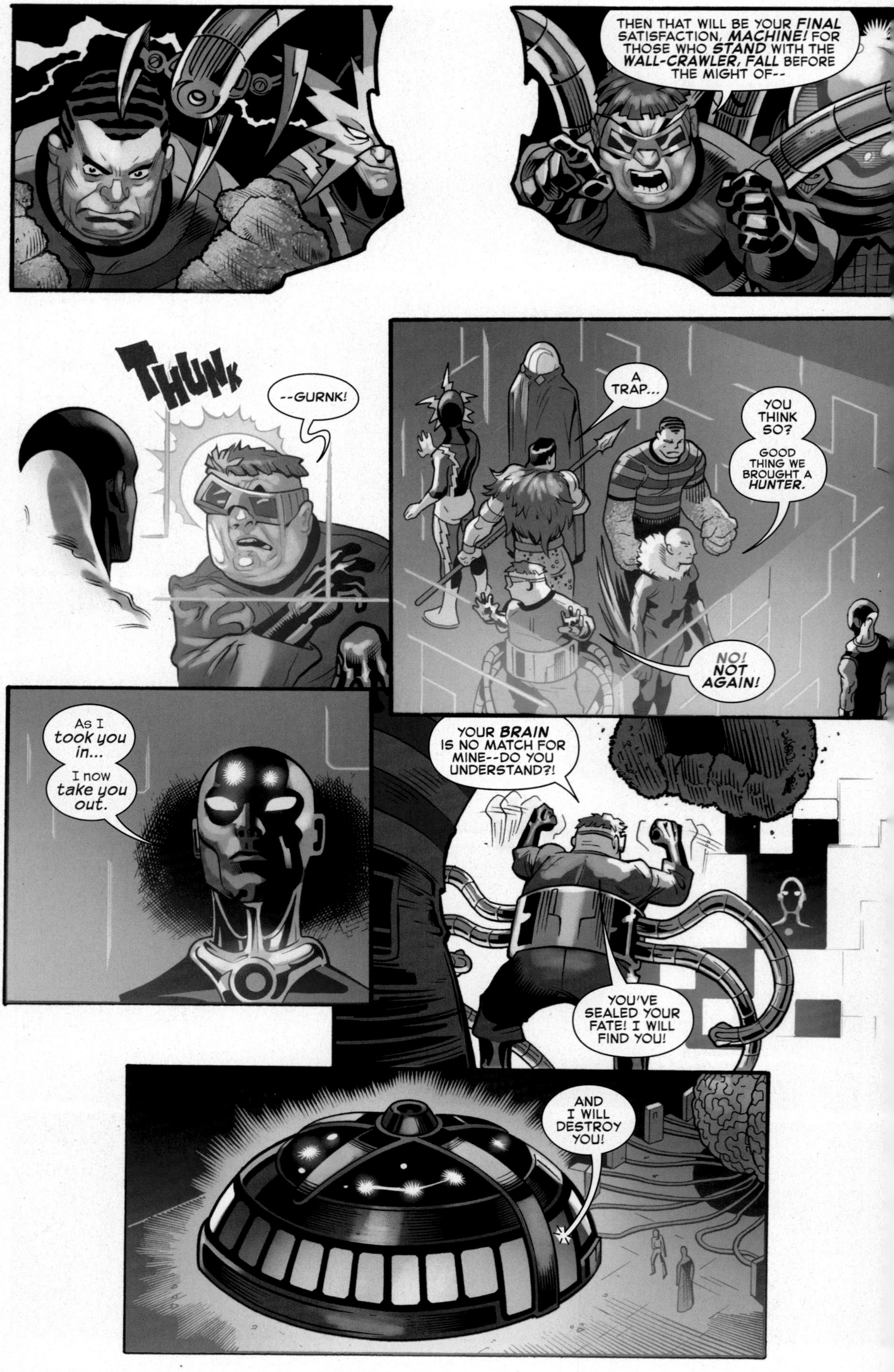
THEN THAT WILL BE YOUR FINAL SATISFACTION, MACHINE! FOR THOSE WHO STAND WITH THE WALL-CRAWLER, FALL BEFORE THE MIGHT OF--
THUNK
--GURNK!
A TRAP...
YOU THINK SO?
GOOD THING WE BROUGHT A HUNTER.
NO! NOT AGAIN!
As I took you in...
I now take you out.
YOUR BRAIN IS NO MATCH FOR MINE--DO YOU UNDERSTAND?!
YOU'VE SEALED YOUR FATE! I WILL FIND YOU!
AND I WILL DESTROY YOU!

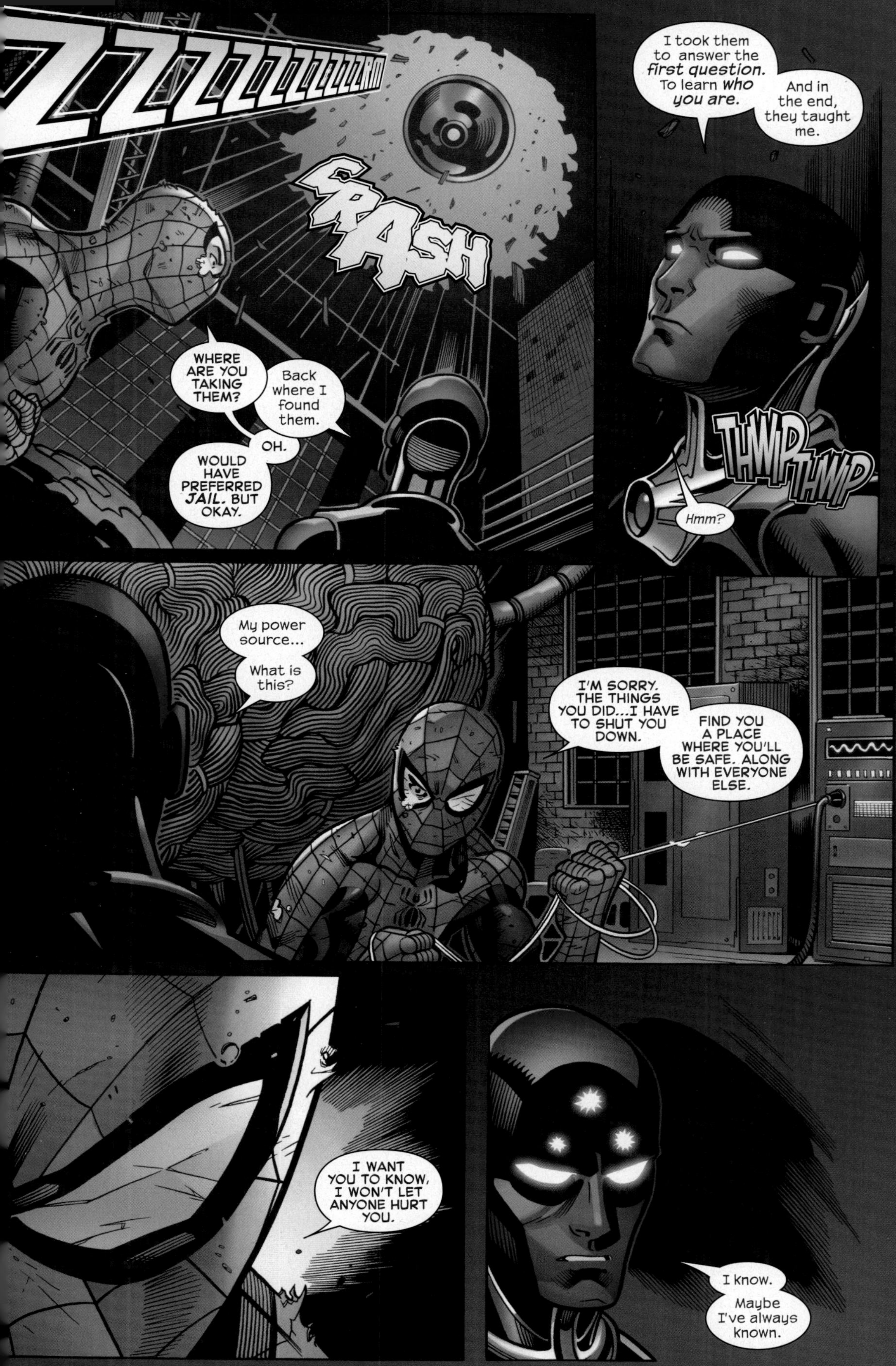
ZZZZZZZZZZZZZRM
CRASH
I took them to answer the *first question.* To learn *who you are.*
And in the end, they taught me.
WHERE ARE YOU TAKING THEM?
Back where I found them.
OH.
WOULD HAVE PREFERRED *JAIL.* BUT OKAY.
THWIP THWIP
Hmm?
My power source...
What is this?
I'M SORRY. THE THINGS YOU DID...I HAVE TO SHUT YOU DOWN.
FIND YOU A PLACE WHERE YOU'LL BE SAFE. ALONG WITH EVERYONE ELSE.
I WANT YOU TO KNOW, I WON'T LET ANYONE HURT YOU.
I know.
Maybe I've always known.

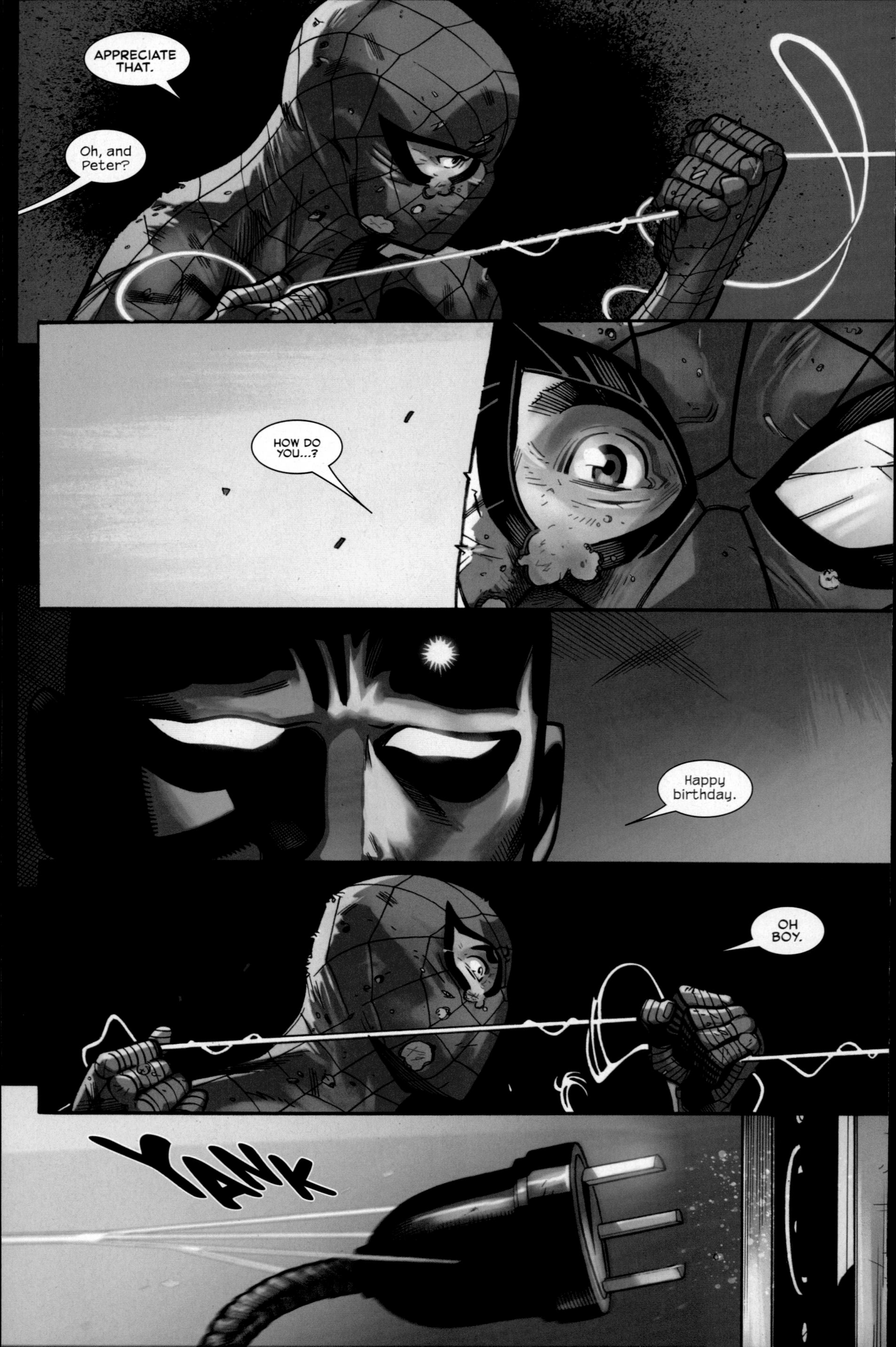
APPRECIATE THAT.
Oh, and Peter?
HOW DO YOU...?
Happy birthday.
OH BOY.
YANK

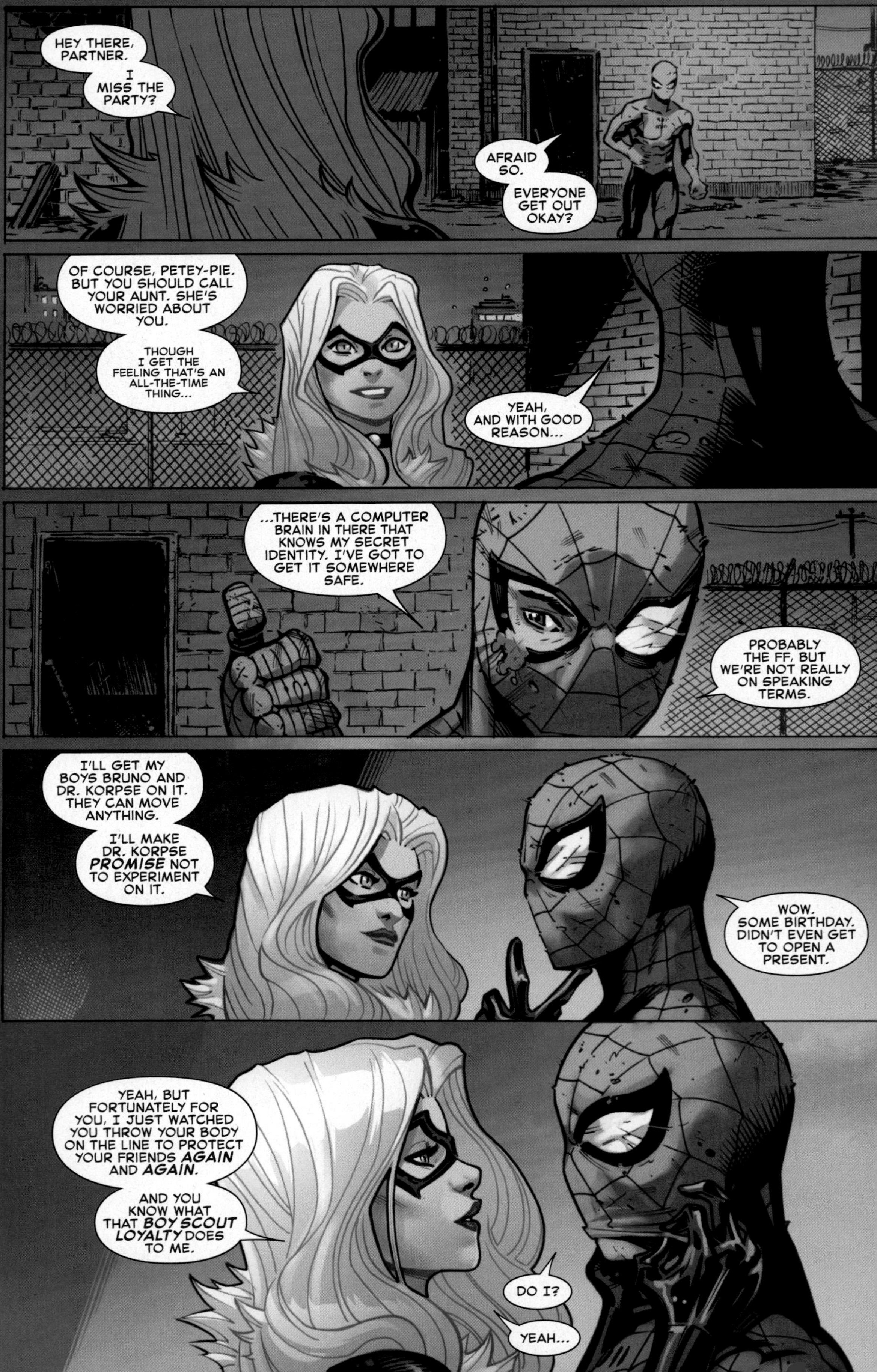
HEY THERE, PARTNER.
I MISS THE PARTY?
AFRAID SO.
EVERYONE GET OUT OKAY?
OF COURSE, PETEY-PIE. BUT YOU SHOULD CALL YOUR AUNT. SHE'S WORRIED ABOUT YOU.
THOUGH I GET THE FEELING THAT'S AN ALL-THE-TIME THING...
YEAH, AND WITH GOOD REASON...
...THERE'S A COMPUTER BRAIN IN THERE THAT KNOWS MY SECRET IDENTITY. I'VE GOT TO GET IT SOMEWHERE SAFE.
PROBABLY THE FF, BUT WE'RE NOT REALLY ON SPEAKING TERMS.
I'LL GET MY BOYS BRUNO AND DR. KORPSE ON IT. THEY CAN MOVE ANYTHING.
I'LL MAKE DR. KORPSE PROMISE NOT TO EXPERIMENT ON IT.
WOW. SOME BIRTHDAY. DIDN'T EVEN GET TO OPEN A PRESENT.
YEAH, BUT FORTUNATELY FOR YOU, I JUST WATCHED YOU THROW YOUR BODY ON THE LINE TO PROTECT YOUR FRIENDS AGAIN AND AGAIN.
AND YOU KNOW WHAT THAT BOY SCOUT LOYALTY DOES TO ME.
DO I?
YEAH...

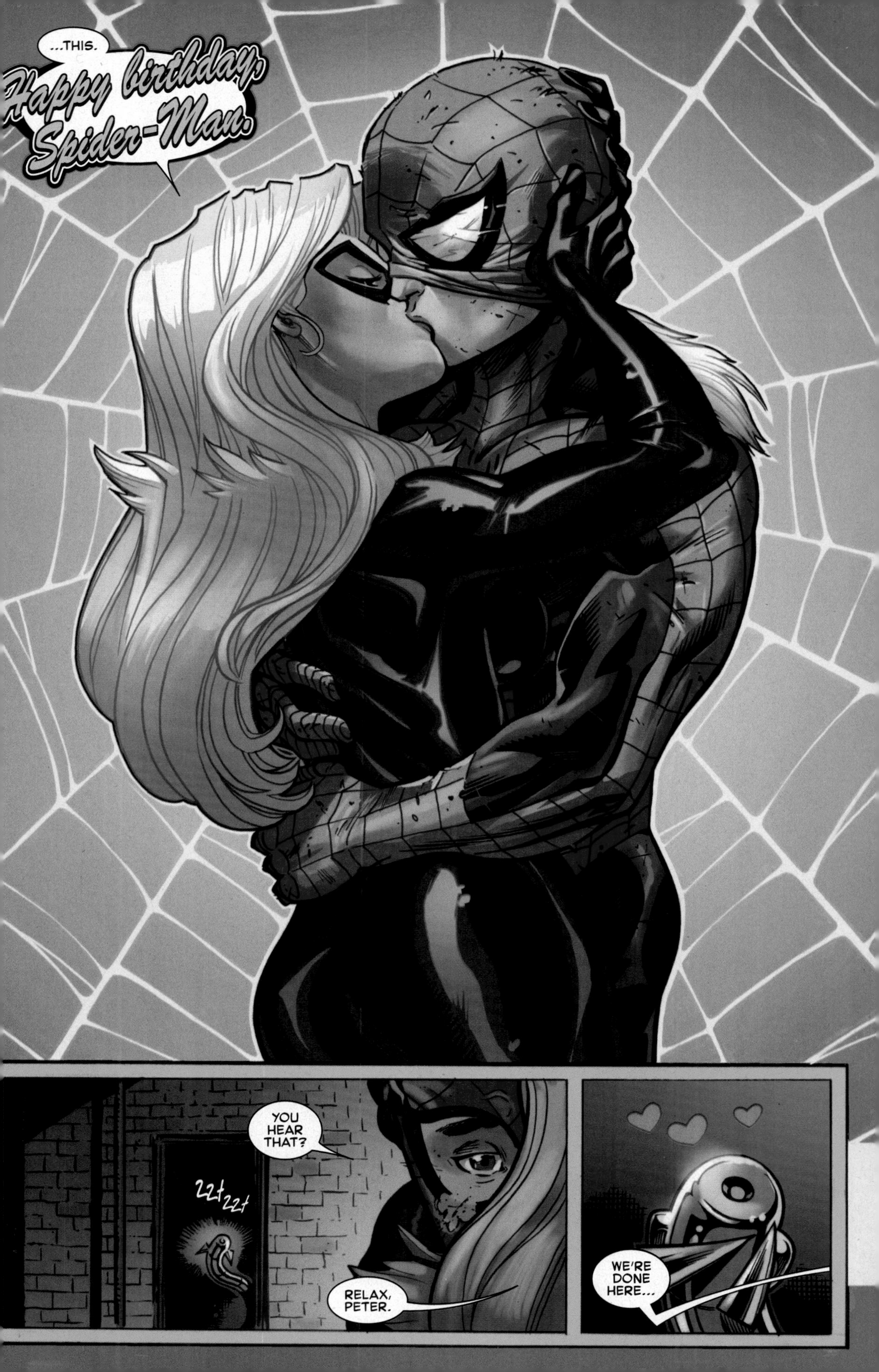
...THIS.
Happy birthday, Spider-Man.
YOU HEAR THAT?
ZZT ZZT
RELAX, PETER.
WE'RE DONE HERE...

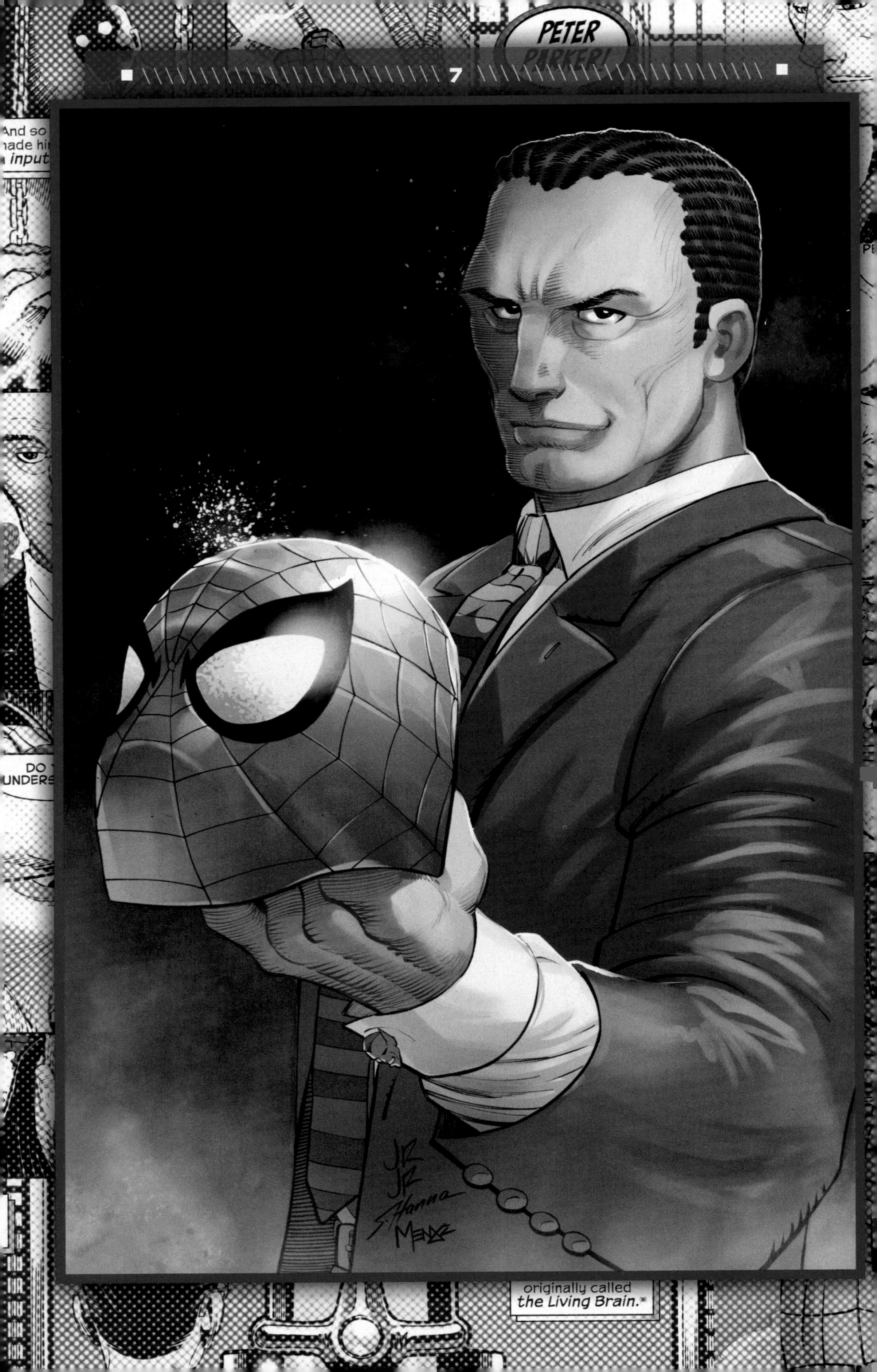
PETER PARKER!
originally called the Living Brain.

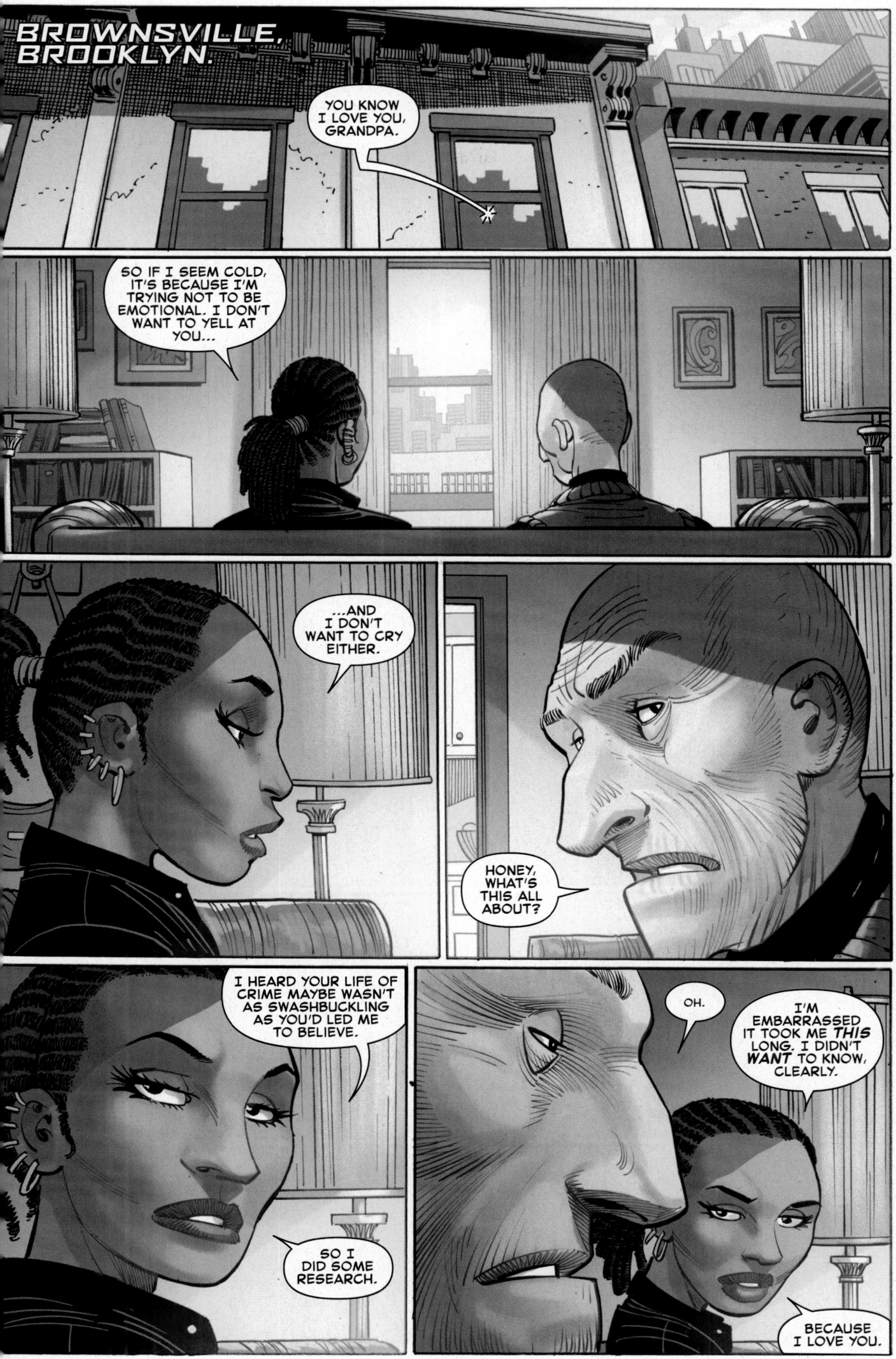
BROWNSVILLE, BROOKLYN.
YOU KNOW I LOVE YOU, GRANDPA.
SO IF I SEEM COLD, IT'S BECAUSE I'M TRYING NOT TO BE EMOTIONAL. I DON'T WANT TO YELL AT YOU...
...AND I DON'T WANT TO CRY EITHER.
HONEY, WHAT'S THIS ALL ABOUT?
I HEARD YOUR LIFE OF CRIME MAYBE WASN'T AS SWASHBUCKLING AS YOU'D LED ME TO BELIEVE.
SO I DID SOME RESEARCH.
OH.
I'M EMBARRASSED IT TOOK ME THIS LONG. I DIDN'T WANT TO KNOW, CLEARLY.
BECAUSE I LOVE YOU.

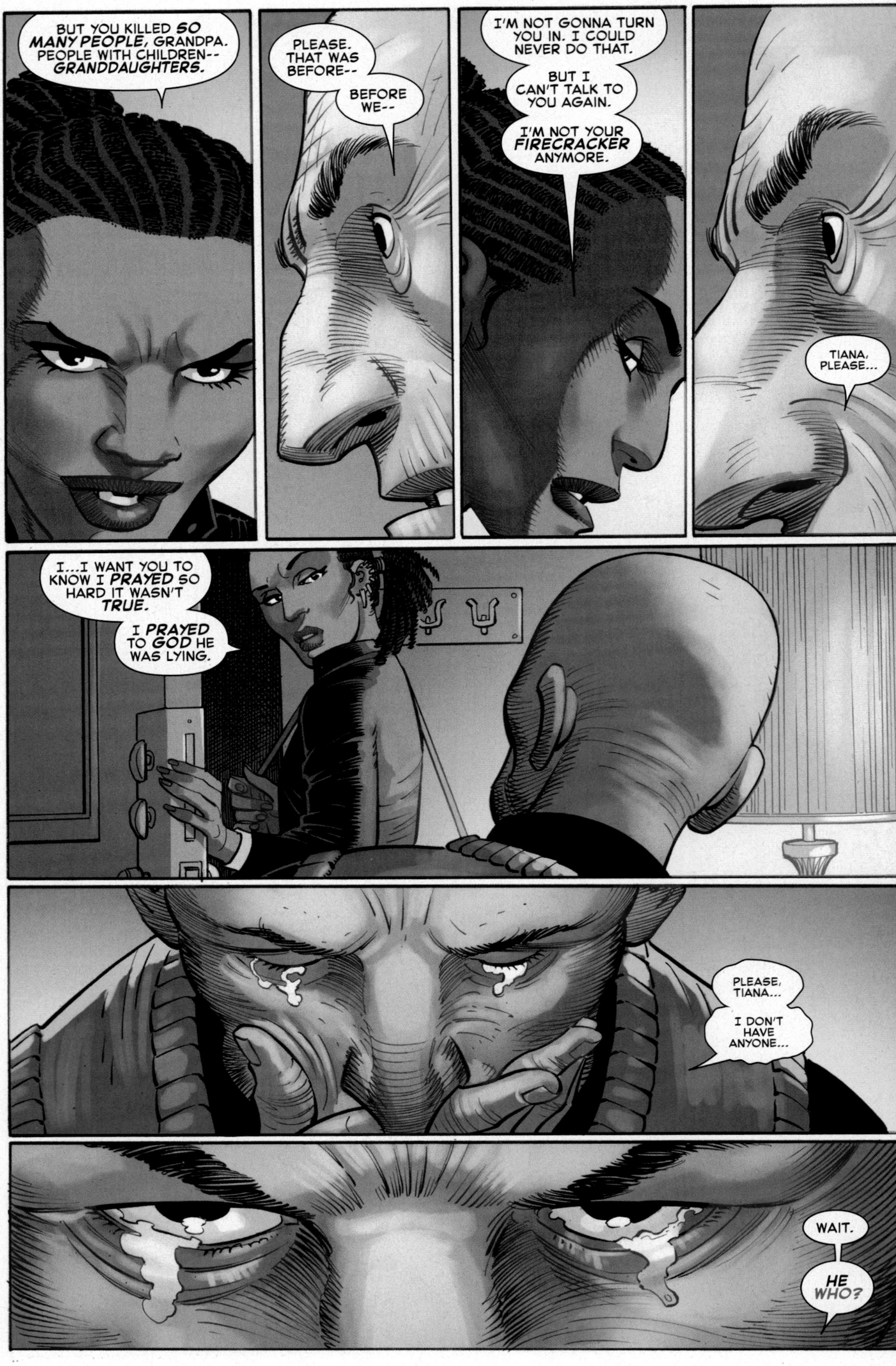
BUT YOU KILLED SO MANY PEOPLE, GRANDPA. PEOPLE WITH CHILDREN-- GRANDDAUGHTERS.
PLEASE. THAT WAS BEFORE--
BEFORE WE--
I'M NOT GONNA TURN YOU IN. I COULD NEVER DO THAT.
BUT I CAN'T TALK TO YOU AGAIN.
I'M NOT YOUR FIRECRACKER ANYMORE.
TIANA, PLEASE...
I...I WANT YOU TO KNOW I PRAYED SO HARD IT WASN'T TRUE.
I PRAYED TO GOD HE WAS LYING.
PLEASE, TIANA...
I DON'T HAVE ANYONE...
WAIT.
HE WHO?

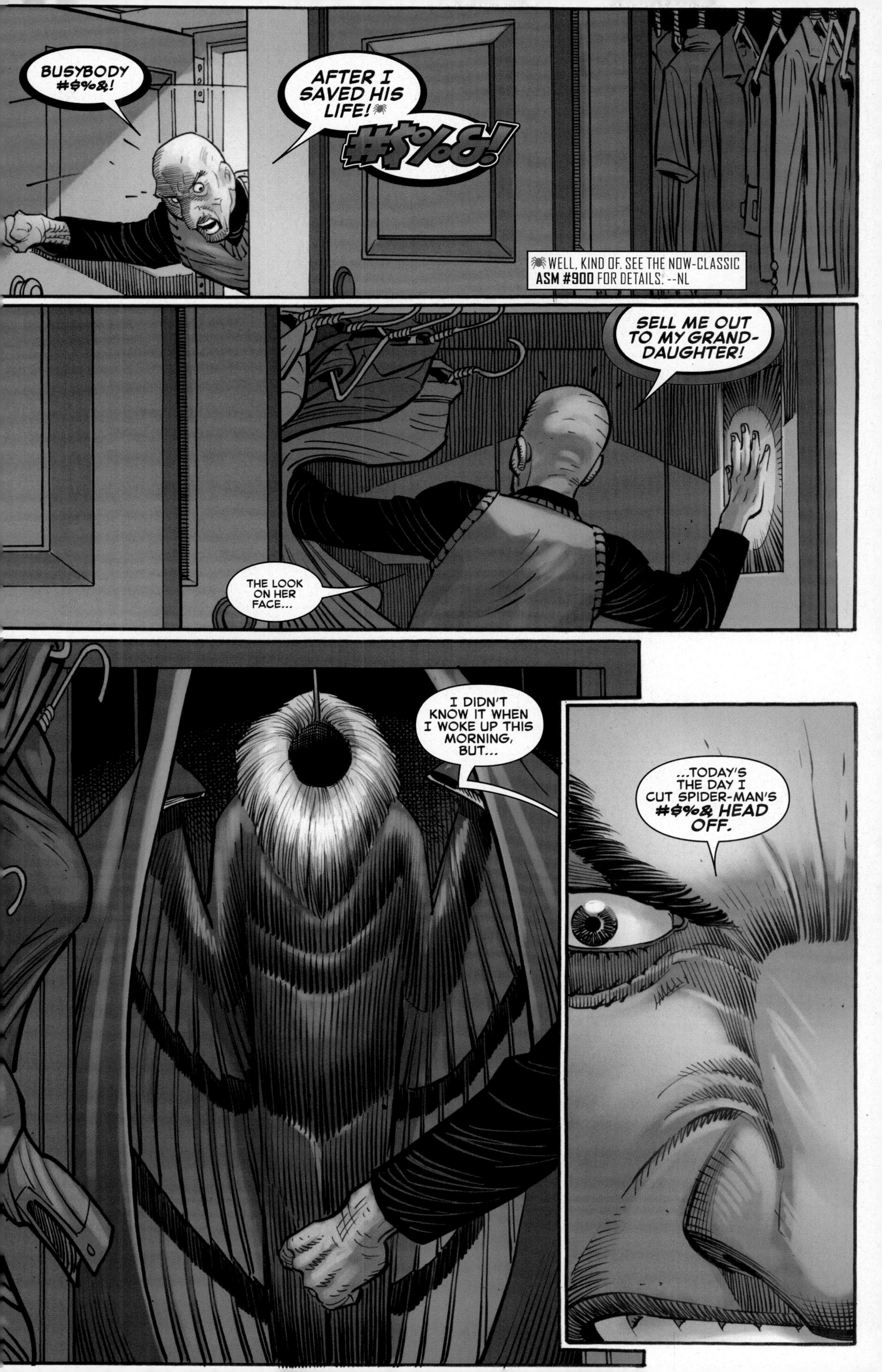
BUSYBODY #$%&!
AFTER I SAVED HIS LIFE!
#$%&!
WELL, KIND OF. SEE THE NOW-CLASSIC ASM #900 FOR DETAILS. --NL
SELL ME OUT TO MY GRAND-DAUGHTER!
THE LOOK ON HER FACE...
I DIDN'T KNOW IT WHEN I WOKE UP THIS MORNING, BUT...
...TODAY'S THE DAY I CUT SPIDER-MAN'S #$%& HEAD OFF.

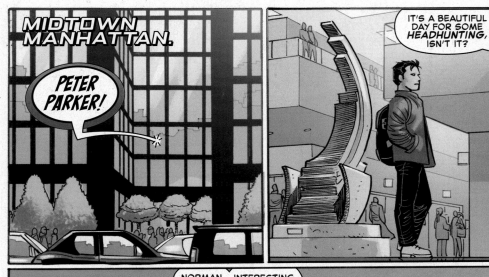

PETER PARKER!

IT'S A BEAUTIFUL DAY FOR SOME *HEADHUNTING*, ISN'T IT?

NORMAN. HELLO. INTERESTING CHOICE OF WORDS.

OH, I KNOW I INVITED YOU FOR A PEEK AT THE NEW OFFICES. BUT *SURELY* YOU KNEW I HAD ULTERIOR MOTIVES.

I TAKE THAT AS A GIVEN, YES.

OKAY, LET'S PUT IT ALL ON THE TABLE. I WOULD LIKE TO OFFER YOU A POSITION AT MY NEW COMPANY.

I KNOW YOU'LL BE A HARD SELL, SO PLEASE EXCUSE THE *HARD SELL*.

THIS OSCORP IS ABOUT FINDING ALTRUISTIC USES FOR MY *ENGINEERING PROFICIENCIES*.

WITH MY BACKGROUND IN... *UNIQUE* AERODYNAMICS, AVIATION SEEMED LIKE THE PLACE TO START.

ELECTRIC PLASMA JET ENGINES...?

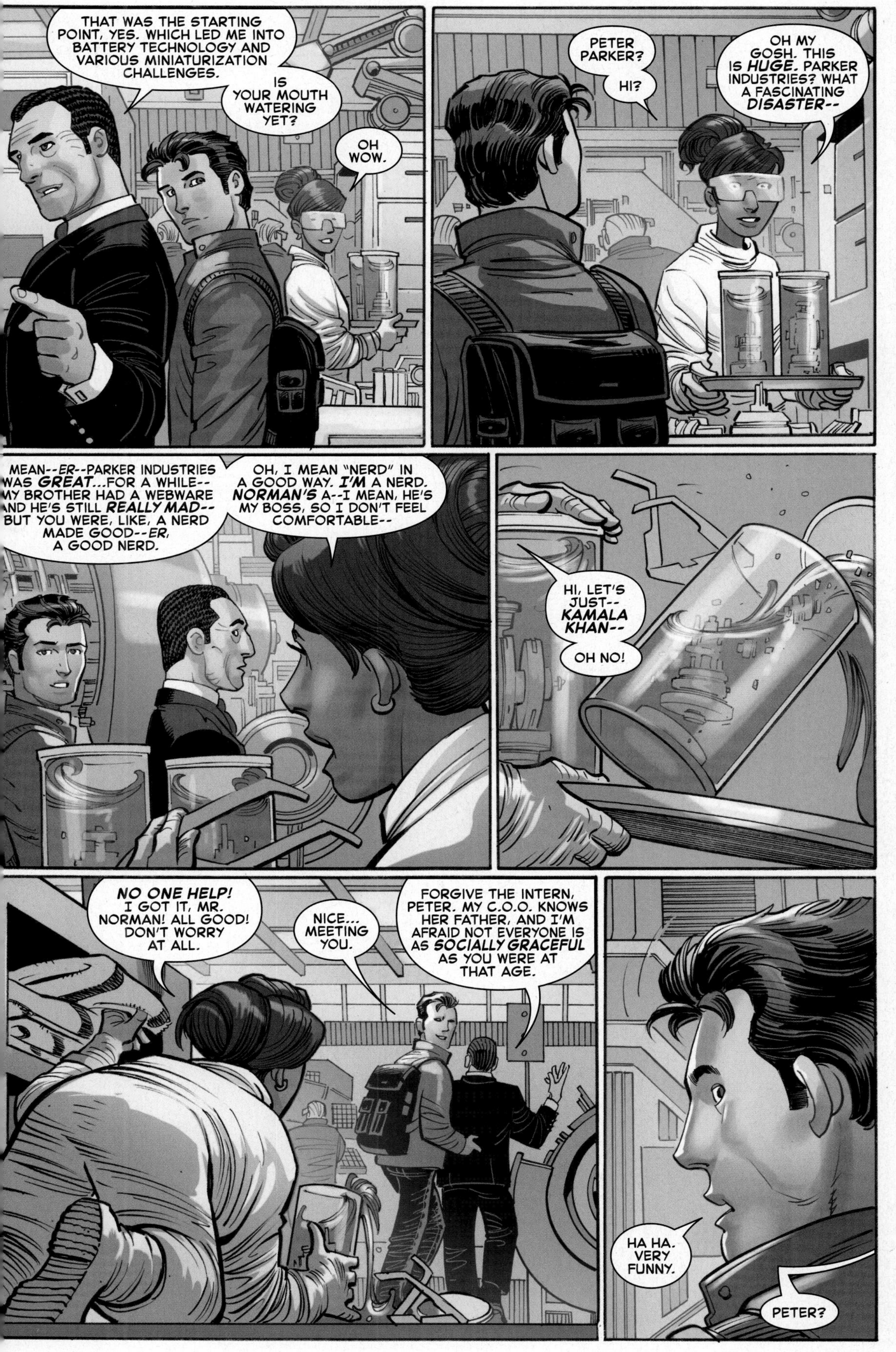
THAT WAS THE STARTING POINT, YES. WHICH LED ME INTO BATTERY TECHNOLOGY AND VARIOUS MINIATURIZATION CHALLENGES.
IS YOUR MOUTH WATERING YET?
OH WOW.
PETER PARKER?
HI?
OH MY GOSH. THIS IS HUGE. PARKER INDUSTRIES? WHAT A FASCINATING DISASTER--
I MEAN--ER--PARKER INDUSTRIES WAS GREAT...FOR A WHILE--MY BROTHER HAD A WEBWARE AND HE'S STILL REALLY MAD--BUT YOU WERE, LIKE, A NERD MADE GOOD--ER, A GOOD NERD.
OH, I MEAN "NERD" IN A GOOD WAY. I'M A NERD. NORMAN'S A--I MEAN, HE'S MY BOSS, SO I DON'T FEEL COMFORTABLE--
HI, LET'S JUST--KAMALA KHAN--
OH NO!
NO ONE HELP! I GOT IT, MR. NORMAN! ALL GOOD! DON'T WORRY AT ALL.
NICE... MEETING YOU.
FORGIVE THE INTERN, PETER. MY C.O.O. KNOWS HER FATHER, AND I'M AFRAID NOT EVERYONE IS AS SOCIALLY GRACEFUL AS YOU WERE AT THAT AGE.
HA HA. VERY FUNNY.
PETER?

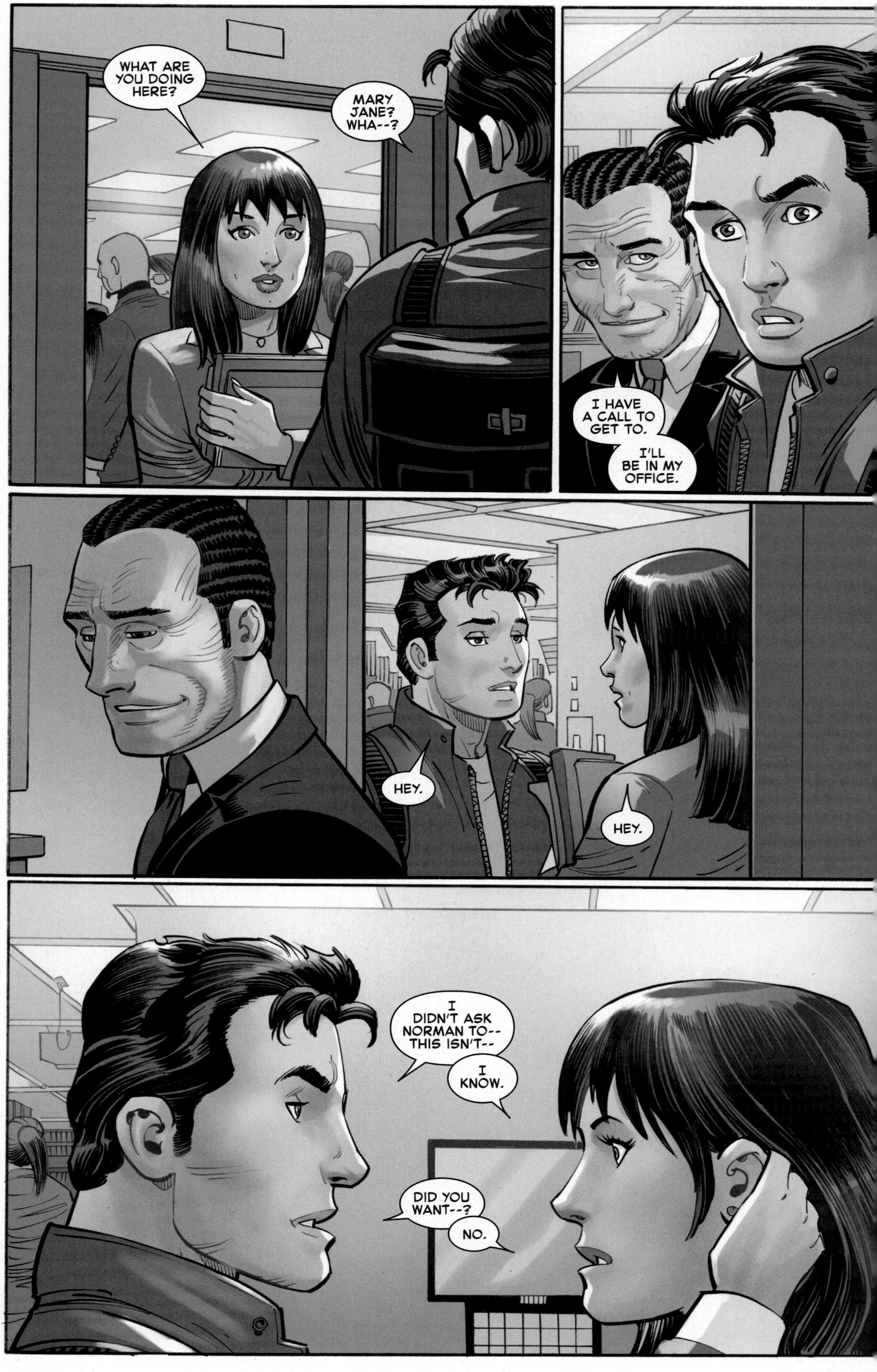
WHAT ARE YOU DOING HERE?
MARY JANE? WHA--?
I HAVE A CALL TO GET TO.
I'LL BE IN MY OFFICE.
HEY.
HEY.
I DIDN'T ASK NORMAN TO-- THIS ISN'T--
I KNOW.
DID YOU WANT--?
NO.

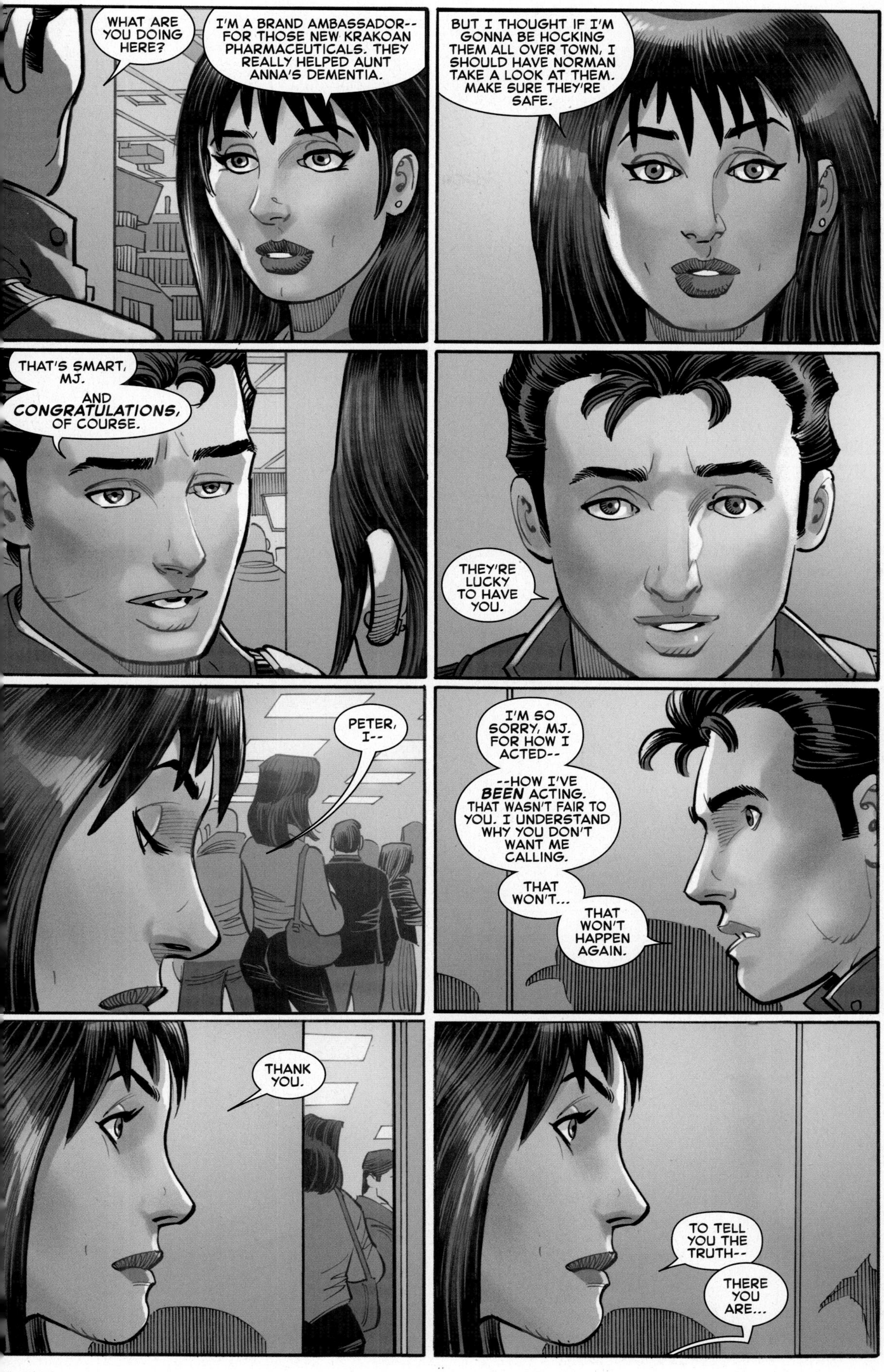
WHAT ARE YOU DOING HERE?
I'M A BRAND AMBASSADOR-- FOR THOSE NEW KRAKOAN PHARMACEUTICALS. THEY REALLY HELPED AUNT ANNA'S DEMENTIA.
BUT I THOUGHT IF I'M GONNA BE HOCKING THEM ALL OVER TOWN, I SHOULD HAVE NORMAN TAKE A LOOK AT THEM. MAKE SURE THEY'RE SAFE.
THAT'S SMART, MJ.
AND *CONGRATULATIONS,* OF COURSE.
THEY'RE LUCKY TO HAVE YOU.
PETER, I--
I'M SO SORRY, MJ. FOR HOW I ACTED--
--HOW I'VE *BEEN* ACTING. THAT WASN'T FAIR TO YOU. I UNDERSTAND WHY YOU DON'T WANT ME CALLING.
THAT WON'T...
THAT WON'T HAPPEN AGAIN.
THANK YOU.
TO TELL YOU THE TRUTH--
THERE YOU ARE...

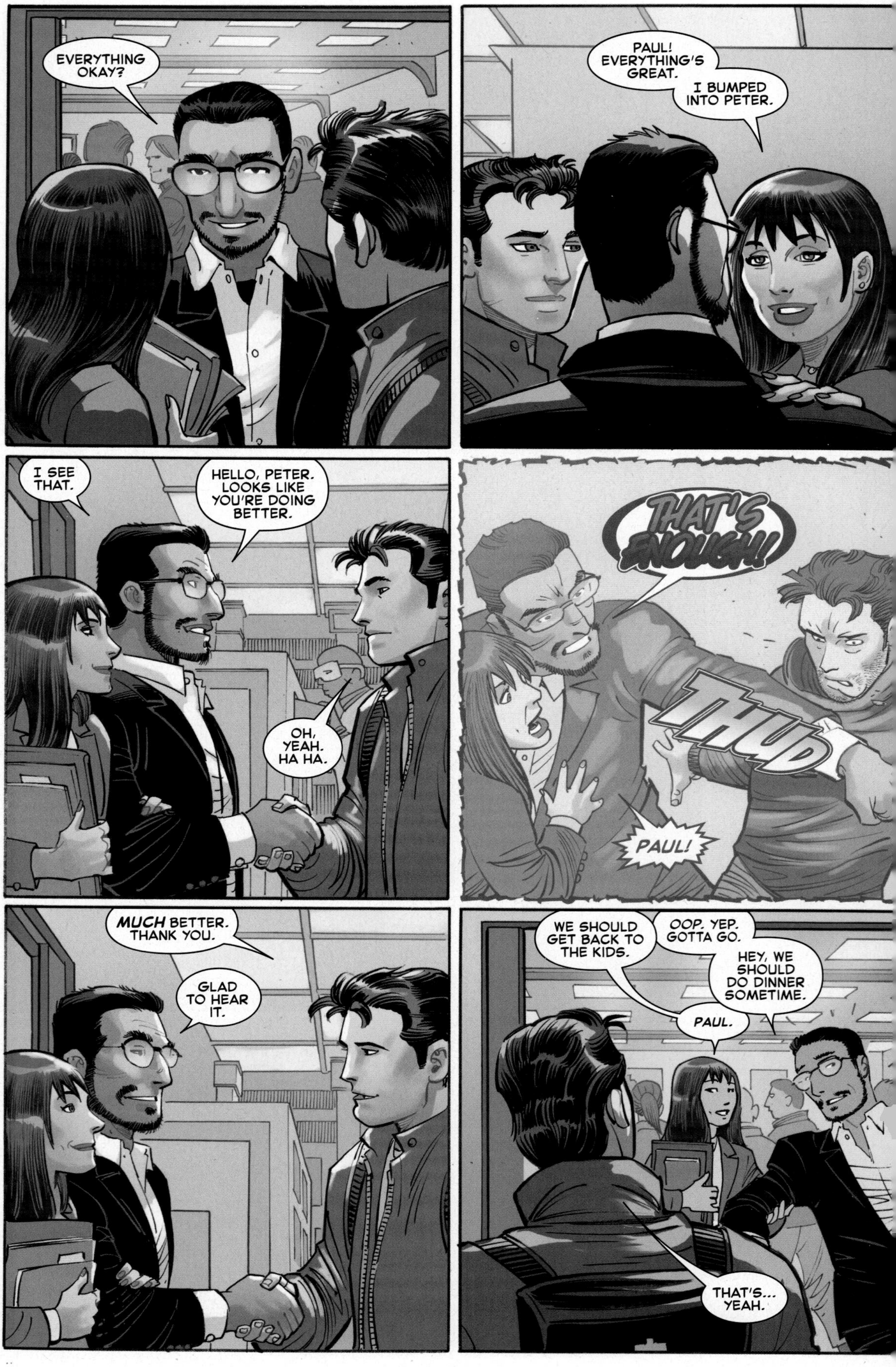
EVERYTHING OKAY?
PAUL! EVERYTHING'S GREAT.
I BUMPED INTO PETER.
I SEE THAT.
HELLO, PETER. LOOKS LIKE YOU'RE DOING BETTER.
OH, YEAH. HA HA.
THAT'S ENOUGH!
THUD
PAUL!
MUCH BETTER. THANK YOU.
GLAD TO HEAR IT.
WE SHOULD GET BACK TO THE KIDS.
PAUL.
OOP. YEP. GOTTA GO.
HEY, WE SHOULD DO DINNER SOMETIME.
THAT'S... YEAH.

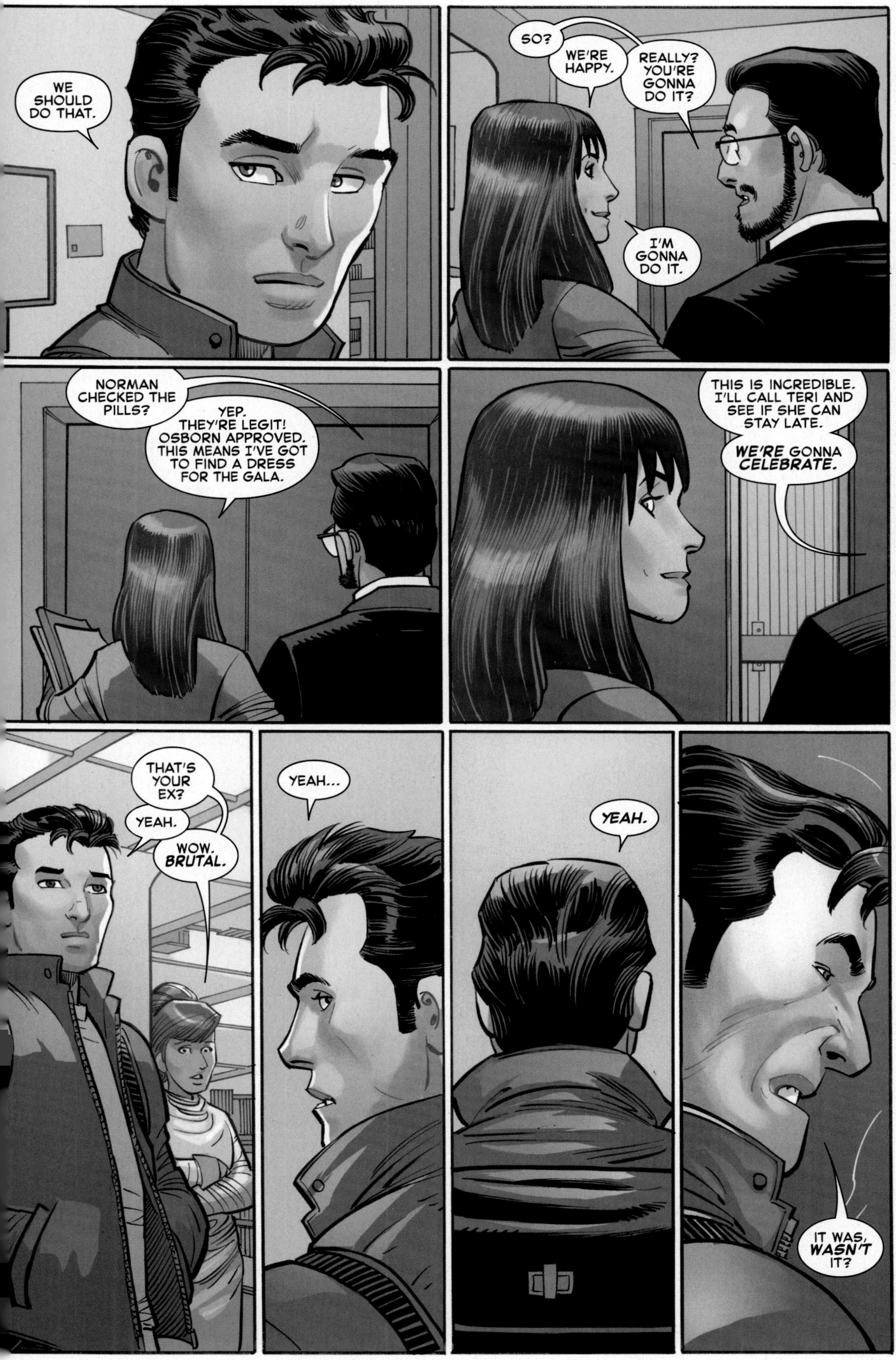
WE SHOULD DO THAT.
SO?
WE'RE HAPPY.
REALLY? YOU'RE GONNA DO IT?
I'M GONNA DO IT.
NORMAN CHECKED THE PILLS?
YEP. THEY'RE LEGIT! OSBORN APPROVED. THIS MEANS I'VE GOT TO FIND A DRESS FOR THE GALA.
THIS IS INCREDIBLE. I'LL CALL TERI AND SEE IF SHE CAN STAY LATE.
WE'RE GONNA CELEBRATE.
THAT'S YOUR EX?
YEAH.
WOW. BRUTAL.
YEAH...
YEAH.
IT WAS, WASN'T IT?

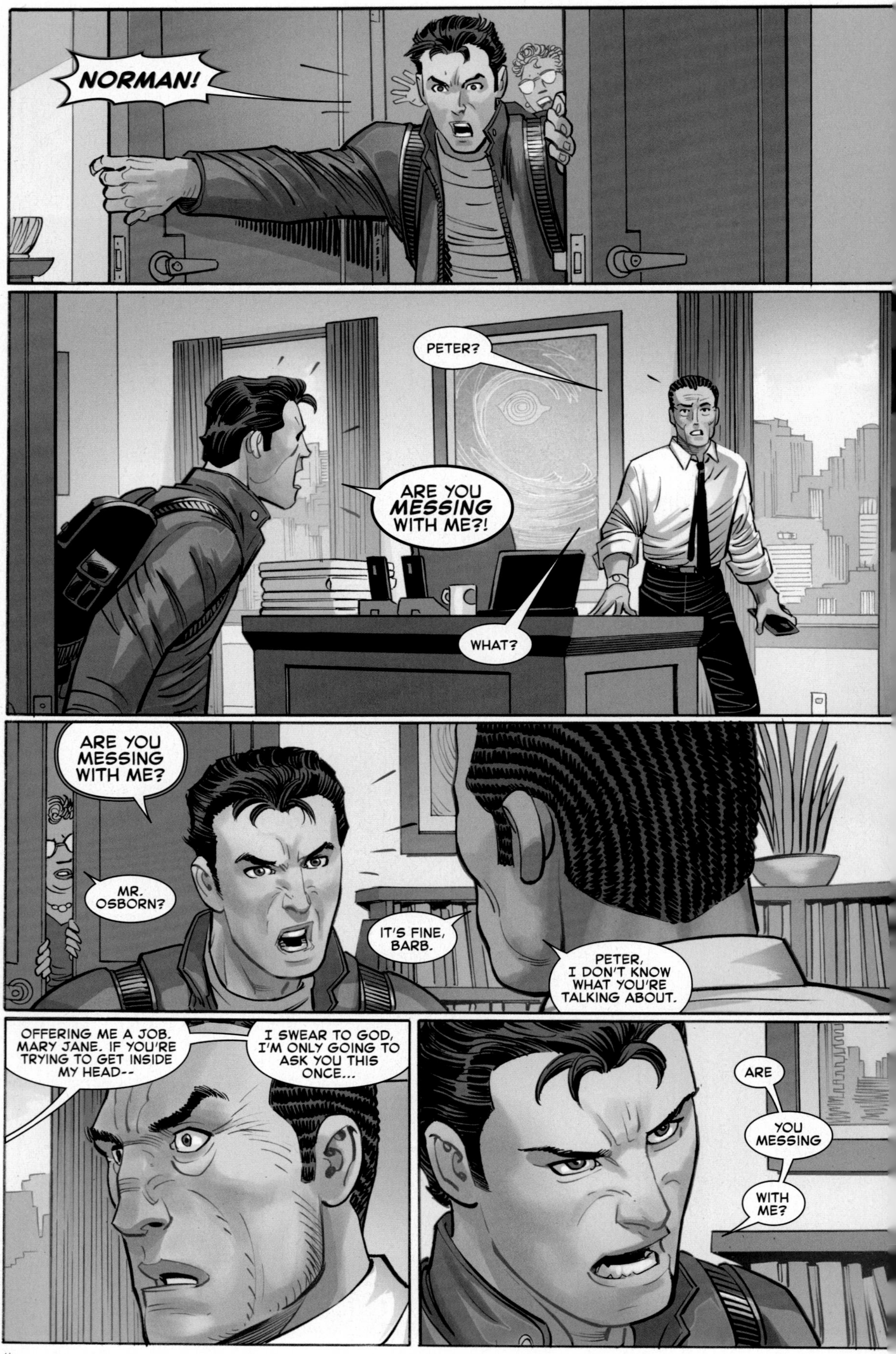
NORMAN!
PETER?
ARE YOU MESSING WITH ME?!
WHAT?
ARE YOU MESSING WITH ME?
MR. OSBORN?
IT'S FINE, BARB.
PETER, I DON'T KNOW WHAT YOU'RE TALKING ABOUT.
I SWEAR TO GOD, I'M ONLY GOING TO ASK YOU THIS ONCE...
OFFERING ME A JOB. MARY JANE. IF YOU'RE TRYING TO GET INSIDE MY HEAD--
ARE
YOU MESSING
WITH ME?

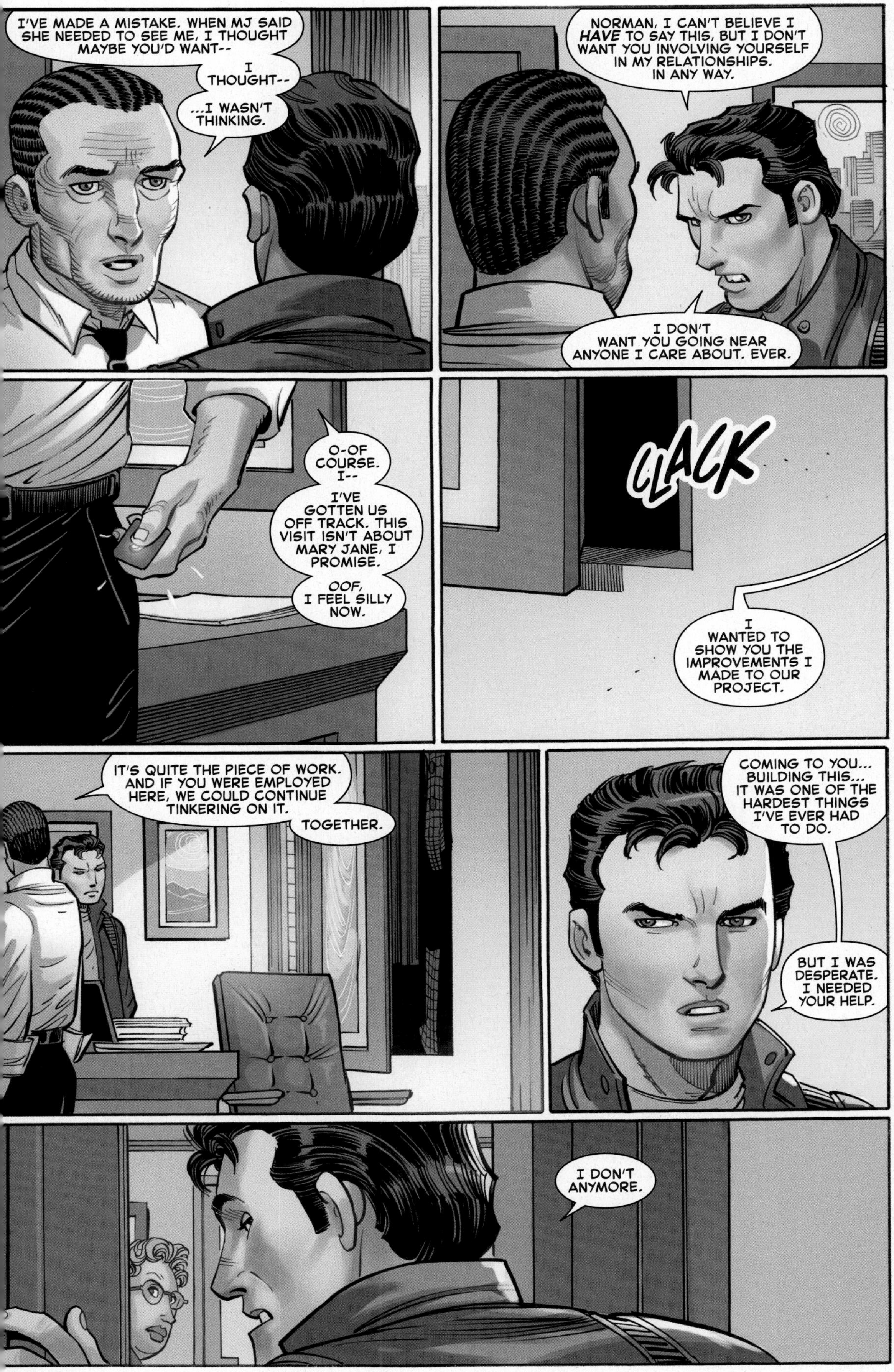
I'VE MADE A MISTAKE. WHEN MJ SAID SHE NEEDED TO SEE ME, I THOUGHT MAYBE YOU'D WANT--
I THOUGHT--
...I WASN'T THINKING.
NORMAN, I CAN'T BELIEVE I *HAVE* TO SAY THIS, BUT I DON'T WANT YOU INVOLVING YOURSELF IN MY RELATIONSHIPS. IN ANY WAY.
I DON'T WANT YOU GOING NEAR ANYONE I CARE ABOUT. EVER.
O-OF COURSE. I--
I'VE GOTTEN US OFF TRACK. THIS VISIT ISN'T ABOUT MARY JANE, I PROMISE.
OOF, I FEEL SILLY NOW.
CLACK
I WANTED TO SHOW YOU THE IMPROVEMENTS I MADE TO OUR PROJECT.
IT'S QUITE THE PIECE OF WORK. AND IF YOU WERE EMPLOYED HERE, WE COULD CONTINUE TINKERING ON IT.
TOGETHER.
COMING TO YOU... BUILDING THIS... IT WAS ONE OF THE HARDEST THINGS I'VE EVER HAD TO DO.
BUT I WAS DESPERATE. I NEEDED YOUR HELP.
I DON'T ANYMORE.

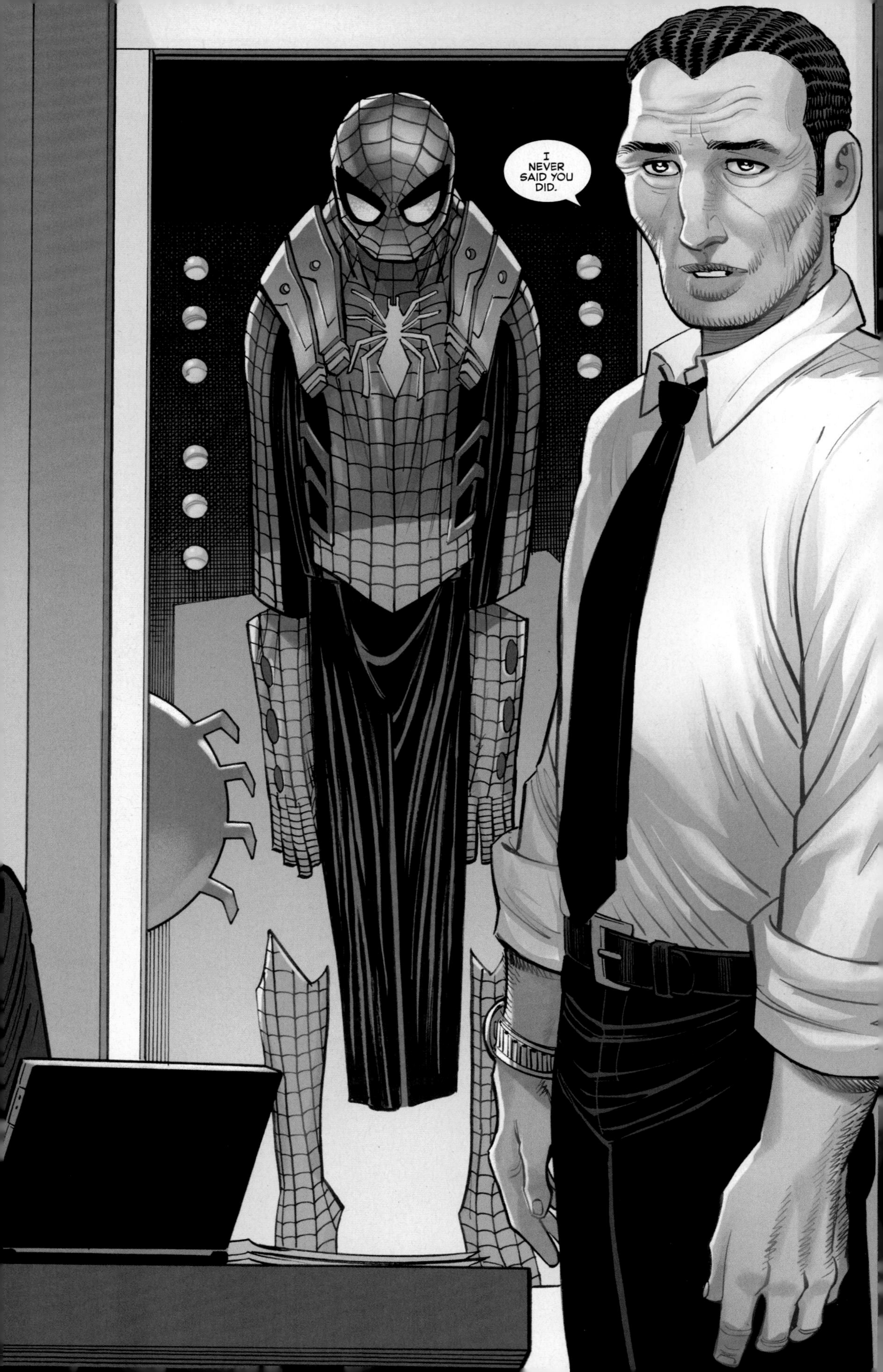
I NEVER SAID YOU DID.

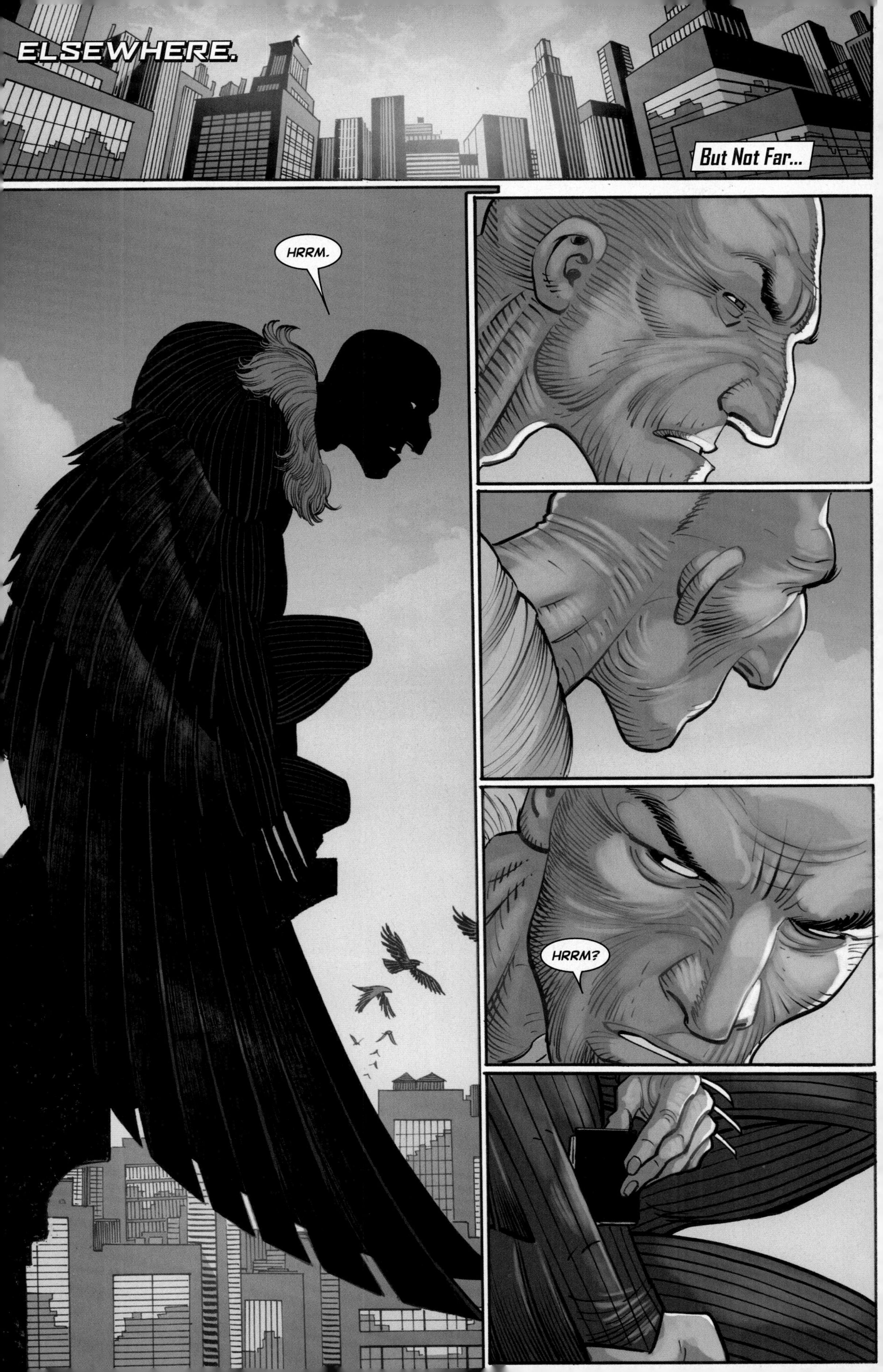
ELSEWHERE.
But Not Far...
HRRM.
HRRM?

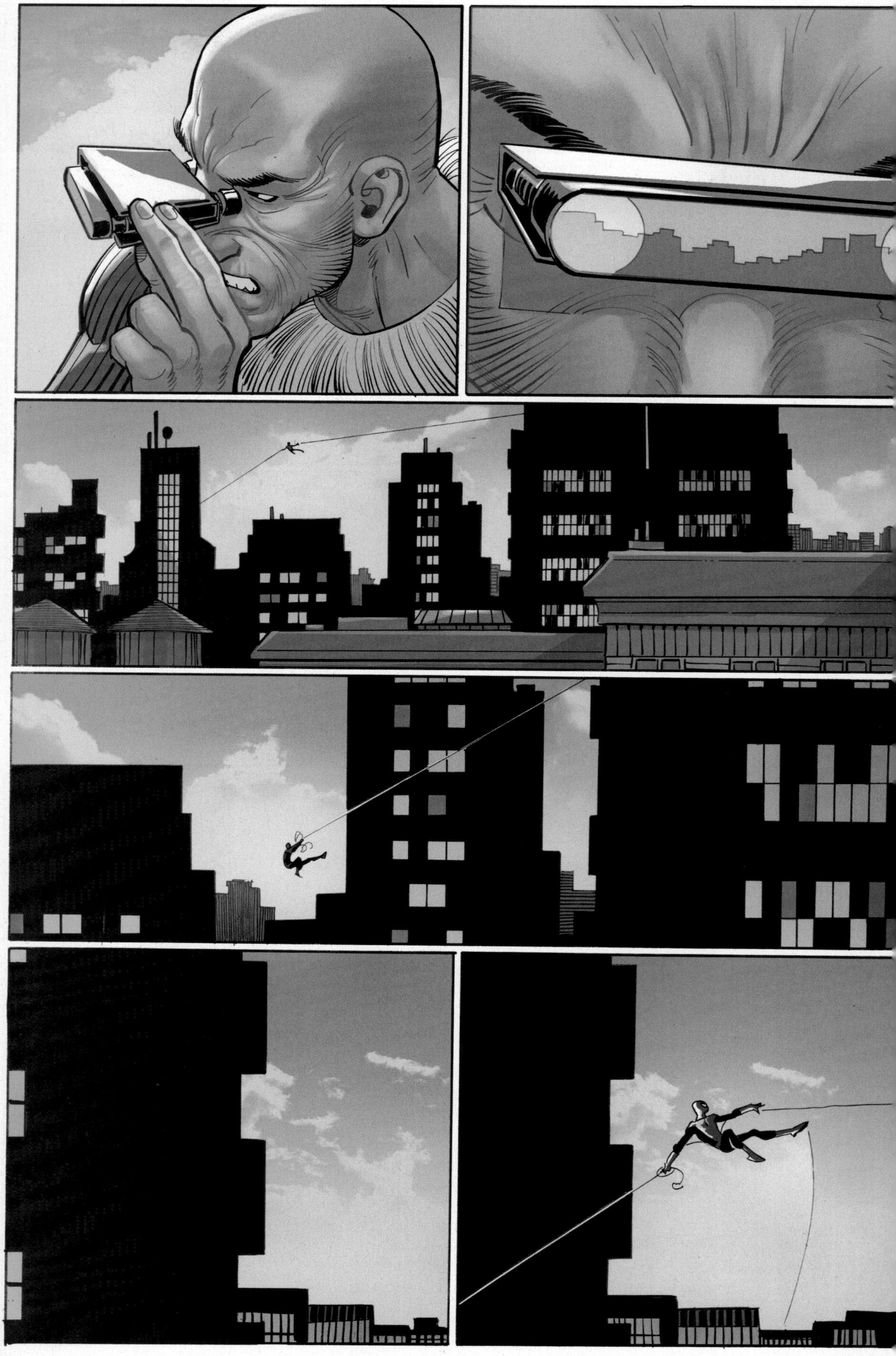

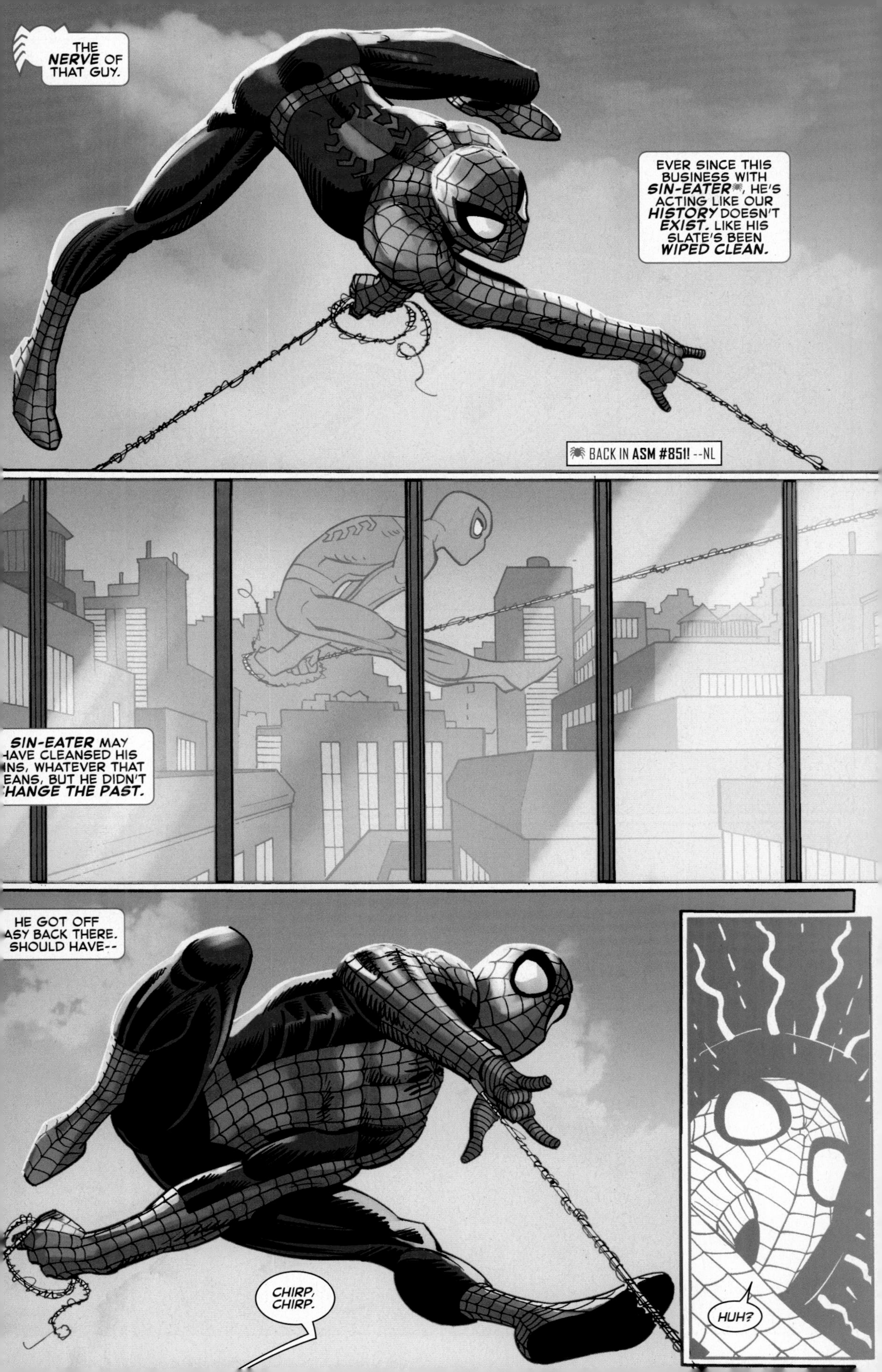
THE NERVE OF THAT GUY.
EVER SINCE THIS BUSINESS WITH SIN-EATER, HE'S ACTING LIKE OUR HISTORY DOESN'T EXIST. LIKE HIS SLATE'S BEEN WIPED CLEAN.
BACK IN ASM #851! --NL
SIN-EATER MAY HAVE CLEANSED HIS INS, WHATEVER THAT EANS, BUT HE DIDN'T HANGE THE PAST.
HE GOT OFF ASY BACK THERE. SHOULD HAVE--
CHIRP, CHIRP.
HUH?

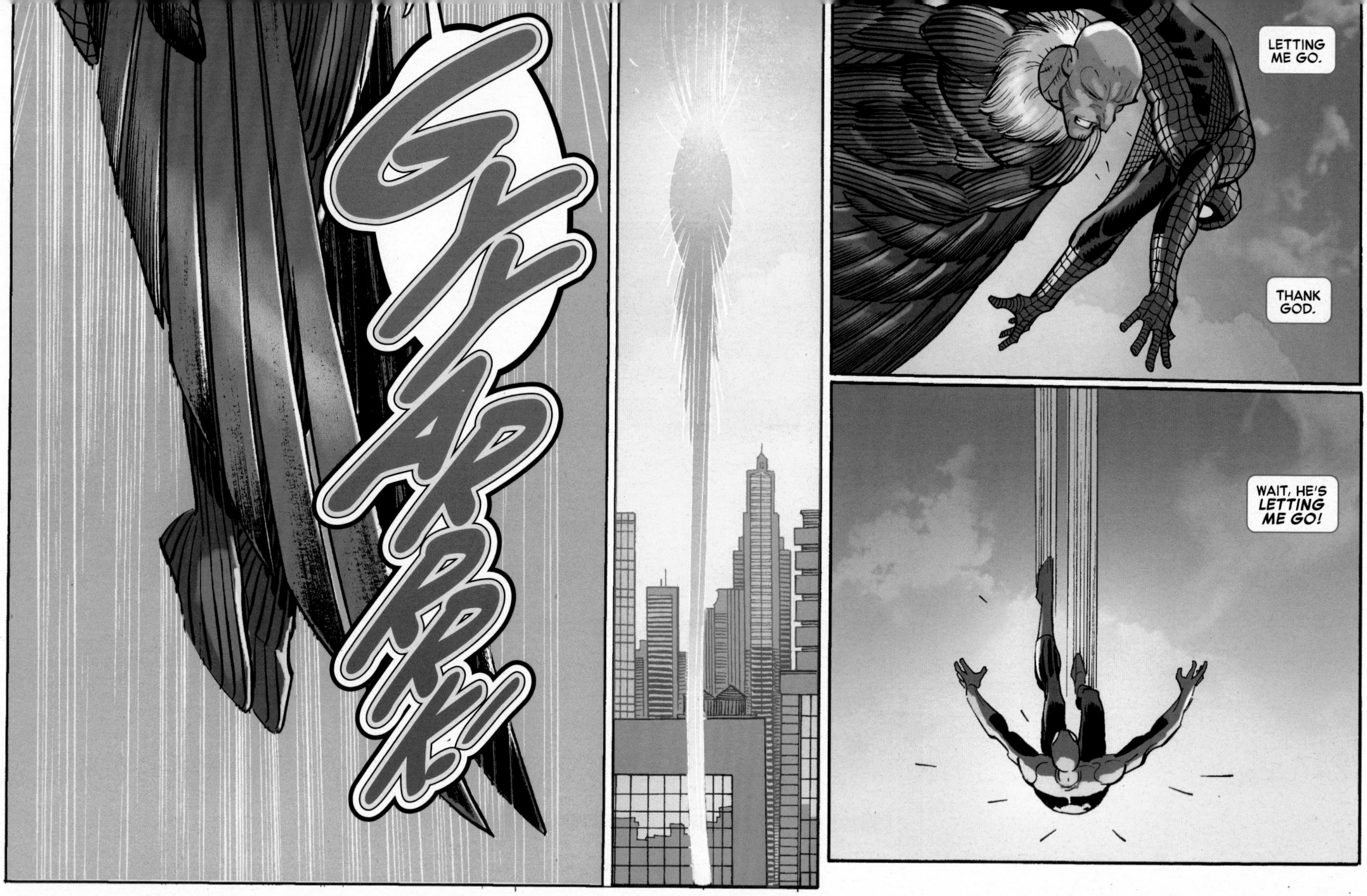
GYYARRK!
LETTING ME GO.
THANK GOD.
WAIT, HE'S *LETTING ME GO!*

CRUNCH

VULTURE.

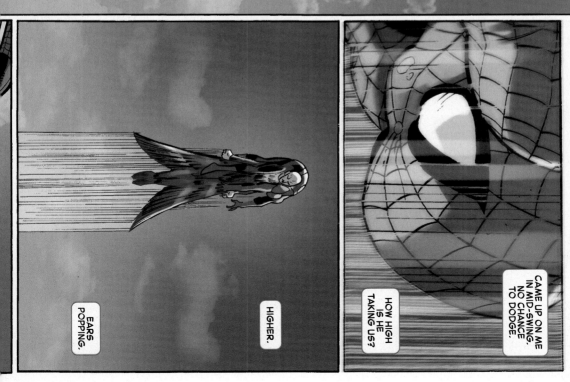

EARS POPPING.

HIGHER.

HOW HIGH IS HE TAKING US?

CAME UP ON ME IN MID-SWING. NO CHANCE TO DODGE.

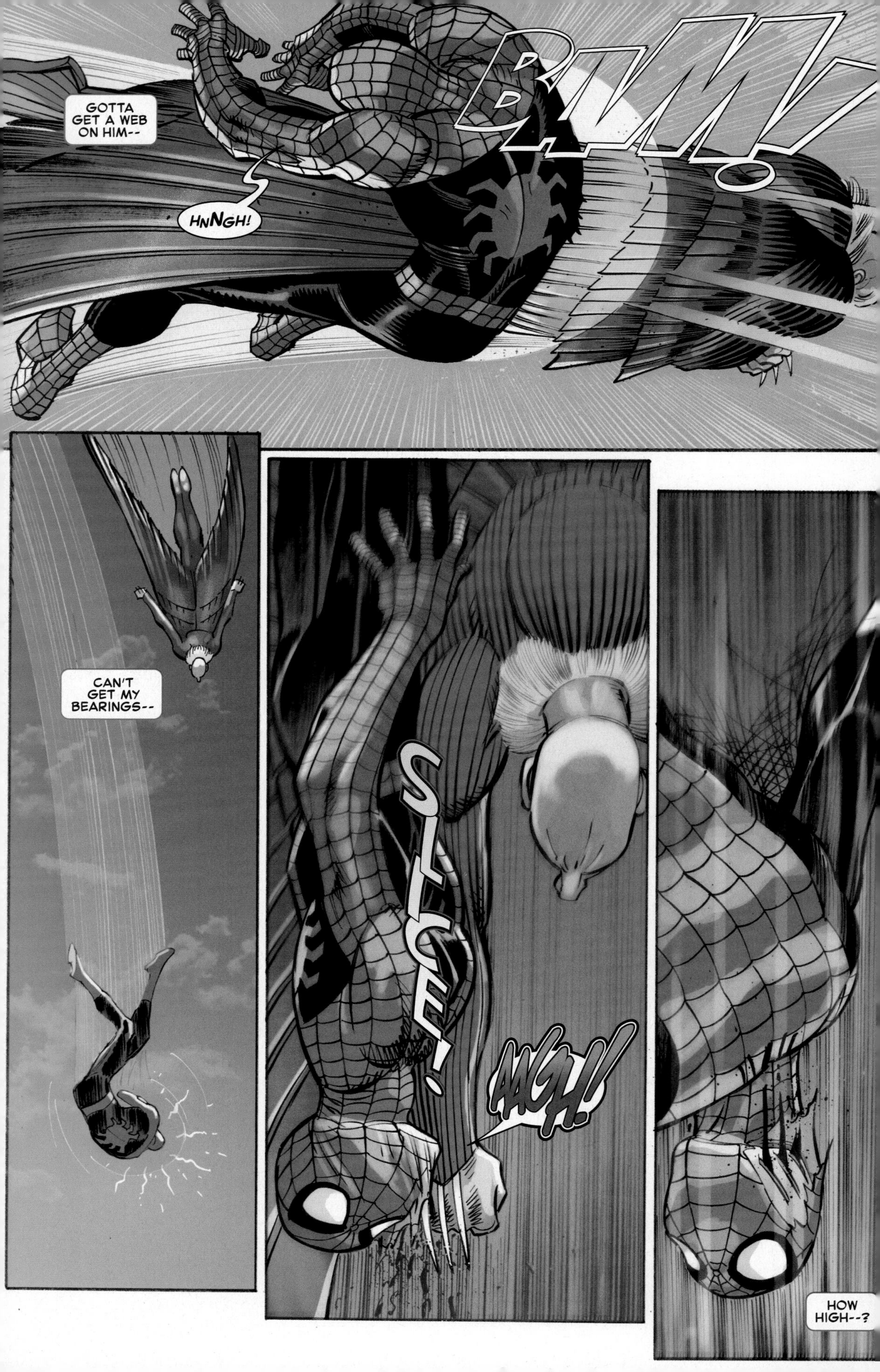
GOTTA GET A WEB ON HIM--
DDAM!
HNNGH!
CAN'T GET MY BEARINGS--
SLICE!
AAGH!!
HOW HIGH--?

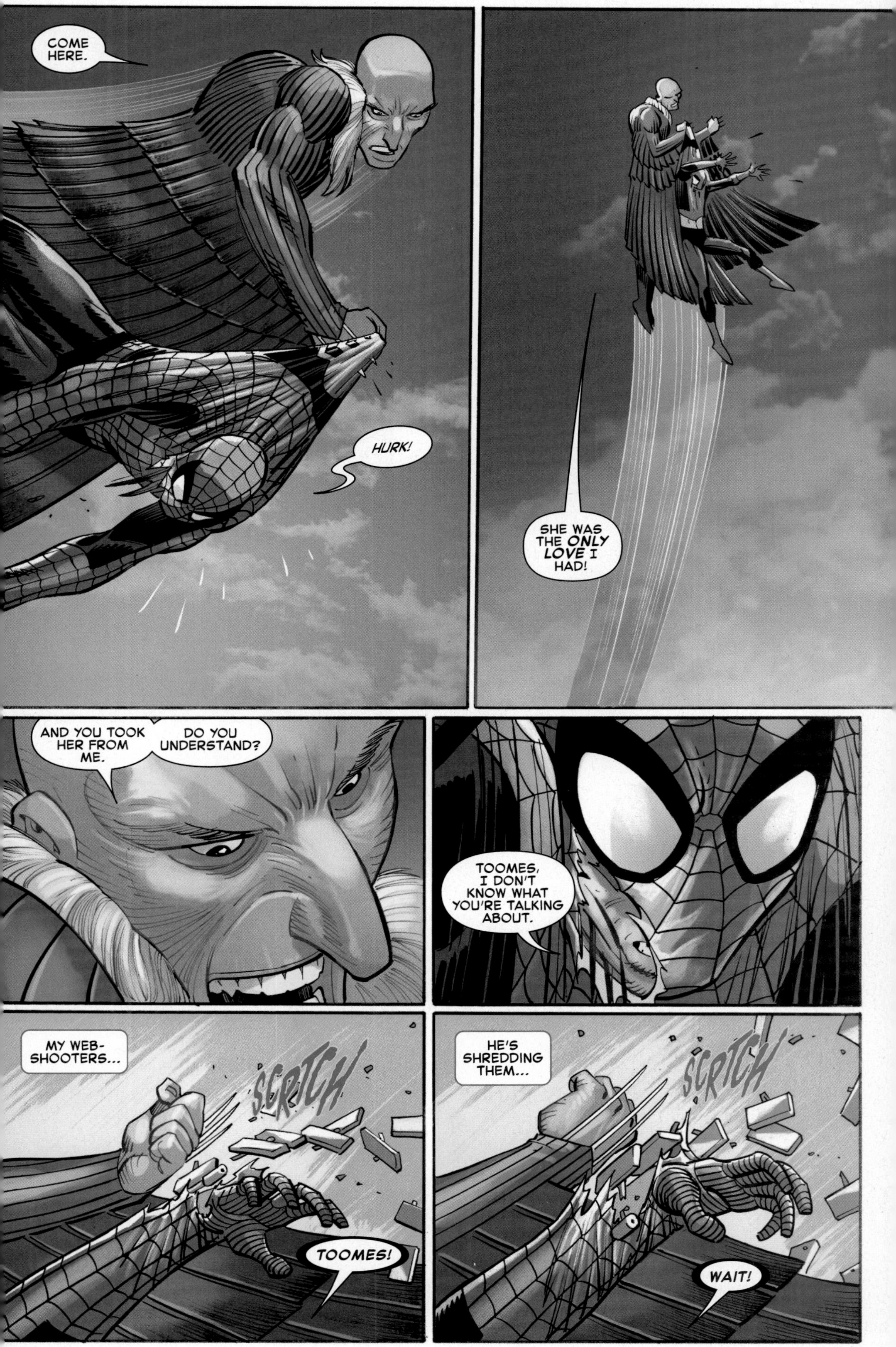
COME HERE.
HURK!
SHE WAS THE ONLY LOVE I HAD!
AND YOU TOOK HER FROM ME.
DO YOU UNDERSTAND?
TOOMES, I DON'T KNOW WHAT YOU'RE TALKING ABOUT.
MY WEB-SHOOTERS...
SCRTCH
TOOMES!
HE'S SHREDDING THEM...
SCRTCH
WAIT!

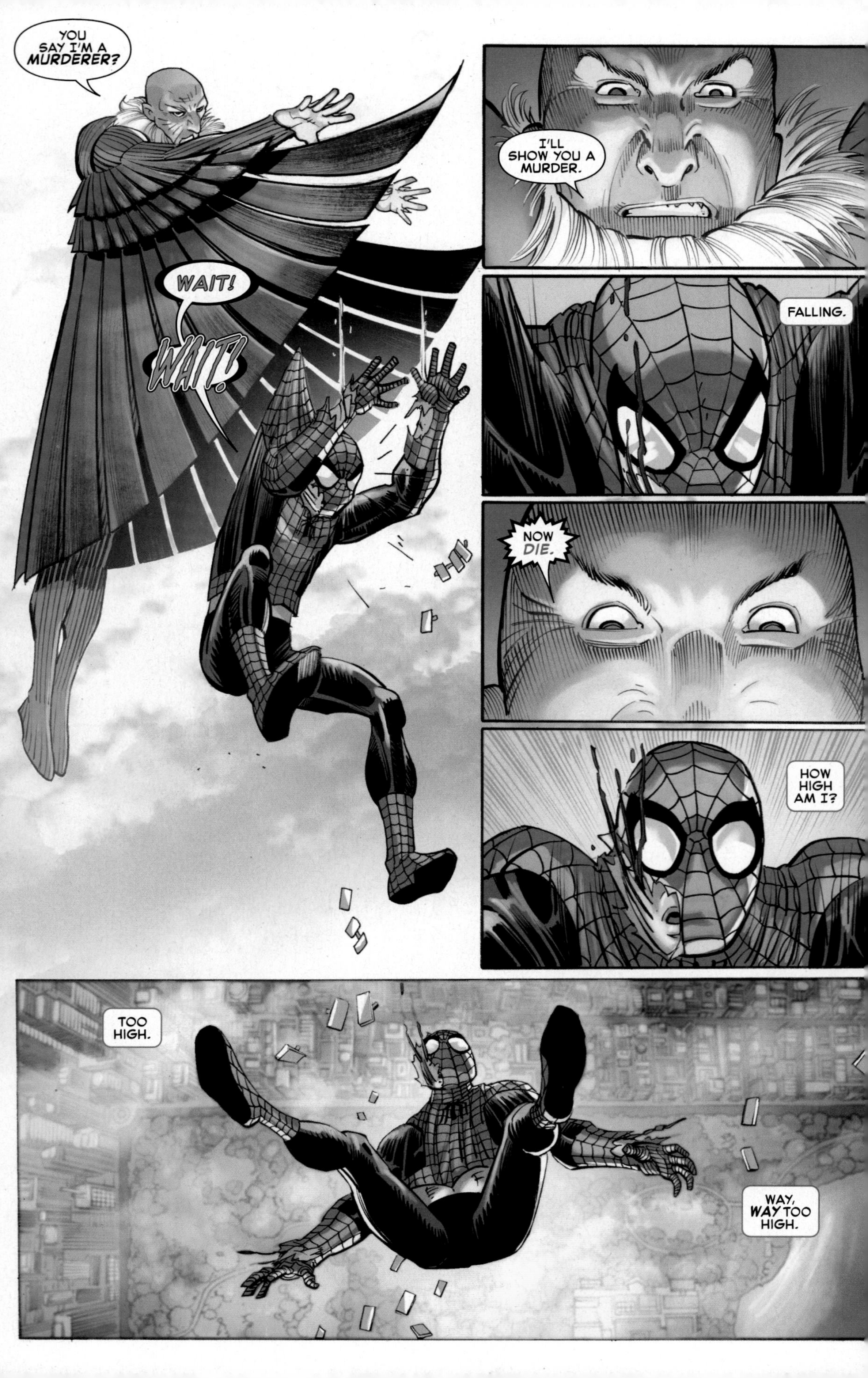
YOU SAY I'M A MURDERER?
I'LL SHOW YOU A MURDER.
WAIT!
WAIT!
FALLING.
NOW DIE.
HOW HIGH AM I?
TOO HIGH.
WAY, WAY TOO HIGH.

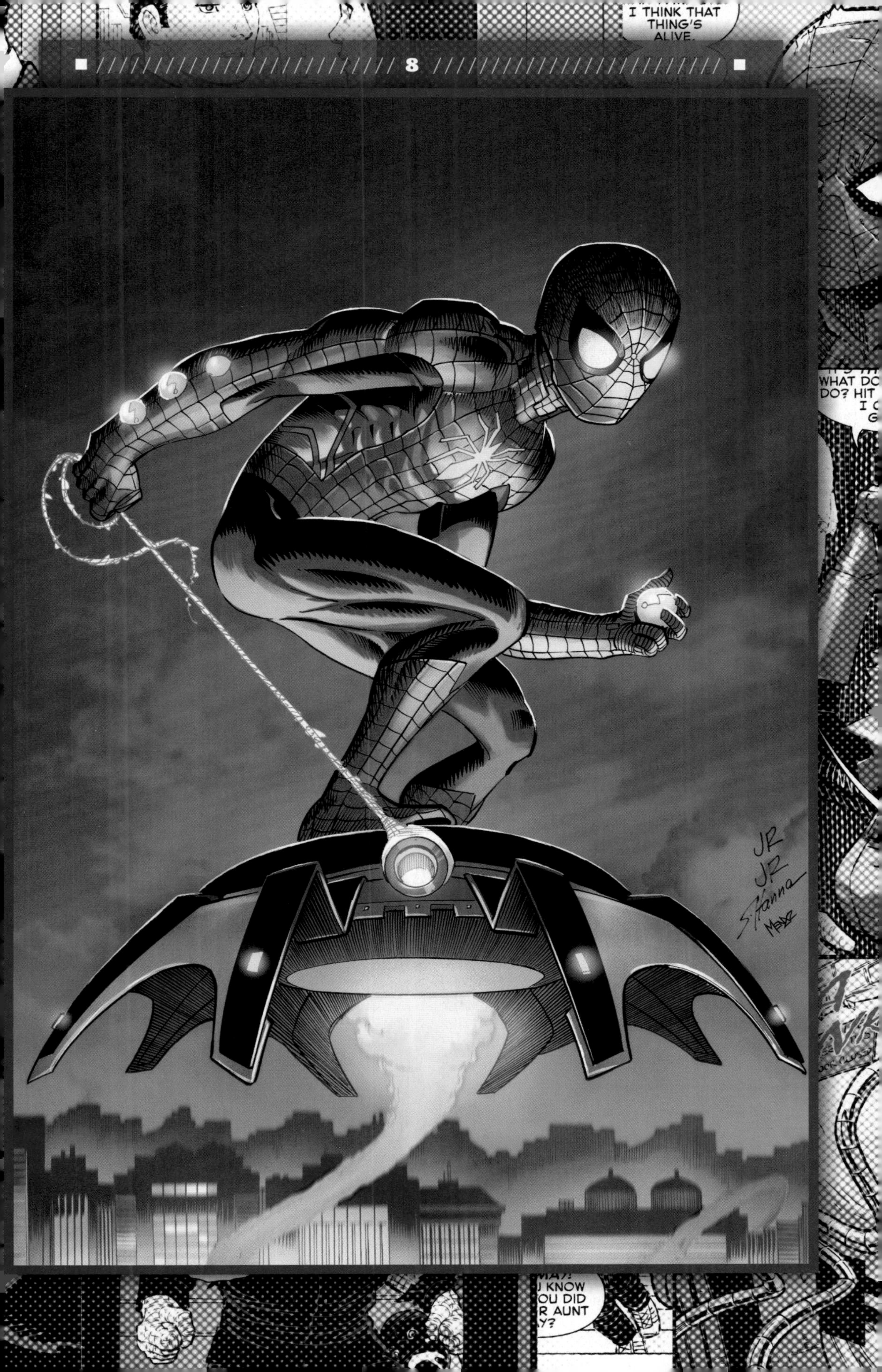
I THINK THAT THING'S ALIVE.
8

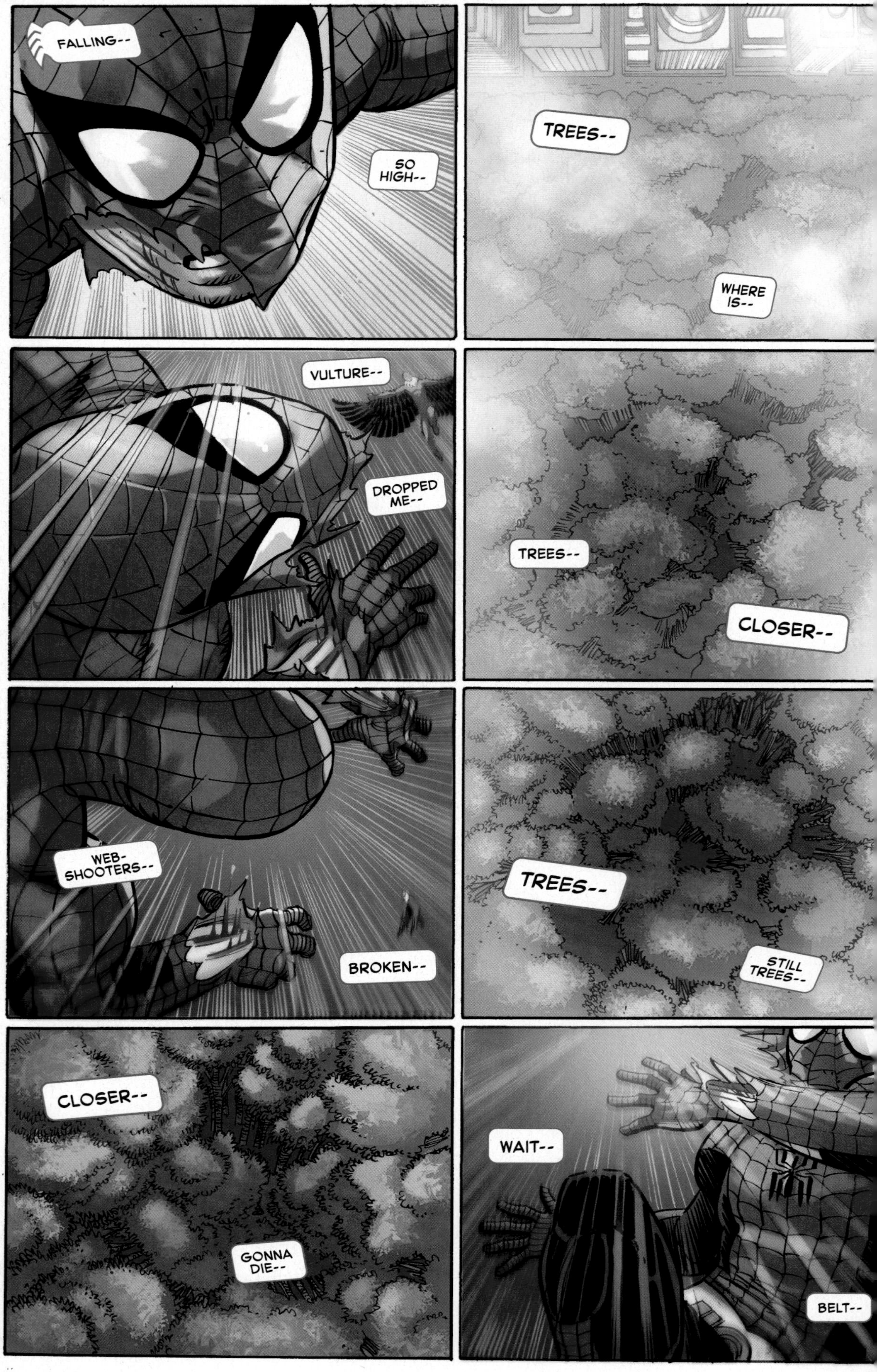
FALLING--
SO HIGH--
TREES--
WHERE IS--
VULTURE--
DROPPED ME--
TREES--
CLOSER--
WEB-SHOOTERS--
BROKEN--
TREES--
STILL TREES--
CLOSER--
GONNA DIE--
WAIT--
BELT--

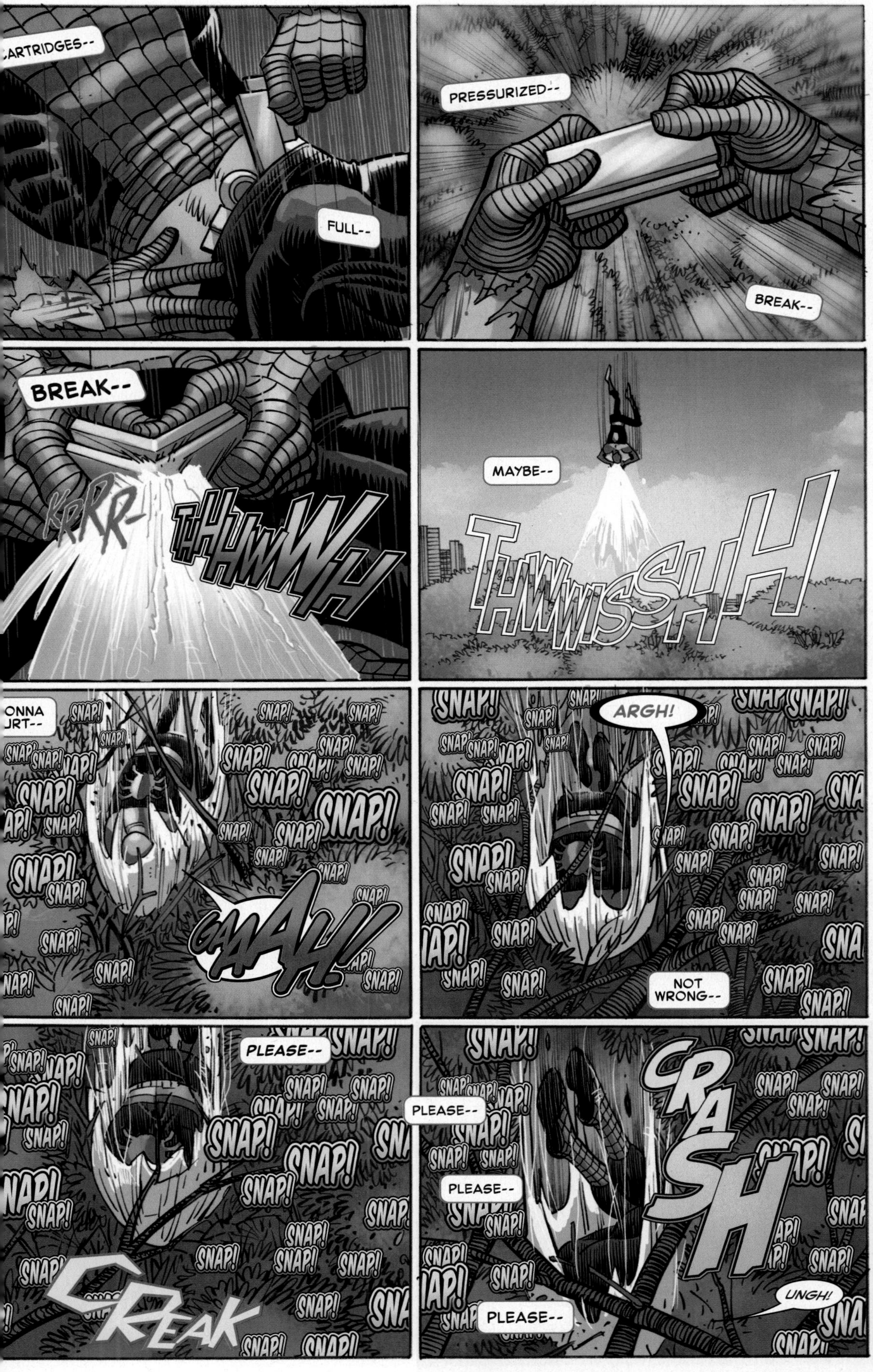
CARTRIDGES--
FULL--
PRESSURIZED--
BREAK--
BREAK--
KRRR-
MAYBE--
THWWISSHH
SNAP!
GAAAH!
ARGH!
SNAP!
NOT WRONG--
PLEASE--
SNAP!
CREAK
PLEASE--
PLEASE--
CRASH
PLEASE--
UNGH!

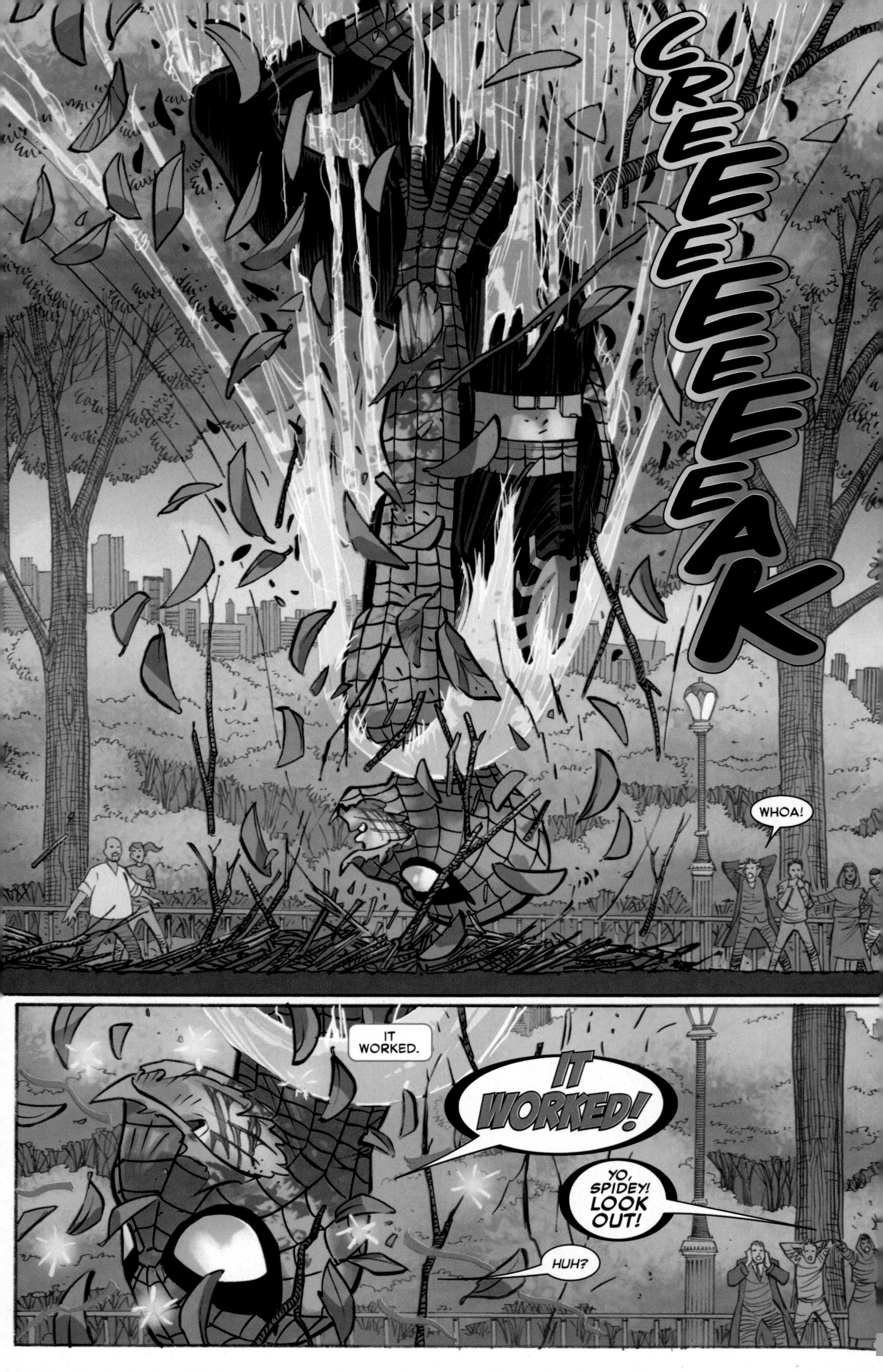
CREEEEEEAK
WHOA!
IT WORKED.
IT WORKED!
YO, SPIDEY! LOOK OUT!
HUH?

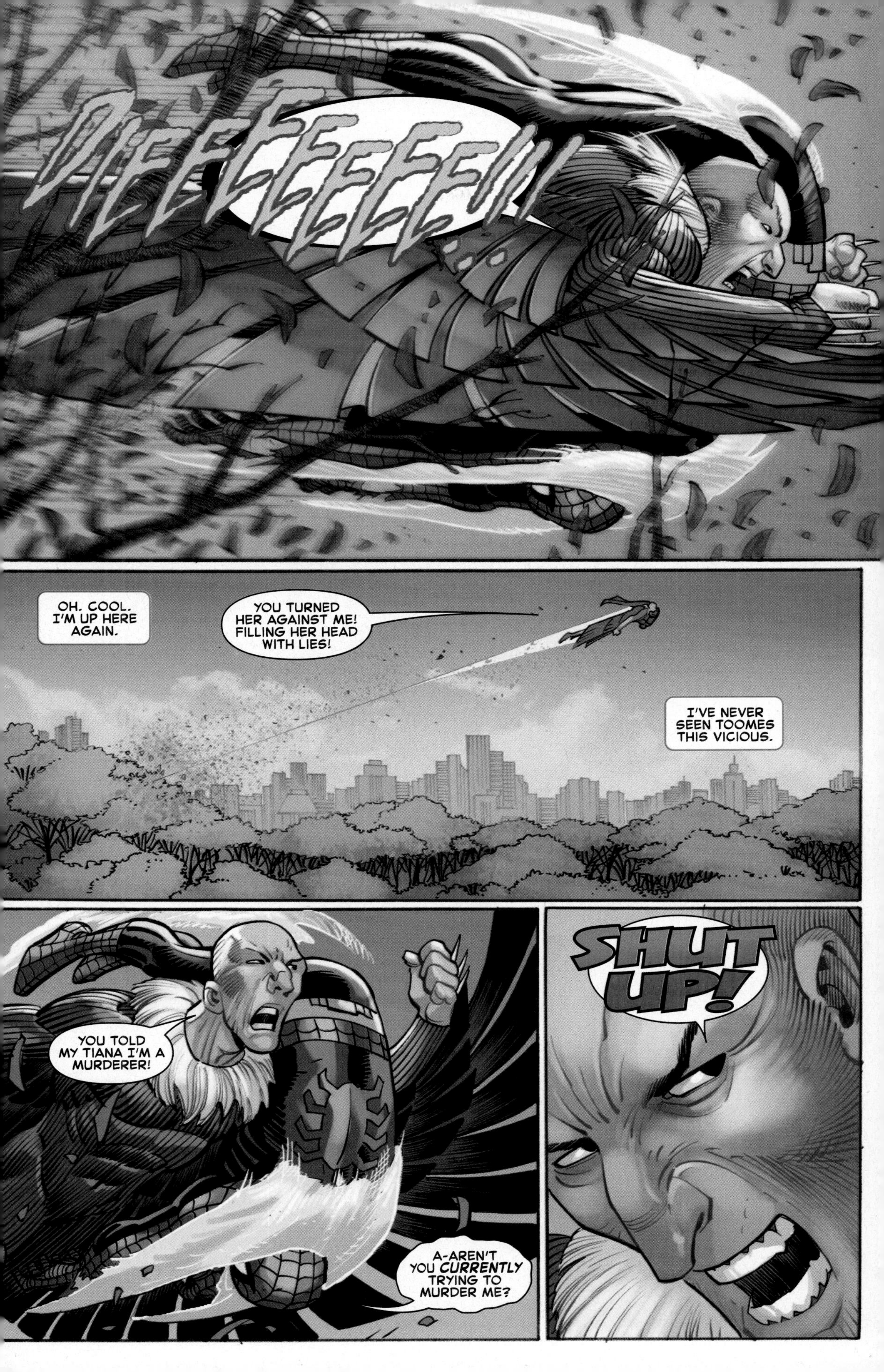
DIEEEEEEEE!!!
OH. COOL. I'M UP HERE AGAIN.
YOU TURNED HER AGAINST ME! FILLING HER HEAD WITH LIES!
I'VE NEVER SEEN TOOMES THIS VICIOUS.
YOU TOLD MY TIANA I'M A MURDERER!
A-AREN'T YOU *CURRENTLY* TRYING TO MURDER ME?
SHUT UP!

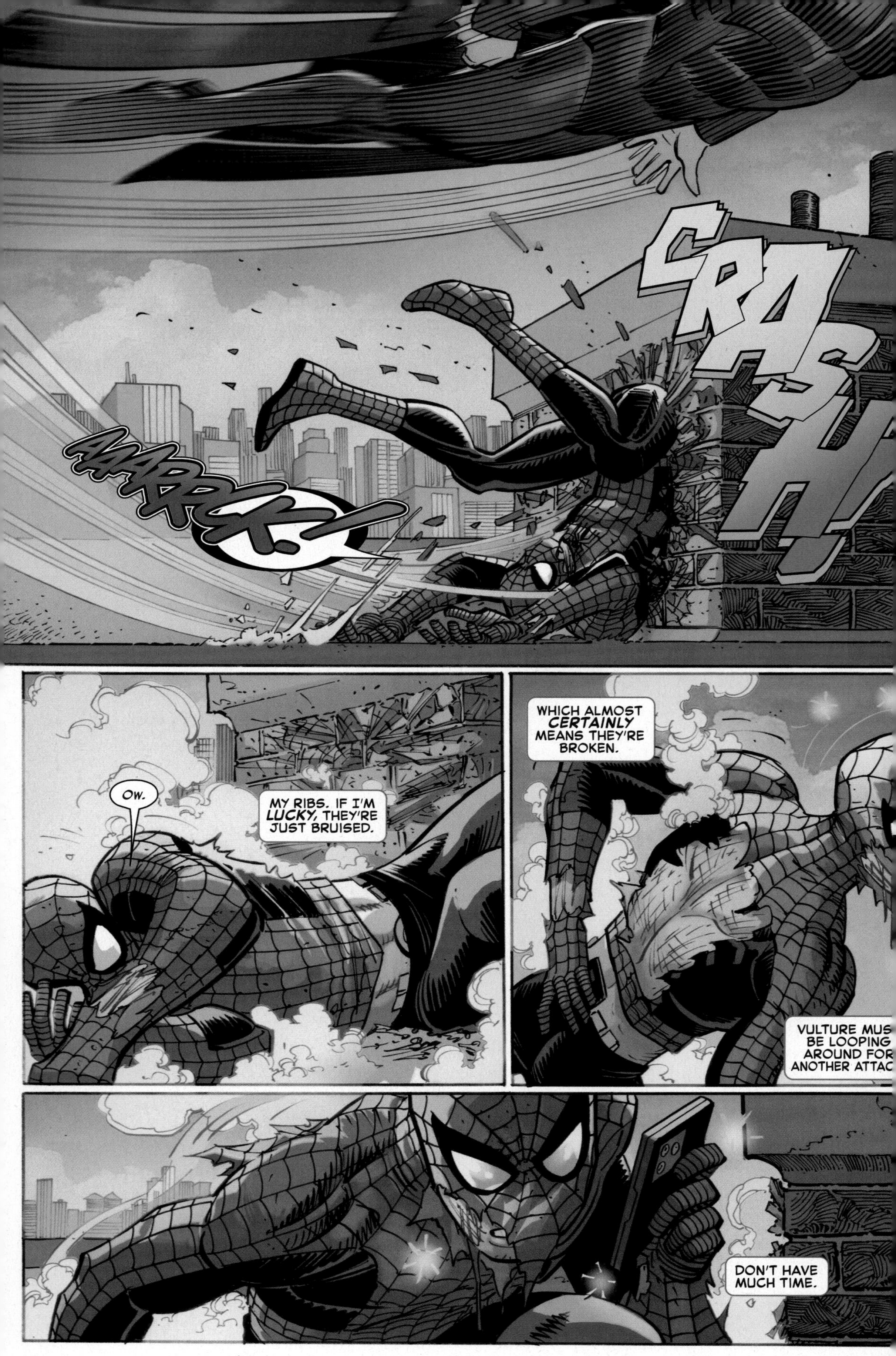

CRASH!
AAARRGK!!
Ow.
MY RIBS. IF I'M *LUCKY,* THEY'RE JUST BRUISED.
WHICH ALMOST *CERTAINLY* MEANS THEY'RE BROKEN.
VULTURE MUS BE LOOPING AROUND FOR ANOTHER ATTAC
DON'T HAVE MUCH TIME.

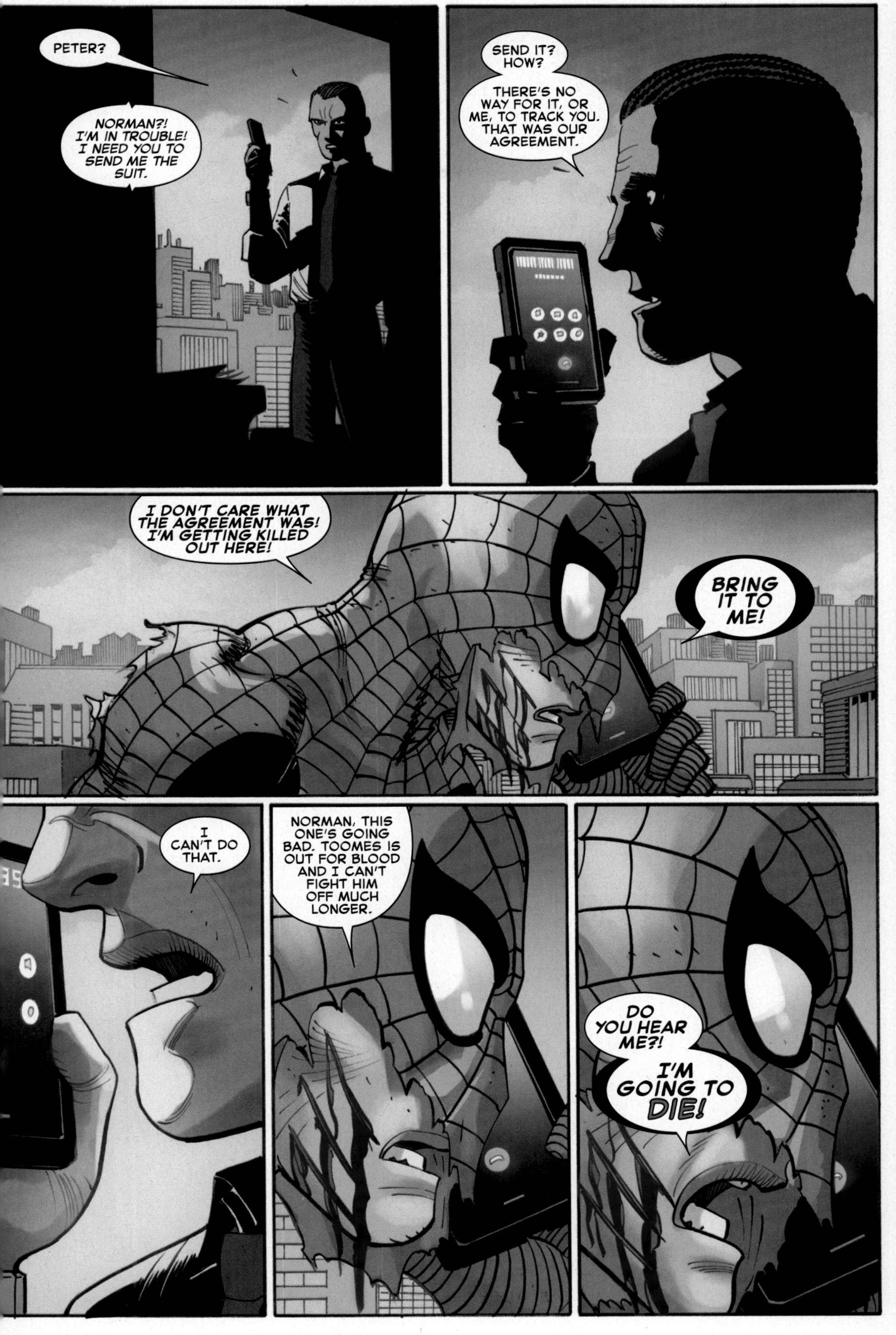
PETER?
NORMAN?! I'M IN TROUBLE! I NEED YOU TO SEND ME THE SUIT.
SEND IT? HOW?
THERE'S NO WAY FOR IT, OR ME, TO TRACK YOU. THAT WAS OUR AGREEMENT.
I DON'T CARE WHAT THE AGREEMENT WAS! I'M GETTING KILLED OUT HERE!
BRING IT TO ME!
I CAN'T DO THAT.
NORMAN, THIS ONE'S GOING BAD. TOOMES IS OUT FOR BLOOD AND I CAN'T FIGHT HIM OFF MUCH LONGER.
DO YOU HEAR ME?!
I'M GOING TO DIE!

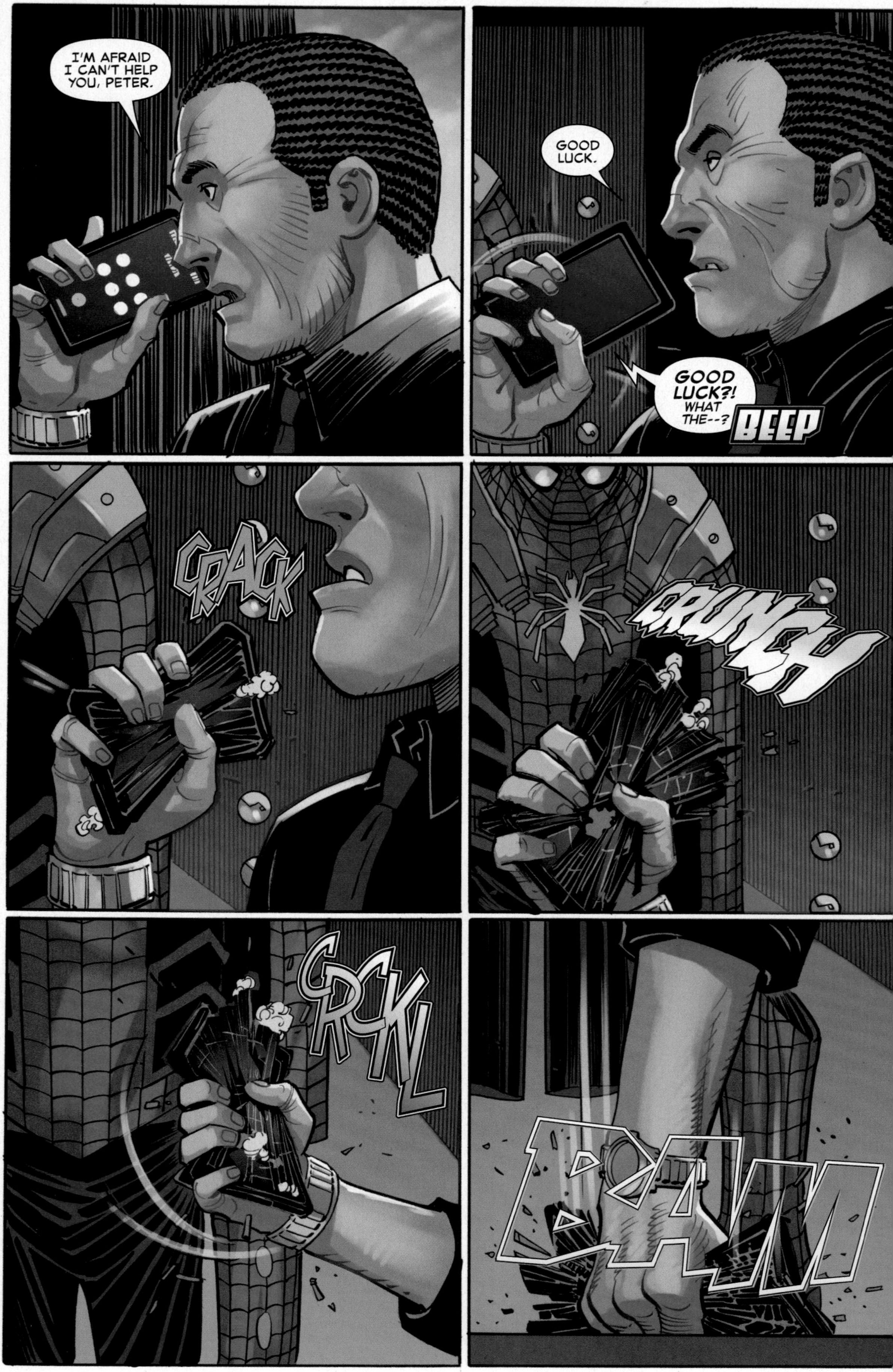
I'M AFRAID I CAN'T HELP YOU, PETER.
GOOD LUCK.
GOOD LUCK?! WHAT THE--?
BEEP
CRACK
CRUNCH
CRCKL
BAM

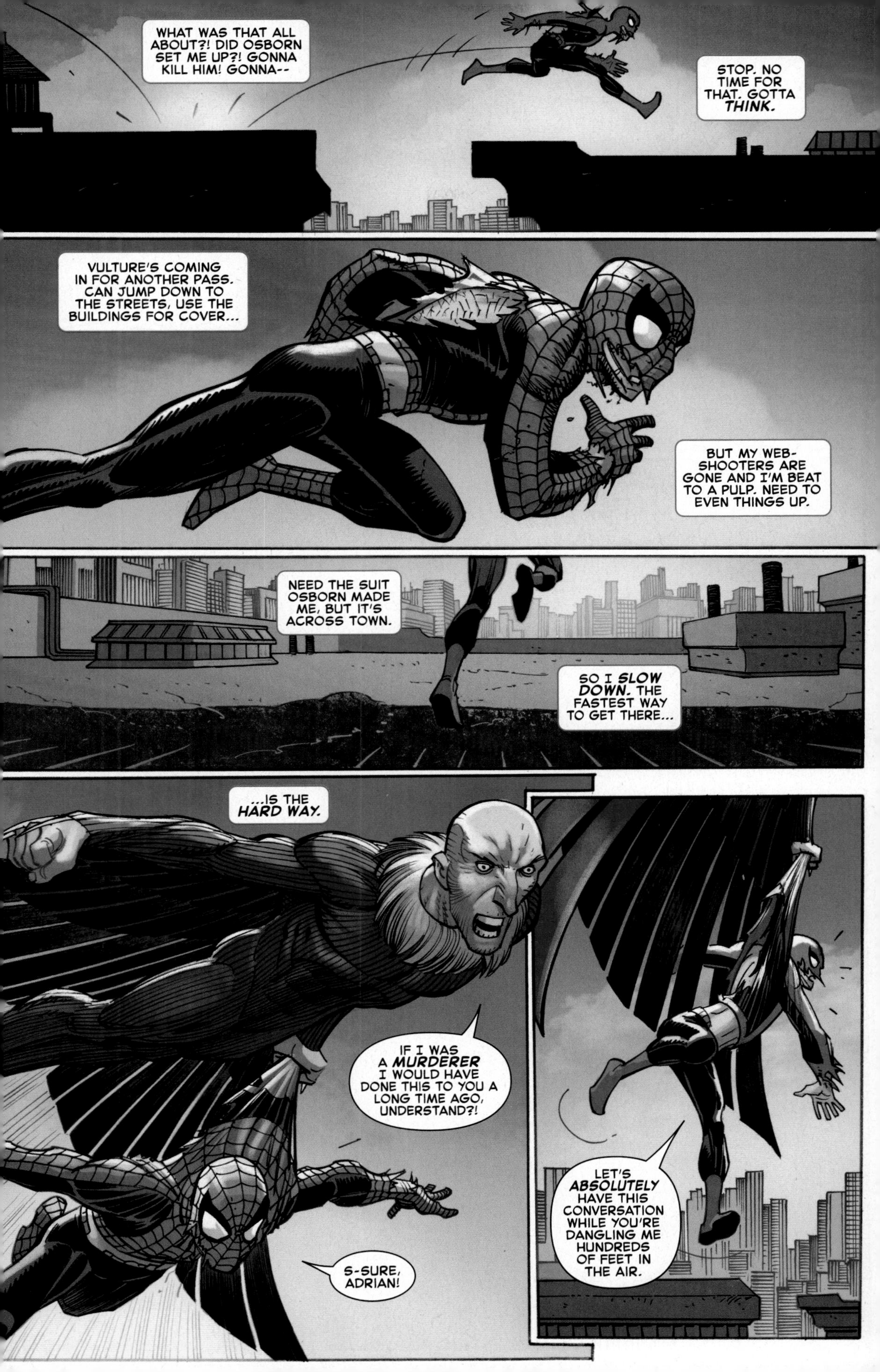
WHAT WAS THAT ALL ABOUT?! DID OSBORN SET ME UP?! GONNA KILL HIM! GONNA--
STOP. NO TIME FOR THAT. GOTTA *THINK.*
VULTURE'S COMING IN FOR ANOTHER PASS. CAN JUMP DOWN TO THE STREETS, USE THE BUILDINGS FOR COVER...
BUT MY WEB-SHOOTERS ARE GONE AND I'M BEAT TO A PULP. NEED TO EVEN THINGS UP.
NEED THE SUIT OSBORN MADE ME, BUT IT'S ACROSS TOWN.
SO I *SLOW DOWN.* THE FASTEST WAY TO GET THERE...
...IS THE *HARD WAY.*
IF I WAS A *MURDERER* I WOULD HAVE DONE THIS TO YOU A LONG TIME AGO, UNDERSTAND?!
S-SURE, ADRIAN!
LET'S *ABSOLUTELY* HAVE THIS CONVERSATION WHILE YOU'RE DANGLING ME HUNDREDS OF FEET IN THE AIR.

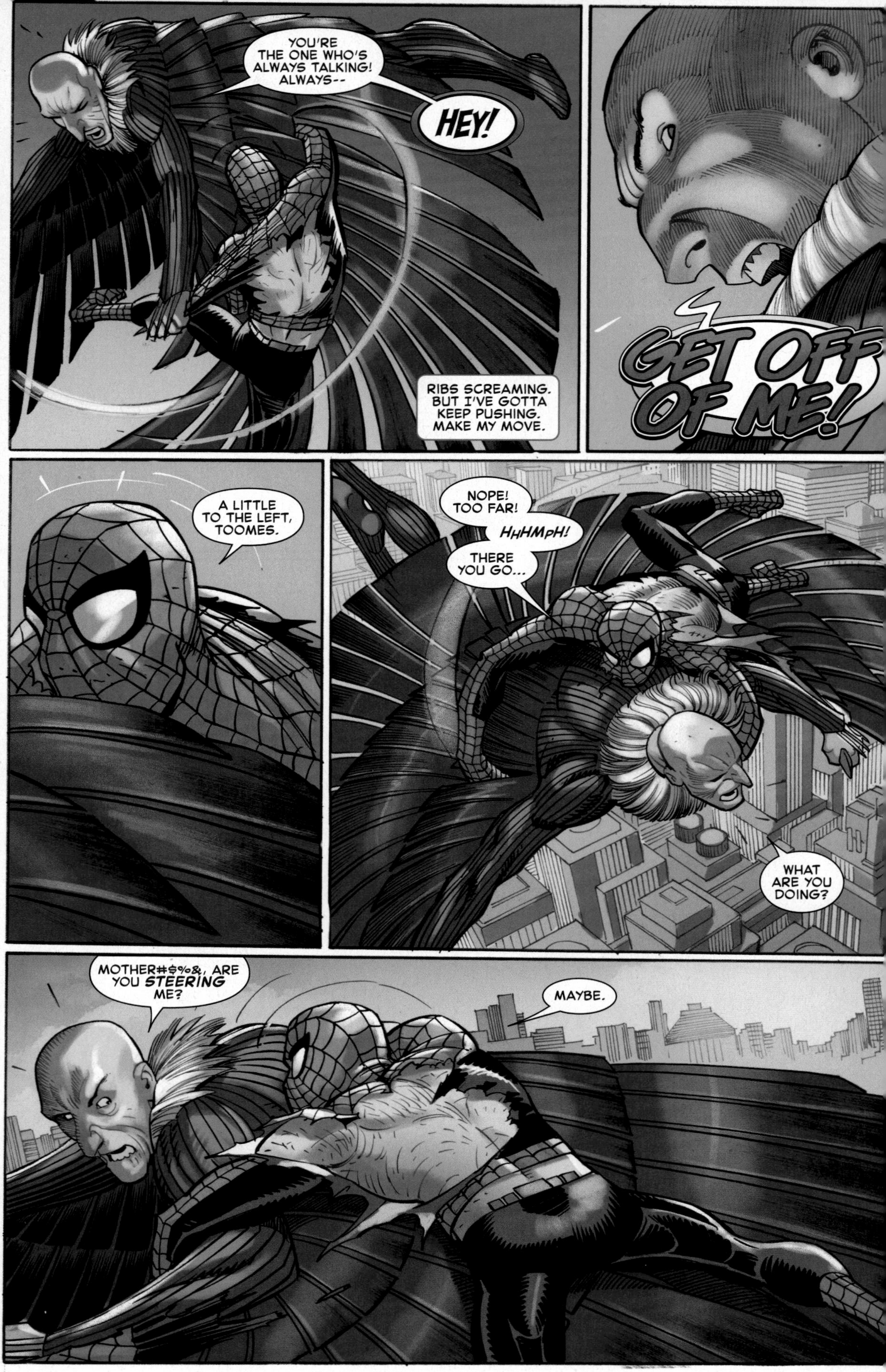
YOU'RE THE ONE WHO'S ALWAYS TALKING! ALWAYS--
HEY!
RIBS SCREAMING. BUT I'VE GOTTA KEEP PUSHING. MAKE MY MOVE.
GET OFF OF ME!
A LITTLE TO THE LEFT, TOOMES.
NOPE! TOO FAR!
HHHMPH!
THERE YOU GO...
WHAT ARE YOU DOING?
MOTHER#$%&, ARE YOU STEERING ME?
MAYBE.

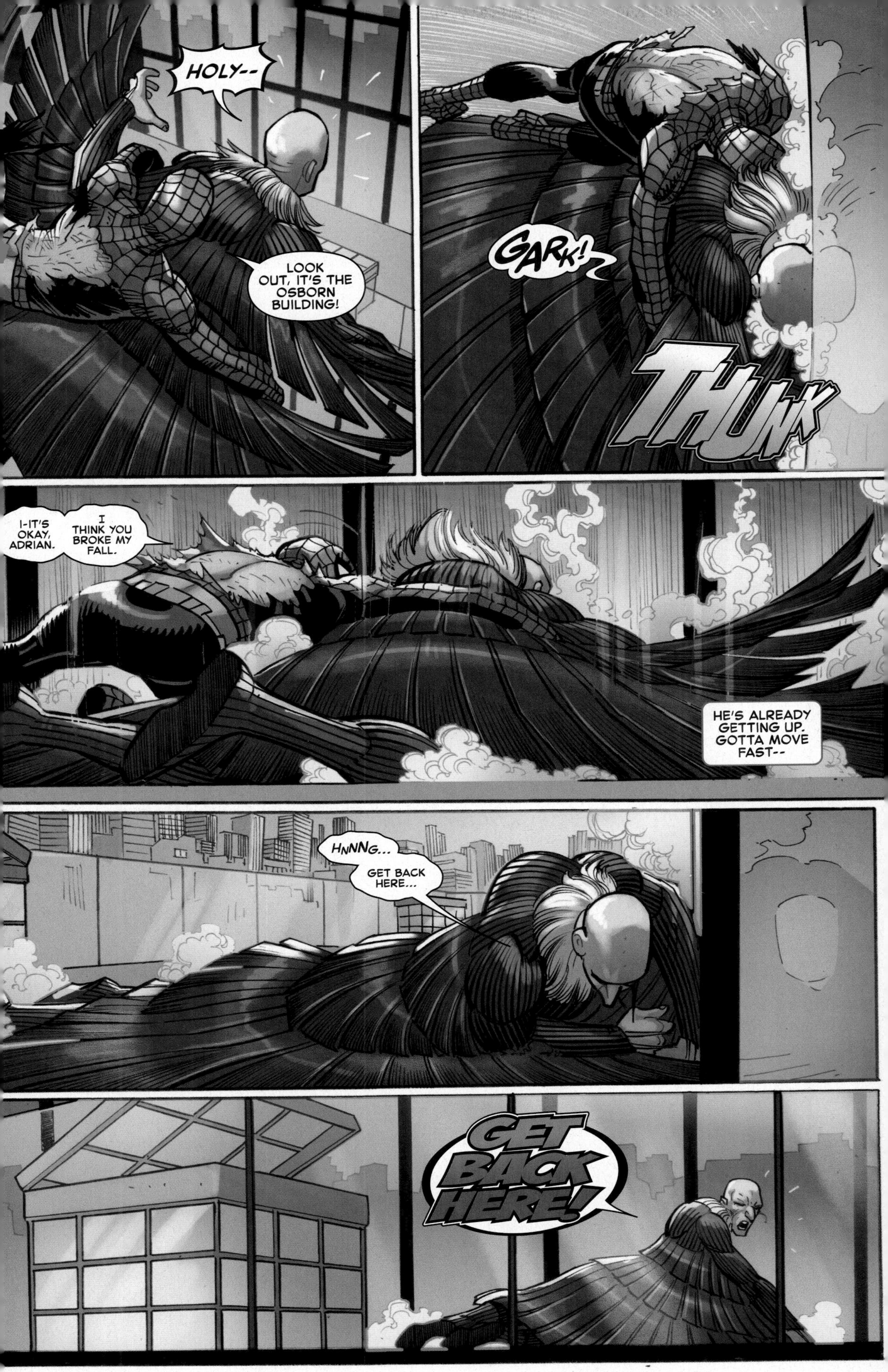
HOLY--
LOOK OUT, IT'S THE OSBORN BUILDING!
GARK!
THUNK
I-IT'S OKAY, ADRIAN.
I THINK YOU BROKE MY FALL.
HE'S ALREADY GETTING UP. GOTTA MOVE FAST--
HNNNG...
GET BACK HERE...
GET BACK HERE!

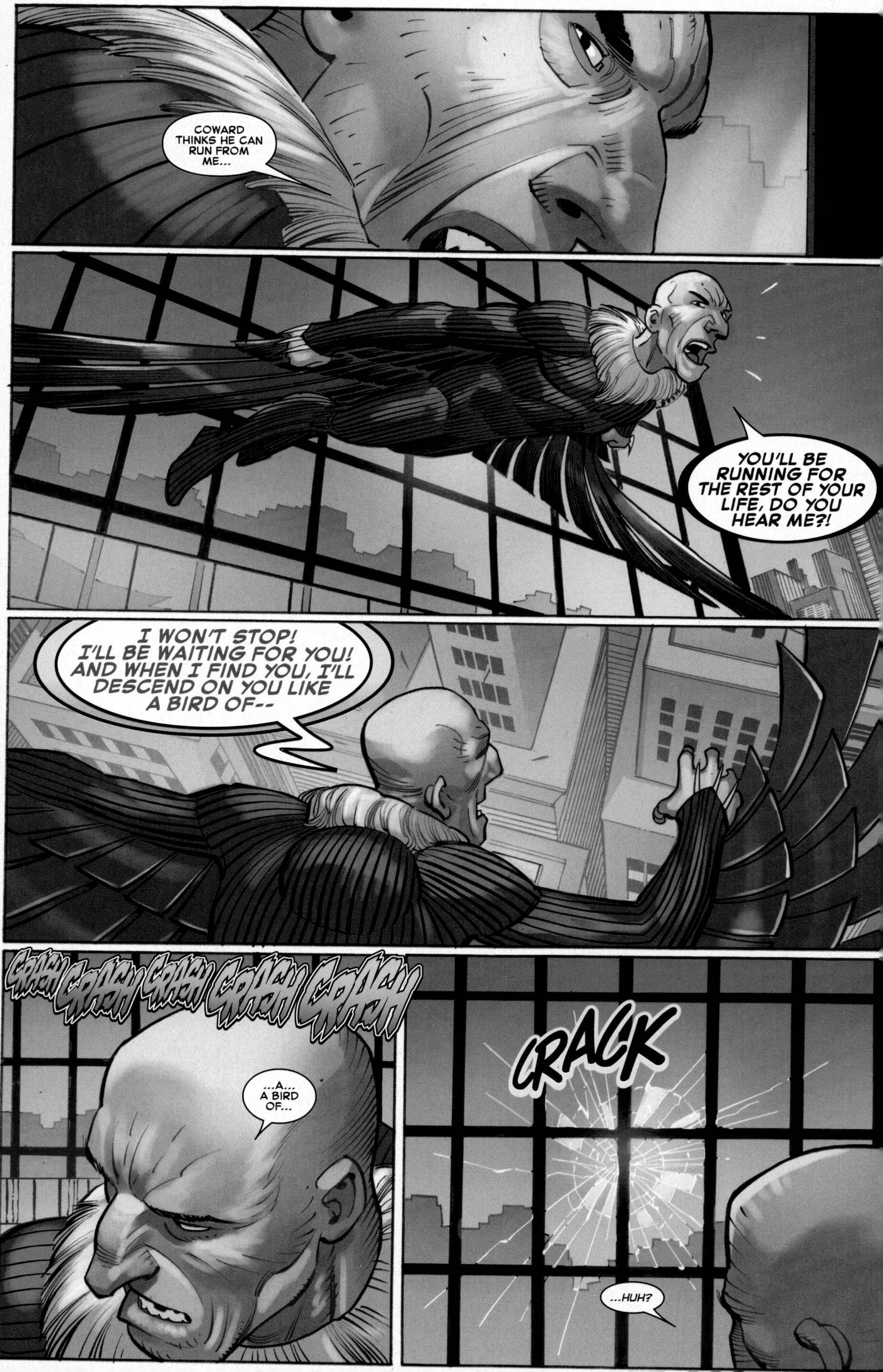
COWARD THINKS HE CAN RUN FROM ME...
YOU'LL BE RUNNING FOR THE REST OF YOUR LIFE, DO YOU HEAR ME?!
I WON'T STOP! I'LL BE WAITING FOR YOU! AND WHEN I FIND YOU, I'LL DESCEND ON YOU LIKE A BIRD OF--
CRASH CRASH CRASH CRASH CRASH
...A... A BIRD OF...
CRACK
...HUH?

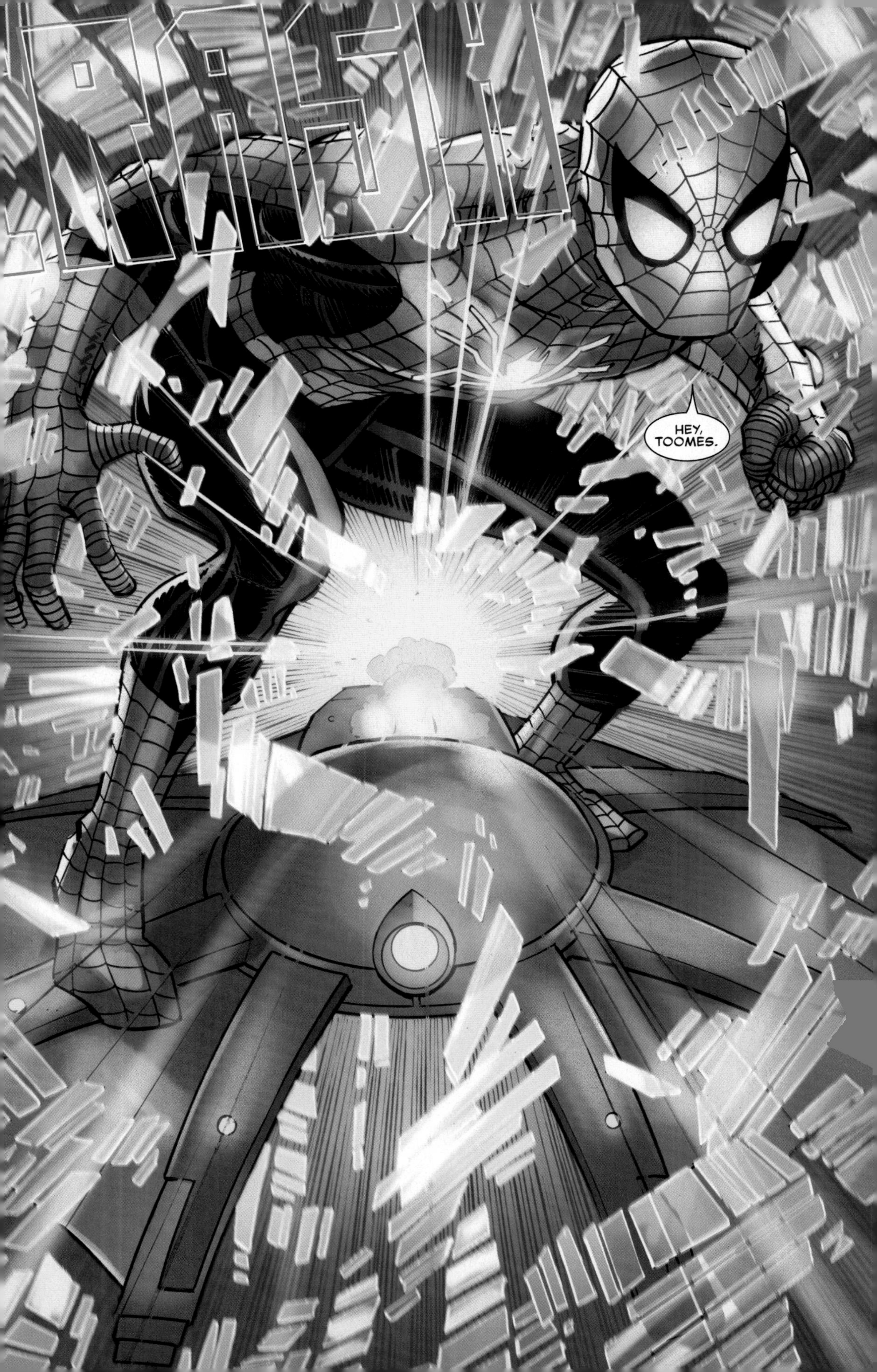
HEY, TOOMES.

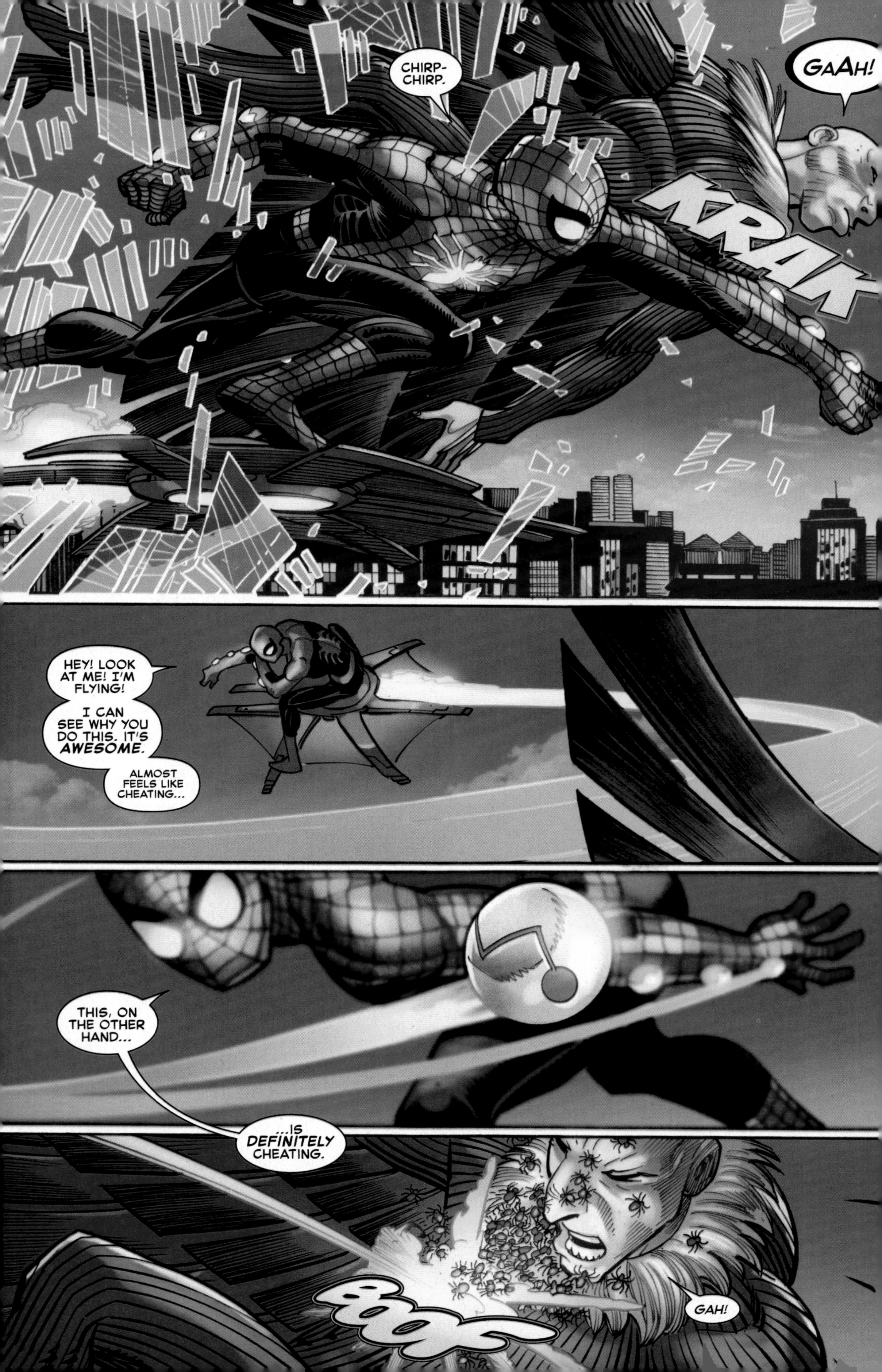
CHIRP-CHIRP.
GAAH!
KRAK
HEY! LOOK AT ME! I'M FLYING!
I CAN SEE WHY YOU DO THIS. IT'S AWESOME.
ALMOST FEELS LIKE CHEATING...
THIS, ON THE OTHER HAND...
...IS DEFINITELY CHEATING.
BOOF
GAH!

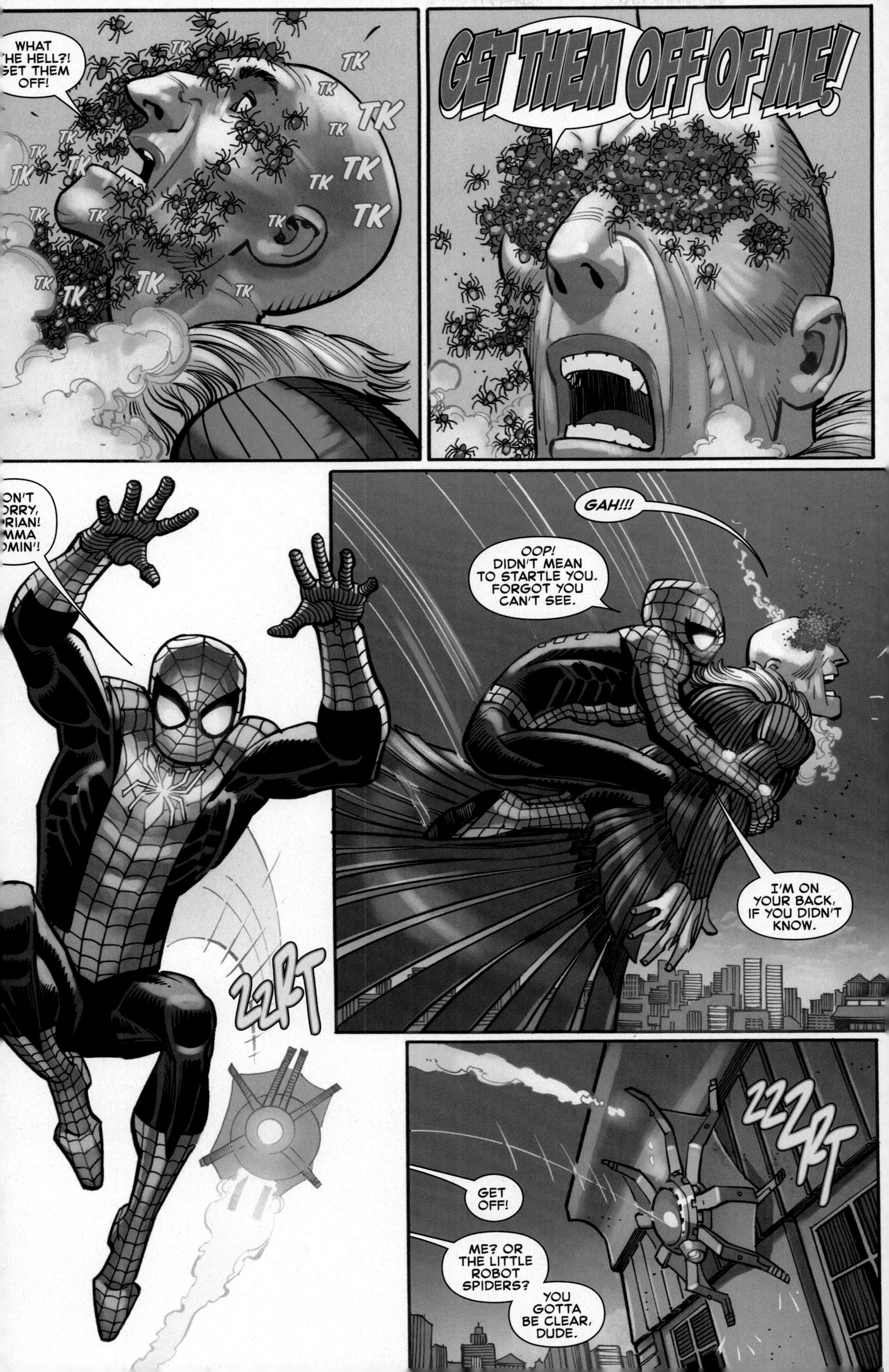

WHAT THE HELL?! GET THEM OFF!
TK TK TK TK TK TK TK TK TK TK TK TK TK TK TK
GET THEM OFF OF ME!
ON'T ORRY, DRIAN! IMMA OMIN'!
GAH!!!
OOP! DIDN'T MEAN TO STARTLE YOU. FORGOT YOU CAN'T SEE.
I'M ON YOUR BACK, IF YOU DIDN'T KNOW.
ZZRT
ZZZRT
GET OFF!
ME? OR THE LITTLE ROBOT SPIDERS?
YOU GOTTA BE CLEAR, DUDE.

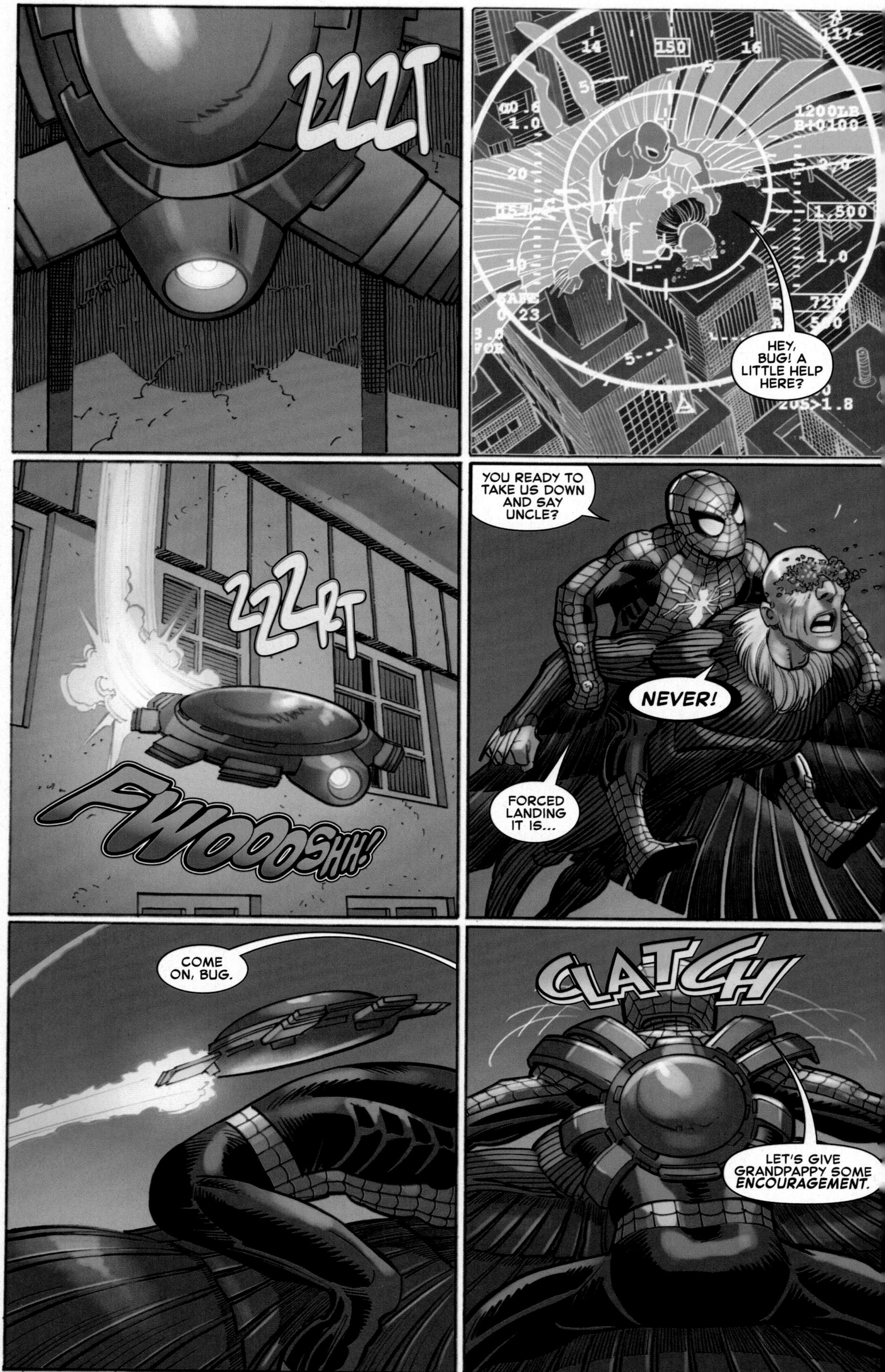
ZZZT
HEY, BUG! A LITTLE HELP HERE?
ZZZRT
FWOOOSHH!
YOU READY TO TAKE US DOWN AND SAY UNCLE?
NEVER!
FORCED LANDING IT IS...
COME ON, BUG.
CLATCH
LET'S GIVE GRANDPAPPY SOME ENCOURAGEMENT.

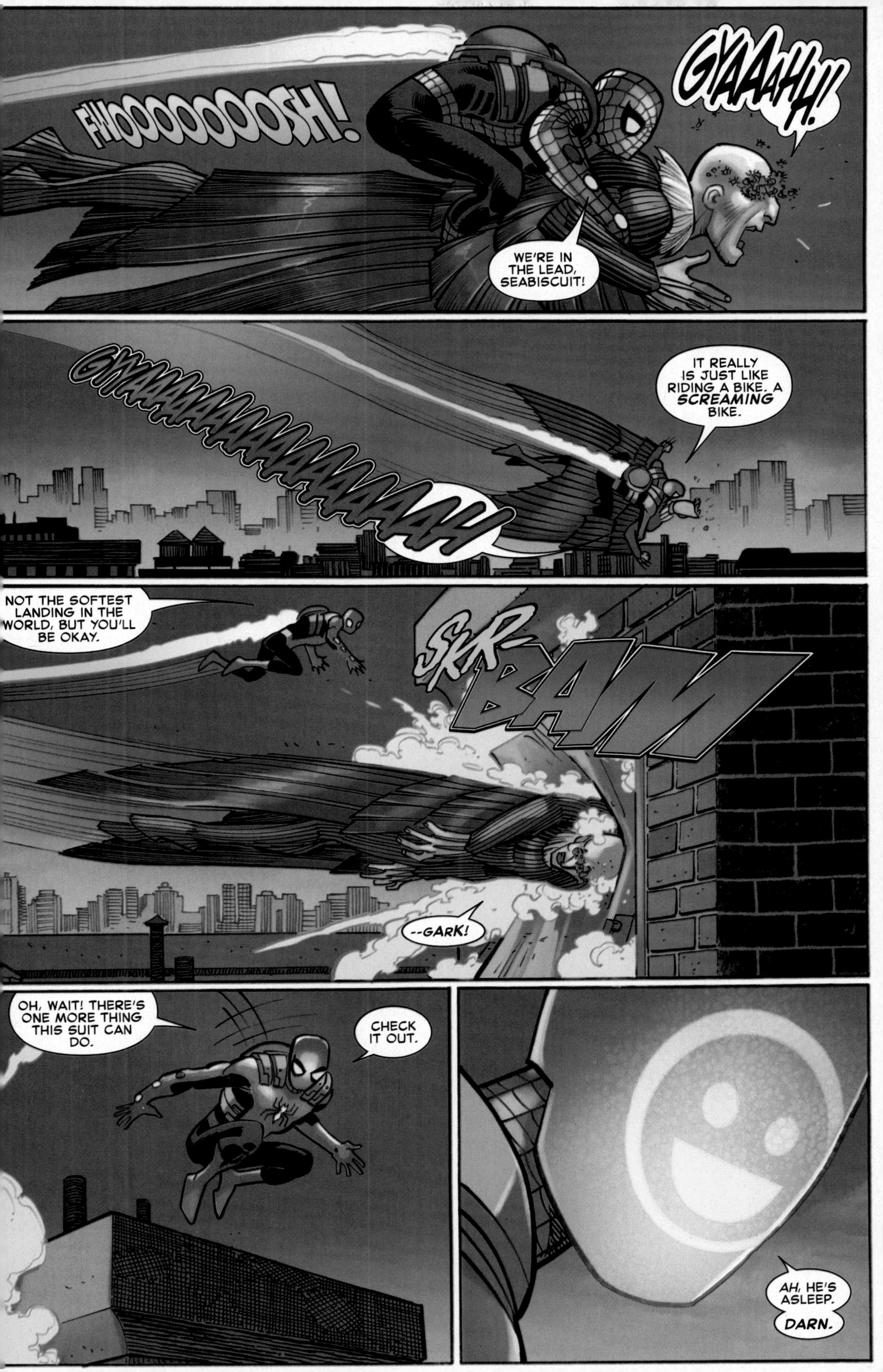
FWOOOOOOOOSH!
GYAAAHH!
WE'RE IN THE LEAD, SEABISCUIT!
GYYAAAAAAAAAAAAAAAAAAAAAAAH
IT REALLY IS JUST LIKE RIDING A BIKE. A SCREAMING BIKE.
NOT THE SOFTEST LANDING IN THE WORLD, BUT YOU'LL BE OKAY.
SKR-BAM
--GARK!
OH, WAIT! THERE'S ONE MORE THING THIS SUIT CAN DO.
CHECK IT OUT.
AH, HE'S ASLEEP.
DARN.

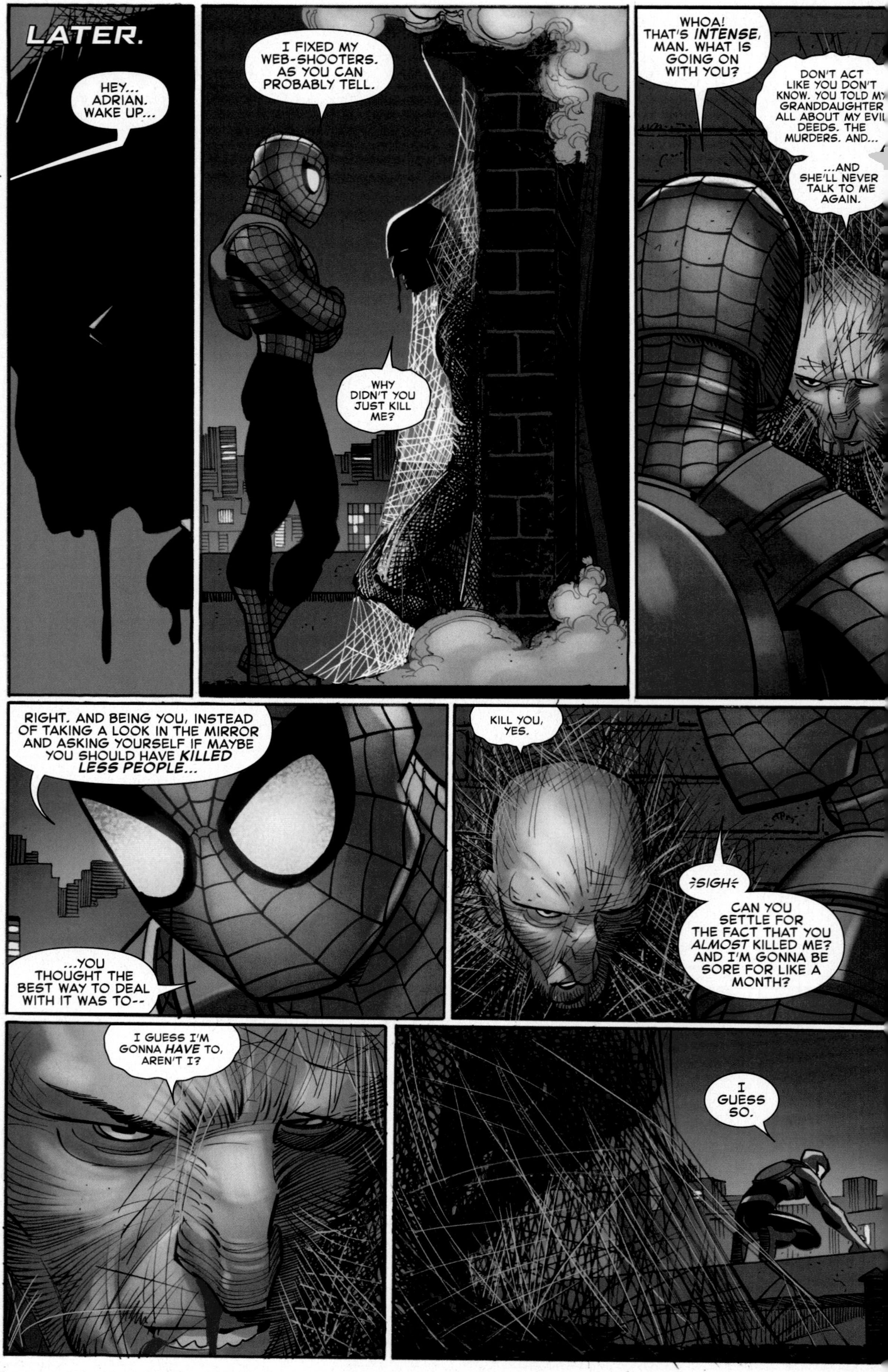
LATER.
HEY... ADRIAN. WAKE UP...
I FIXED MY WEB-SHOOTERS. AS YOU CAN PROBABLY TELL.
WHY DIDN'T YOU JUST KILL ME?
WHOA! THAT'S INTENSE, MAN. WHAT IS GOING ON WITH YOU?
DON'T ACT LIKE YOU DON'T KNOW. YOU TOLD MY GRANDDAUGHTER ALL ABOUT MY EVIL DEEDS. THE MURDERS. AND...
...AND SHE'LL NEVER TALK TO ME AGAIN.
RIGHT. AND BEING YOU, INSTEAD OF TAKING A LOOK IN THE MIRROR AND ASKING YOURSELF IF MAYBE YOU SHOULD HAVE KILLED LESS PEOPLE...
...YOU THOUGHT THE BEST WAY TO DEAL WITH IT WAS TO--
KILL YOU, YES.
SIGH
CAN YOU SETTLE FOR THE FACT THAT YOU ALMOST KILLED ME? AND I'M GONNA BE SORE FOR LIKE A MONTH?
I GUESS I'M GONNA HAVE TO, AREN'T I?
I GUESS SO.

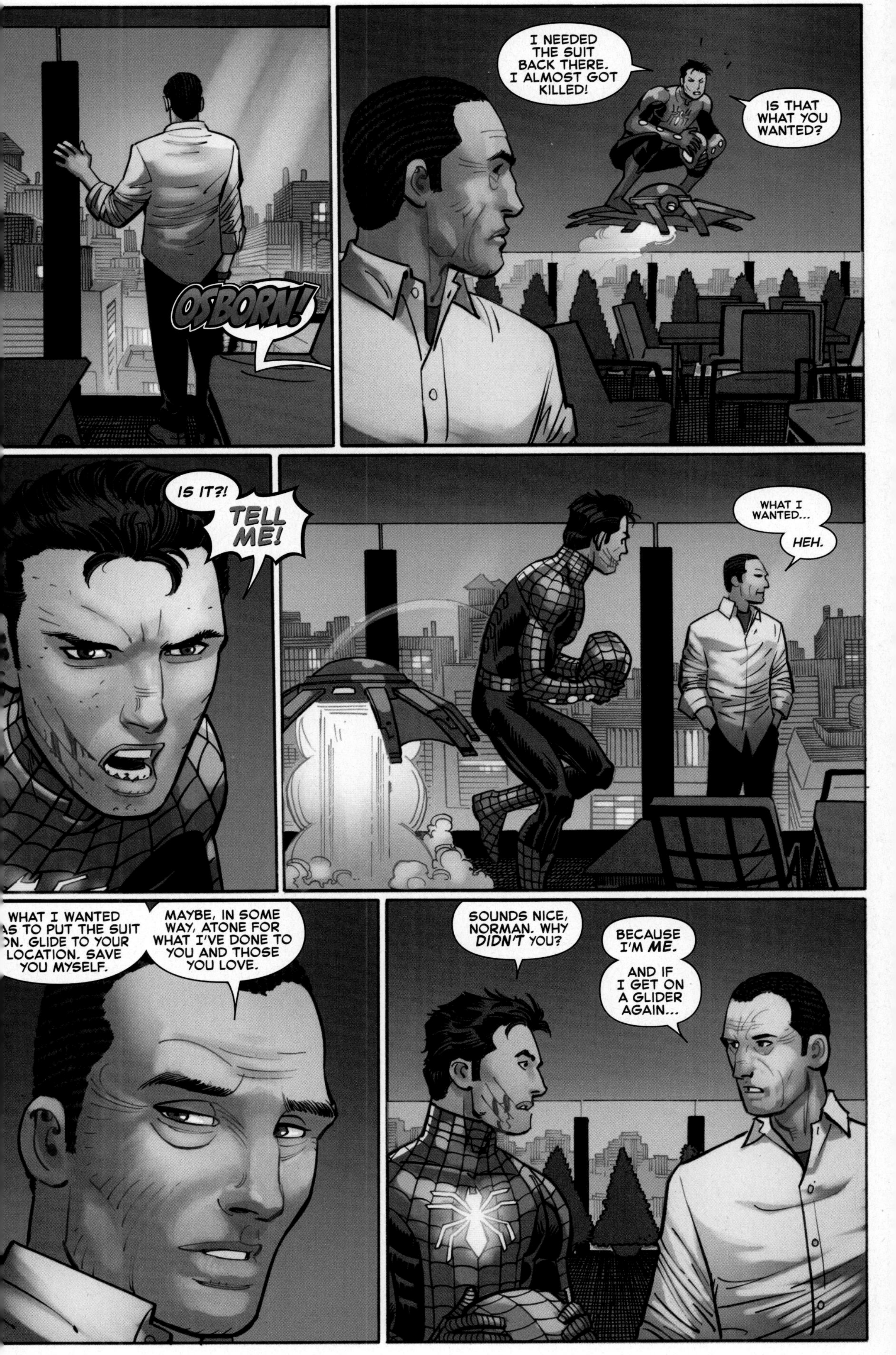
OSBORN!
I NEEDED THE SUIT BACK THERE. I ALMOST GOT KILLED!
IS THAT WHAT YOU WANTED?
IS IT?!
TELL ME!
WHAT I WANTED...
HEH.
WHAT I WANTED
AS TO PUT THE SUIT
ON. GLIDE TO YOUR LOCATION. SAVE YOU MYSELF.
MAYBE, IN SOME WAY, ATONE FOR WHAT I'VE DONE TO YOU AND THOSE YOU LOVE.
SOUNDS NICE, NORMAN. WHY DIDN'T YOU?
BECAUSE I'M ME.
AND IF I GET ON A GLIDER AGAIN...

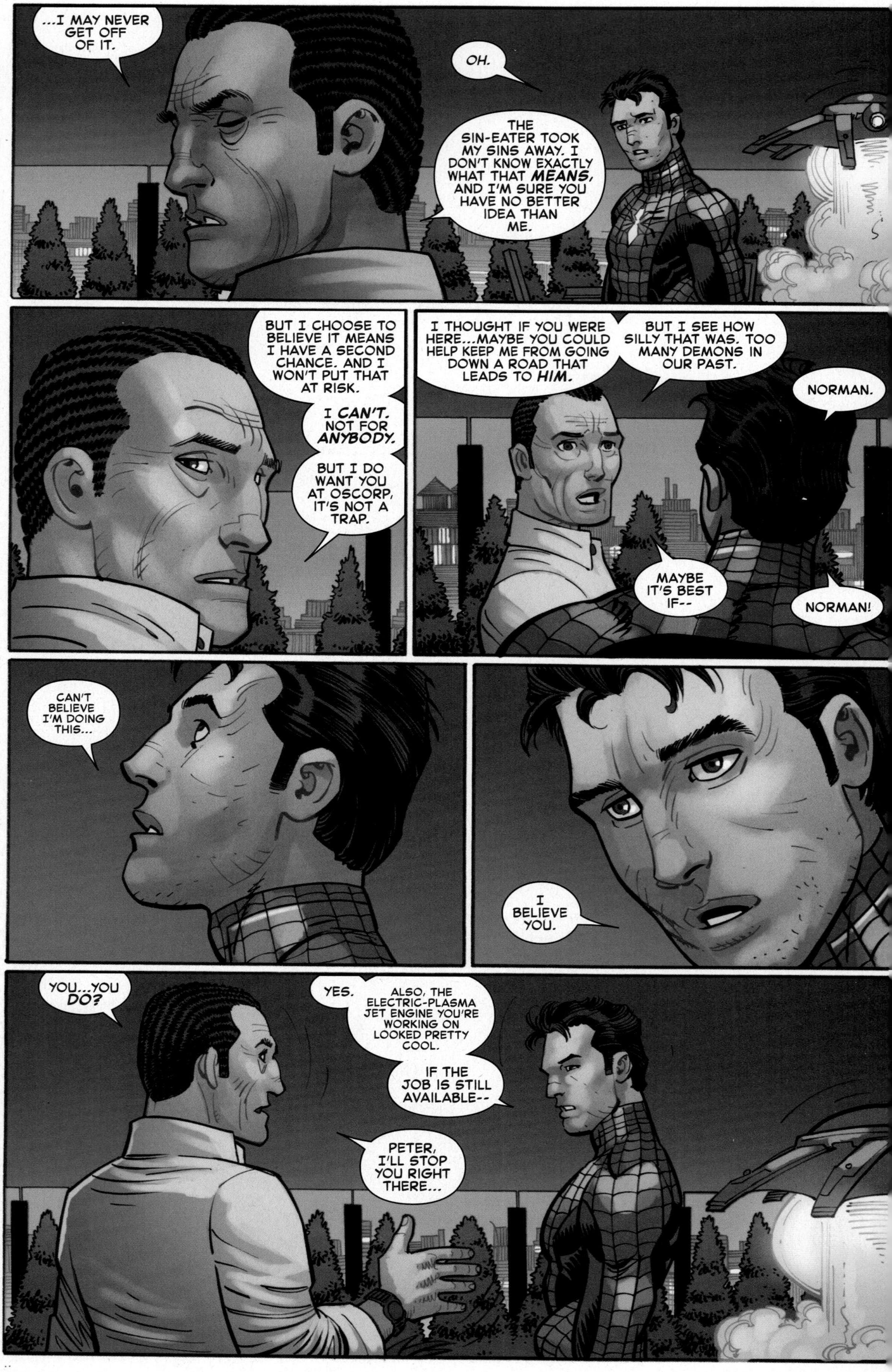
...I MAY NEVER GET OFF OF IT.
OH.
THE SIN-EATER TOOK MY SINS AWAY. I DON'T KNOW EXACTLY WHAT THAT *MEANS*, AND I'M SURE YOU HAVE NO BETTER IDEA THAN ME.
BUT I CHOOSE TO BELIEVE IT MEANS I HAVE A SECOND CHANCE. AND I WON'T PUT THAT AT RISK.
I *CAN'T.* NOT FOR *ANYBODY.*
BUT I DO WANT YOU AT OSCORP, IT'S NOT A TRAP.
I THOUGHT IF YOU WERE HERE...MAYBE YOU COULD HELP KEEP ME FROM GOING DOWN A ROAD THAT LEADS TO *HIM.*
BUT I SEE HOW SILLY THAT WAS. TOO MANY DEMONS IN OUR PAST.
NORMAN.
MAYBE IT'S BEST IF--
NORMAN!
CAN'T BELIEVE I'M DOING THIS...
I BELIEVE YOU.
YOU...YOU *DO?*
YES.
ALSO, THE ELECTRIC-PLASMA JET ENGINE YOU'RE WORKING ON LOOKED PRETTY COOL.
IF THE JOB IS STILL AVAILABLE--
PETER, I'LL STOP YOU RIGHT THERE...

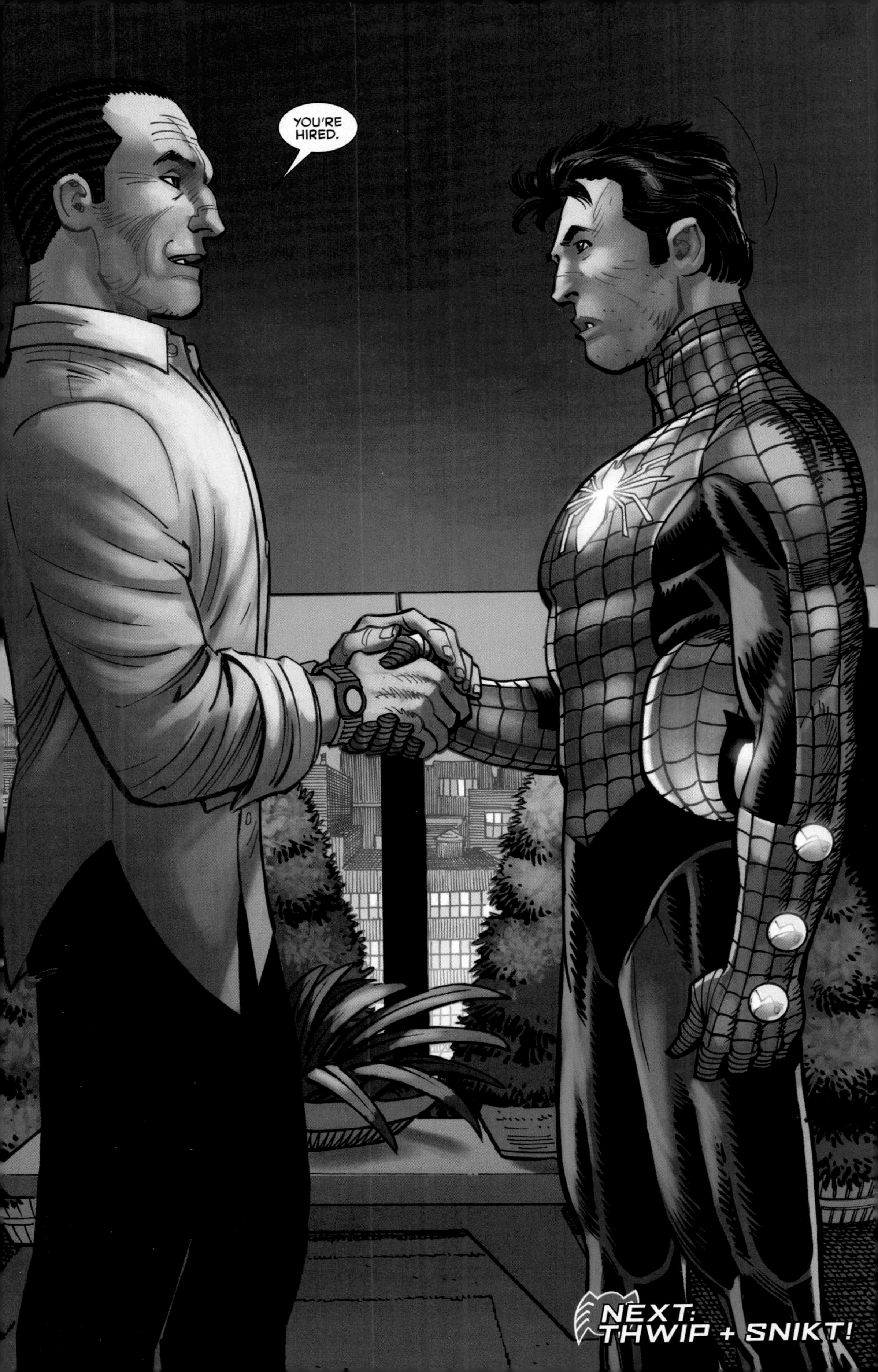
YOU'RE HIRED.
NEXT: THWIP + SNIKT!

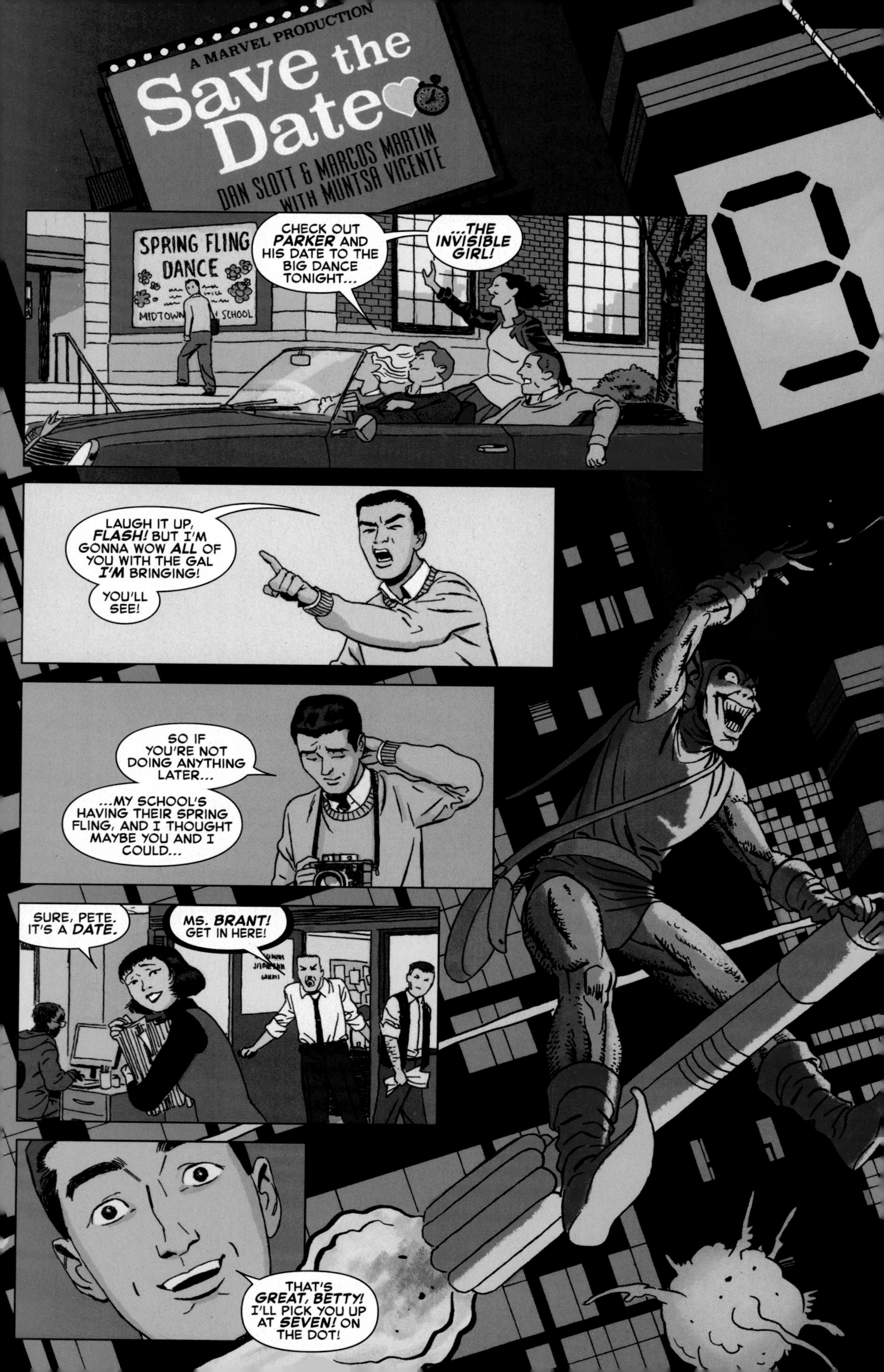
A MARVEL PRODUCTION
Save the Date
DAN SLOTT & MARCOS MARTIN
WITH MUNTSA VICENTE
9
SPRING FLING DANCE
MIDTOWN
SCHOOL
CHECK OUT PARKER AND HIS DATE TO THE BIG DANCE TONIGHT...
...THE INVISIBLE GIRL!
LAUGH IT UP, FLASH! BUT I'M GONNA WOW ALL OF YOU WITH THE GAL I'M BRINGING!
YOU'LL SEE!
SO IF YOU'RE NOT DOING ANYTHING LATER...
...MY SCHOOL'S HAVING THEIR SPRING FLING, AND I THOUGHT MAYBE YOU AND I COULD...
SURE, PETE. IT'S A DATE.
MS. BRANT! GET IN HERE!
THAT'S GREAT, BETTY! I'LL PICK YOU UP AT SEVEN! ON THE DOT!

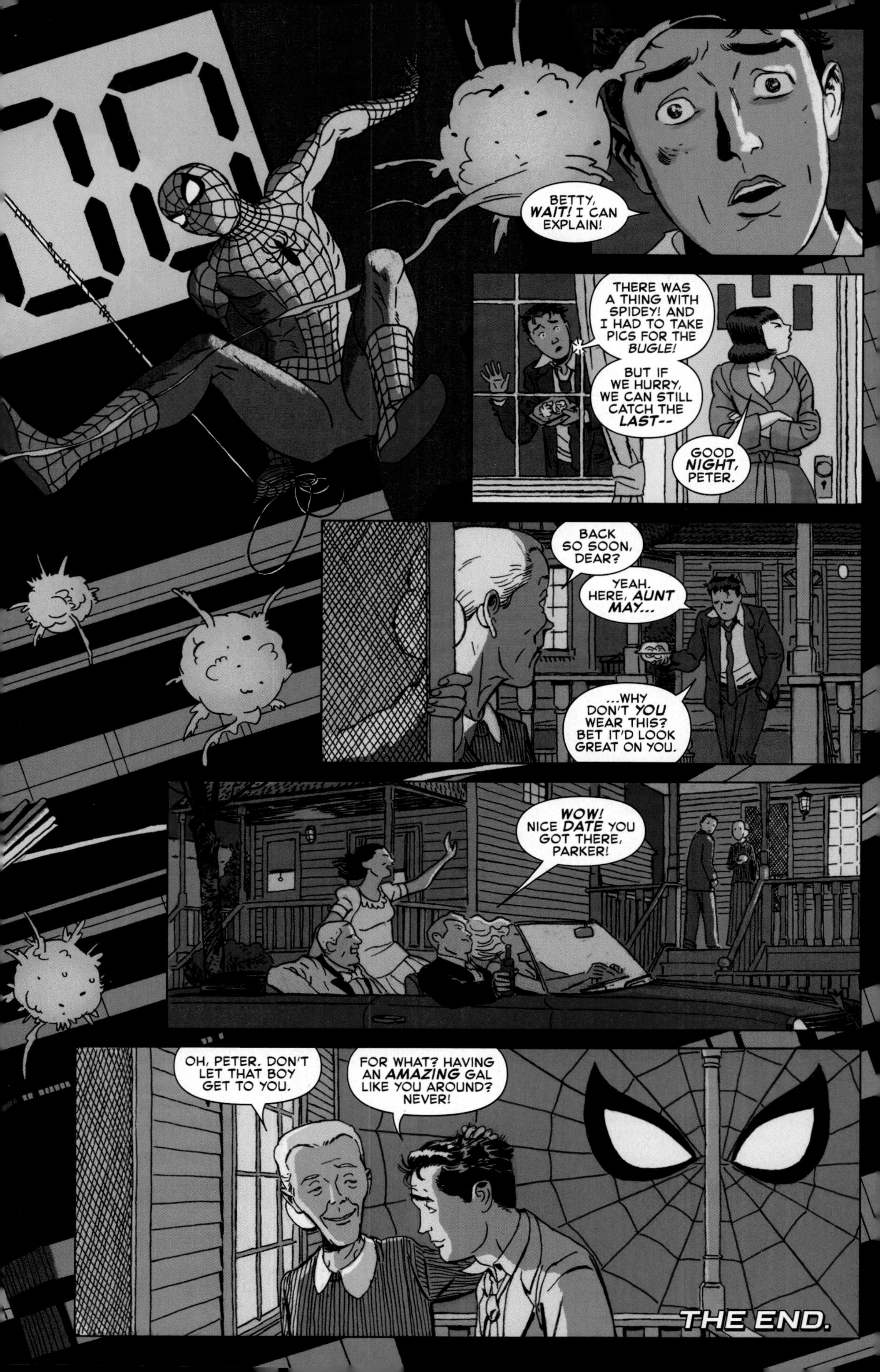
BETTY, WAIT! I CAN EXPLAIN!
THERE WAS A THING WITH SPIDEY! AND I HAD TO TAKE PICS FOR THE BUGLE!
BUT IF WE HURRY, WE CAN STILL CATCH THE LAST--
GOOD NIGHT, PETER.
BACK SO SOON, DEAR?
YEAH. HERE, AUNT MAY...
...WHY DON'T YOU WEAR THIS? BET IT'D LOOK GREAT ON YOU.
WOW! NICE DATE YOU GOT THERE, PARKER!
OH, PETER. DON'T LET THAT BOY GET TO YOU.
FOR WHAT? HAVING AN AMAZING GAL LIKE YOU AROUND? NEVER!
THE END.

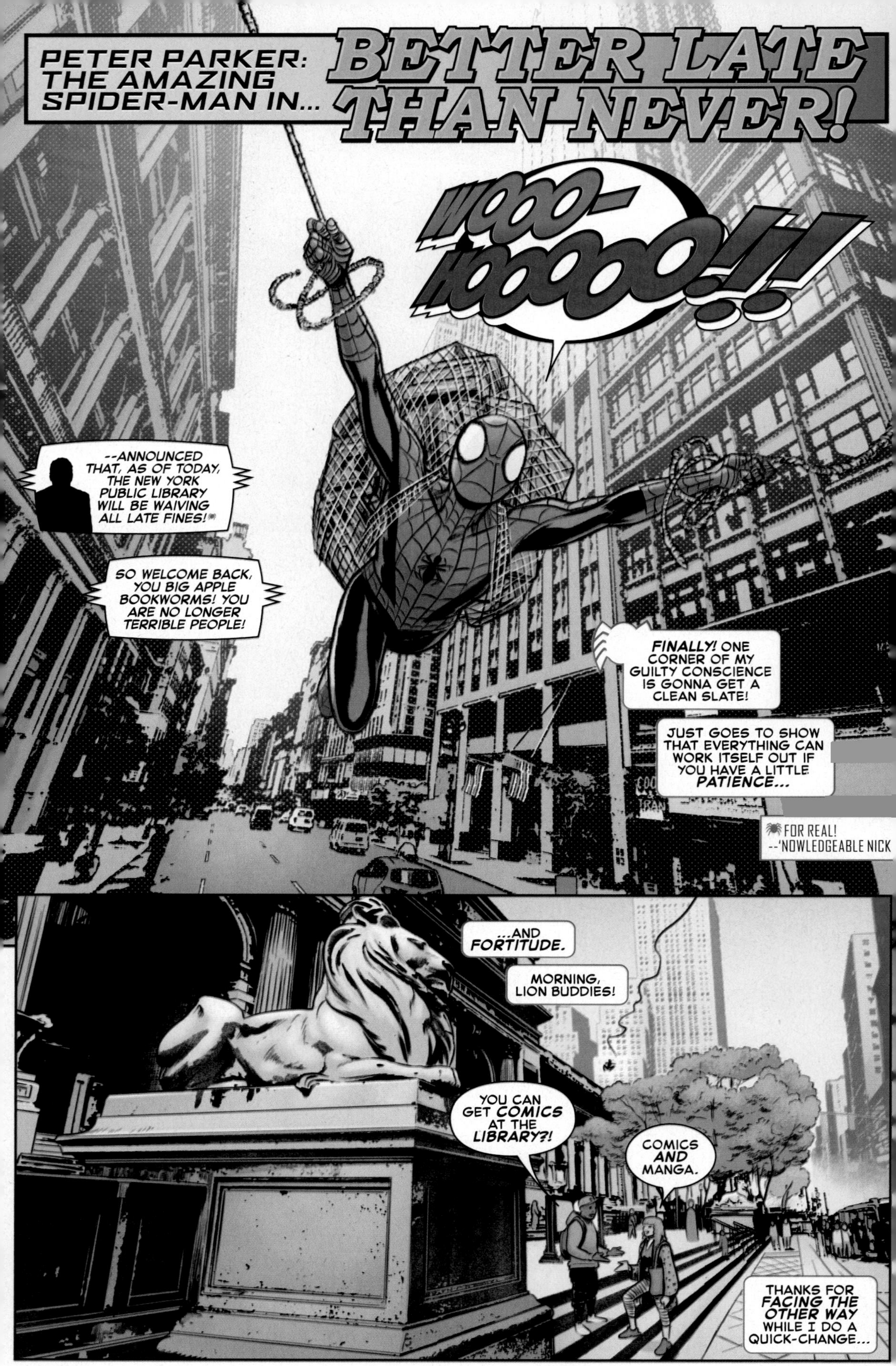
PETER PARKER: THE AMAZING SPIDER-MAN IN...
BETTER LATE THAN NEVER!
WOOO-HOOOOO!!!
--ANNOUNCED THAT, AS OF TODAY, THE NEW YORK PUBLIC LIBRARY WILL BE WAIVING ALL LATE FINES!
SO WELCOME BACK, YOU BIG APPLE BOOKWORMS! YOU ARE NO LONGER TERRIBLE PEOPLE!
FINALLY! ONE CORNER OF MY GUILTY CONSCIENCE IS GONNA GET A CLEAN SLATE!
JUST GOES TO SHOW THAT EVERYTHING CAN WORK ITSELF OUT IF YOU HAVE A LITTLE PATIENCE...
FOR REAL! --'NOWLEDGEABLE NICK
...AND FORTITUDE.
MORNING, LION BUDDIES!
YOU CAN GET COMICS AT THE LIBRARY?!
COMICS AND MANGA.
THANKS FOR FACING THE OTHER WAY WHILE I DO A QUICK-CHANGE...

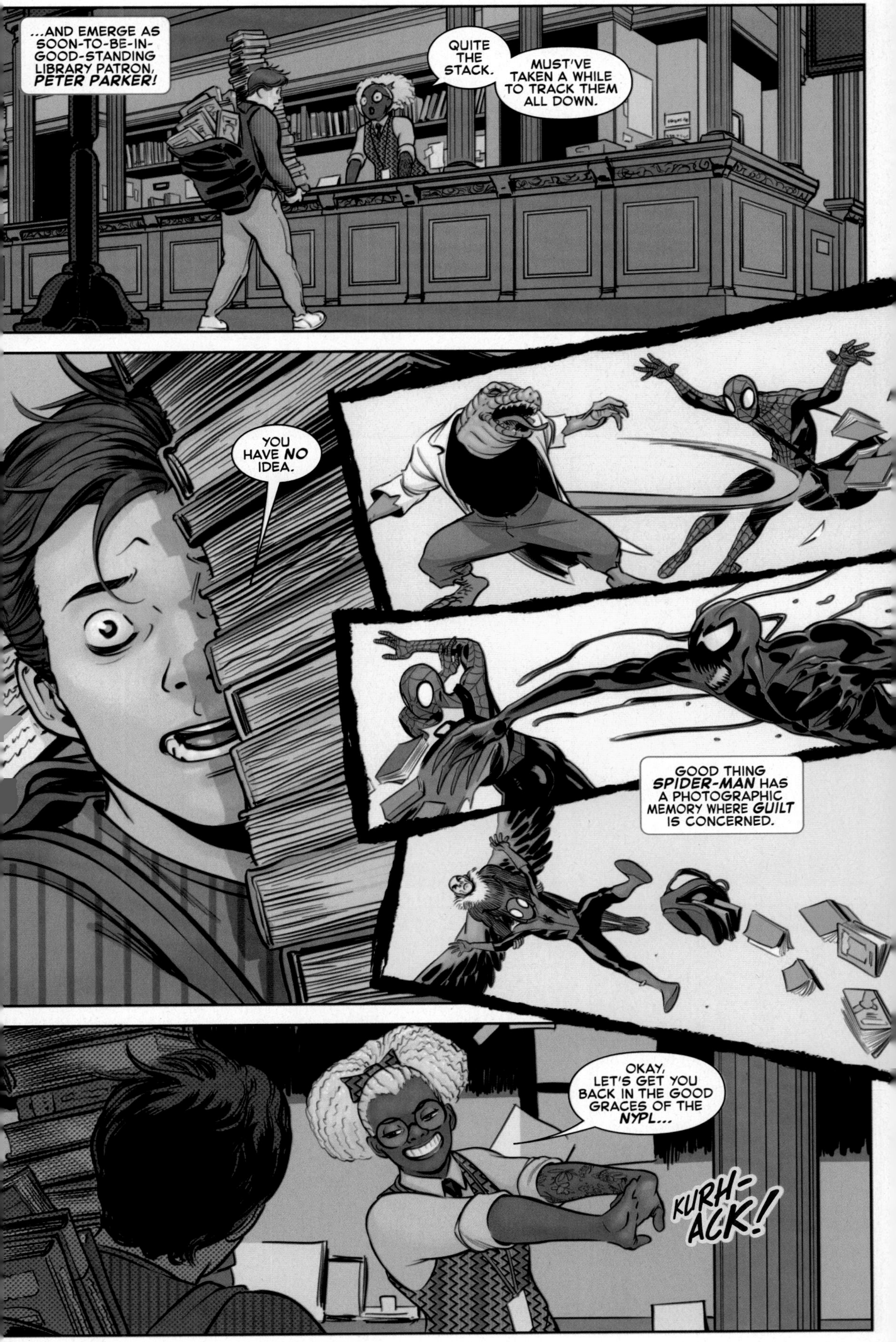
...AND EMERGE AS SOON-TO-BE-IN-GOOD-STANDING LIBRARY PATRON, PETER PARKER!
QUITE THE STACK.
MUST'VE TAKEN A WHILE TO TRACK THEM ALL DOWN.
YOU HAVE NO IDEA.
GOOD THING SPIDER-MAN HAS A PHOTOGRAPHIC MEMORY WHERE GUILT IS CONCERNED.
OKAY, LET'S GET YOU BACK IN THE GOOD GRACES OF THE NYPL...
KURH-ACK!

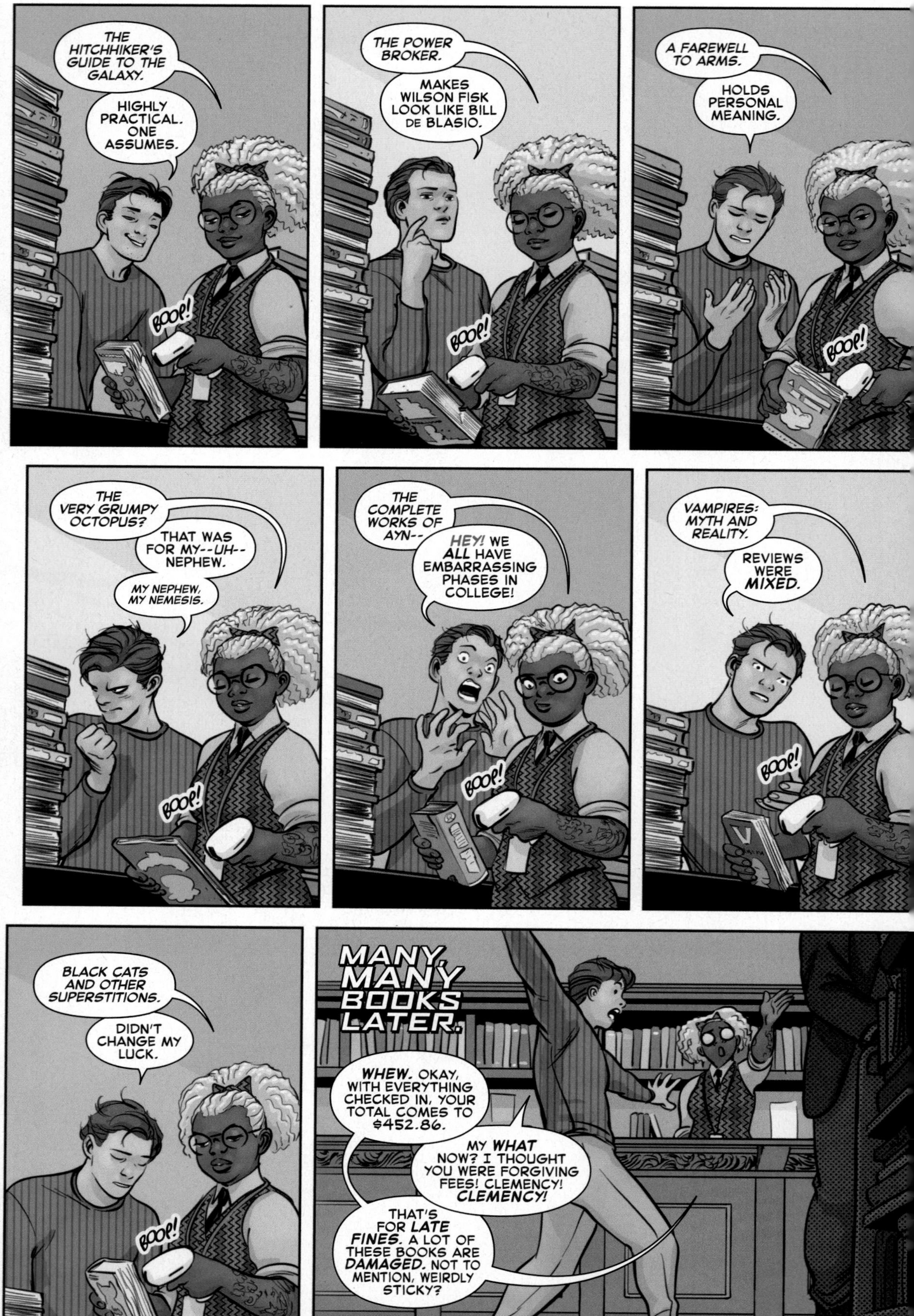

THE HITCHHIKER'S GUIDE TO THE GALAXY.
HIGHLY PRACTICAL. ONE ASSUMES.
BOOP!
THE POWER BROKER.
MAKES WILSON FISK LOOK LIKE BILL DE BLASIO.
BOOP!
A FAREWELL TO ARMS.
HOLDS PERSONAL MEANING.
BOOP!
THE VERY GRUMPY OCTOPUS?
THAT WAS FOR MY--UH--NEPHEW.
MY NEPHEW, MY NEMESIS.
BOOP!
THE COMPLETE WORKS OF AYN--
HEY! WE ALL HAVE EMBARRASSING PHASES IN COLLEGE!
BOOP!
VAMPIRES: MYTH AND REALITY.
REVIEWS WERE MIXED.
BOOP!
BLACK CATS AND OTHER SUPERSTITIONS.
DIDN'T CHANGE MY LUCK.
BOOP!
MANY, MANY BOOKS LATER.
WHEW. OKAY, WITH EVERYTHING CHECKED IN, YOUR TOTAL COMES TO $452.86.
MY WHAT NOW? I THOUGHT YOU WERE FORGIVING FEES! CLEMENCY! CLEMENCY!
THAT'S FOR LATE FINES. A LOT OF THESE BOOKS ARE DAMAGED. NOT TO MENTION, WEIRDLY STICKY?

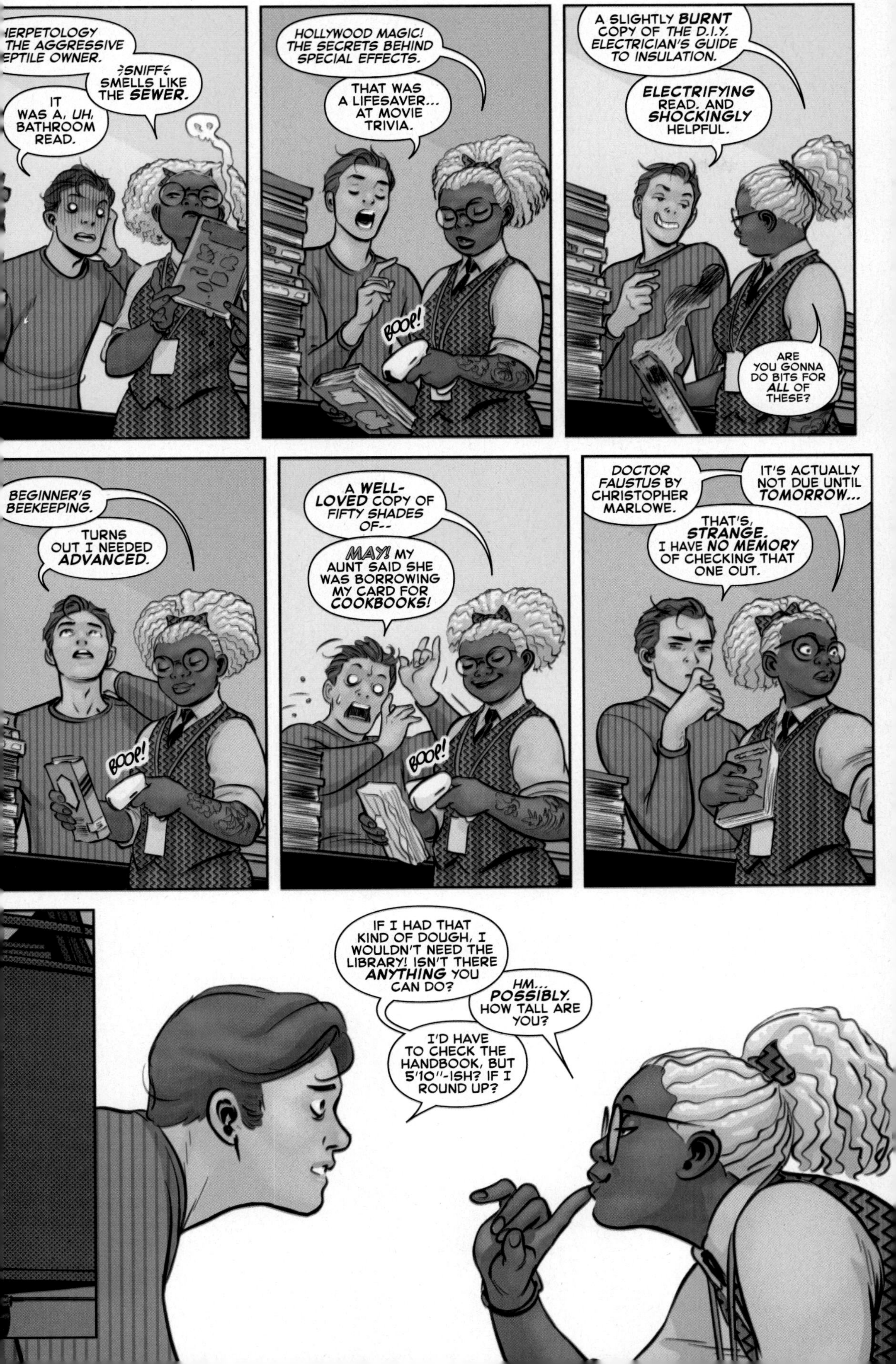

HERPETOLOGY THE AGGRESSIVE EPTILE OWNER.
SNIFF SMELLS LIKE THE SEWER.
IT WAS A, UH, BATHROOM READ.
HOLLYWOOD MAGIC! THE SECRETS BEHIND SPECIAL EFFECTS.
THAT WAS A LIFESAVER... AT MOVIE TRIVIA.
BOOP!
A SLIGHTLY BURNT COPY OF THE D.I.Y. ELECTRICIAN'S GUIDE TO INSULATION.
ELECTRIFYING READ. AND SHOCKINGLY HELPFUL.
ARE YOU GONNA DO BITS FOR ALL OF THESE?
BEGINNER'S BEEKEEPING.
TURNS OUT I NEEDED ADVANCED.
BOOP!
A WELL-LOVED COPY OF FIFTY SHADES OF--
MAY! MY AUNT SAID SHE WAS BORROWING MY CARD FOR COOKBOOKS!
BOOP!
DOCTOR FAUSTUS BY CHRISTOPHER MARLOWE.
IT'S ACTUALLY NOT DUE UNTIL TOMORROW...
THAT'S, STRANGE. I HAVE NO MEMORY OF CHECKING THAT ONE OUT.
IF I HAD THAT KIND OF DOUGH, I WOULDN'T NEED THE LIBRARY! ISN'T THERE ANYTHING YOU CAN DO?
HM... POSSIBLY. HOW TALL ARE YOU?
I'D HAVE TO CHECK THE HANDBOOK, BUT 5'10"-ISH? IF I ROUND UP?

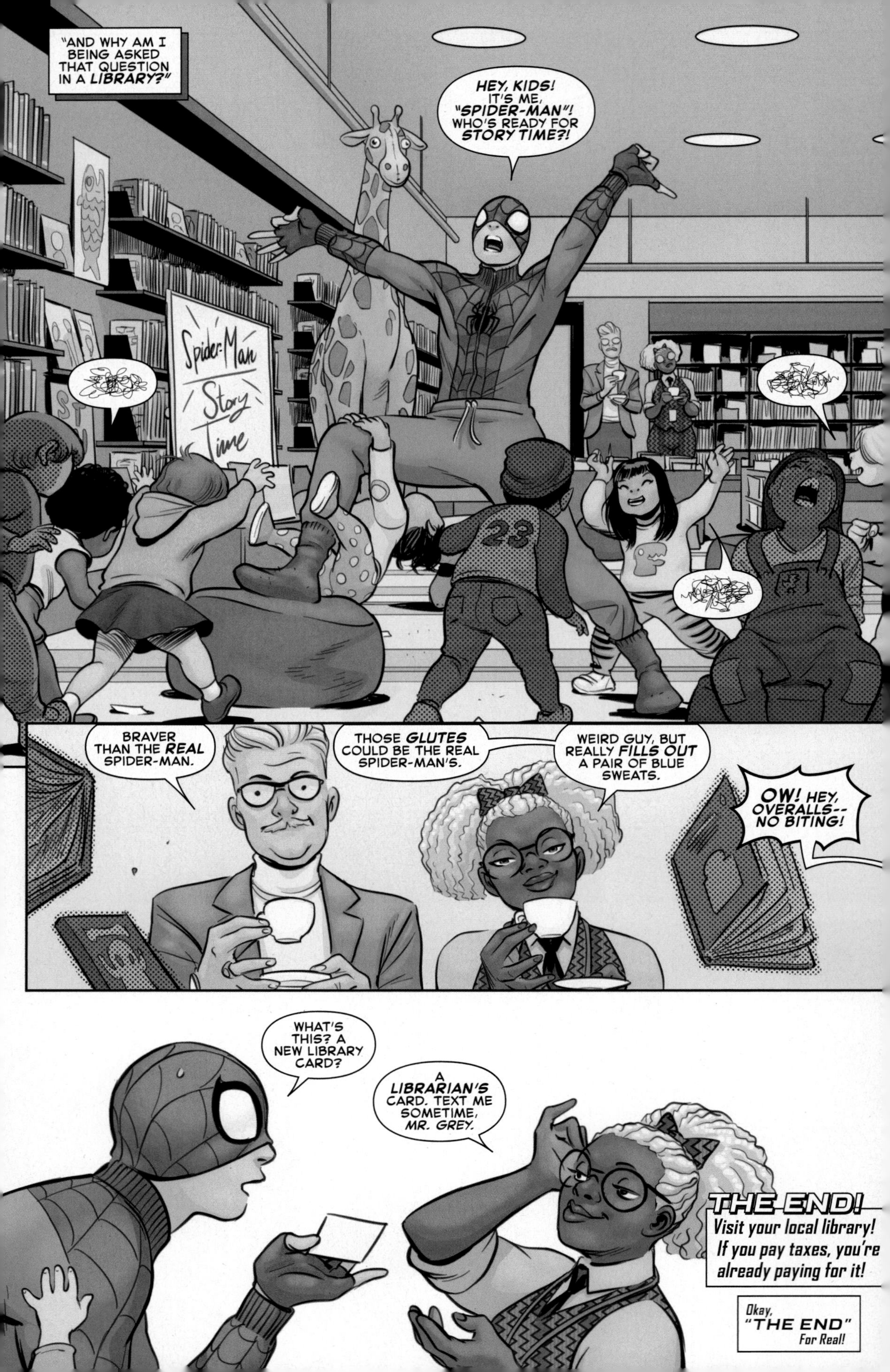
"AND WHY AM I BEING ASKED THAT QUESTION IN A LIBRARY?"
HEY, KIDS! IT'S ME, "SPIDER-MAN"! WHO'S READY FOR STORY TIME?!
Spider-Man Story Time
23
BRAVER THAN THE REAL SPIDER-MAN.
THOSE GLUTES COULD BE THE REAL SPIDER-MAN'S.
WEIRD GUY, BUT REALLY FILLS OUT A PAIR OF BLUE SWEATS.
OW! HEY, OVERALLS--NO BITING!
WHAT'S THIS? A NEW LIBRARY CARD?
A LIBRARIAN'S CARD. TEXT ME SOMETIME, MR. GREY.
THE END!
Visit your local library! If you pay taxes, you're already paying for it!
Okay, "THE END" For Real!

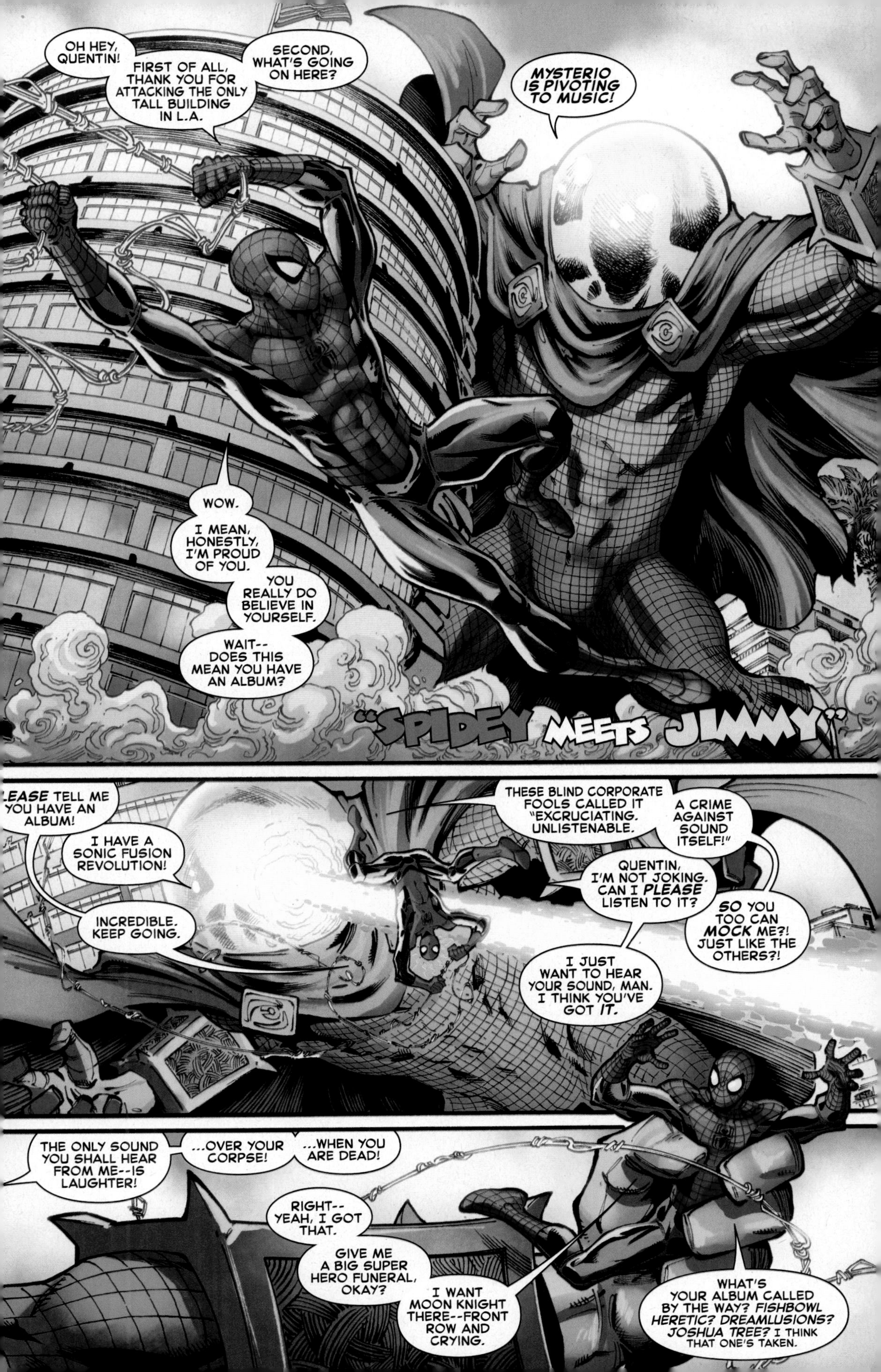
OH HEY, QUENTIN!
FIRST OF ALL, THANK YOU FOR ATTACKING THE ONLY TALL BUILDING IN L.A.
SECOND, WHAT'S GOING ON HERE?
MYSTERIO IS PIVOTING TO MUSIC!
WOW.
I MEAN, HONESTLY, I'M PROUD OF YOU.
YOU REALLY DO BELIEVE IN YOURSELF.
WAIT-- DOES THIS MEAN YOU HAVE AN ALBUM?
"SPIDEY MEETS JIMMY"
LEASE TELL ME YOU HAVE AN ALBUM!
I HAVE A SONIC FUSION REVOLUTION!
INCREDIBLE. KEEP GOING.
THESE BLIND CORPORATE FOOLS CALLED IT "EXCRUCIATING. UNLISTENABLE.
A CRIME AGAINST SOUND ITSELF!"
QUENTIN, I'M NOT JOKING. CAN I PLEASE LISTEN TO IT?
SO YOU TOO CAN MOCK ME?! JUST LIKE THE OTHERS?!
I JUST WANT TO HEAR YOUR SOUND, MAN. I THINK YOU'VE GOT IT.
THE ONLY SOUND YOU SHALL HEAR FROM ME--IS LAUGHTER!
...OVER YOUR CORPSE!
...WHEN YOU ARE DEAD!
RIGHT-- YEAH, I GOT THAT.
GIVE ME A BIG SUPER HERO FUNERAL, OKAY?
I WANT MOON KNIGHT THERE--FRONT ROW AND CRYING.
WHAT'S YOUR ALBUM CALLED BY THE WAY? FISHBOWL HERETIC? DREAMLUSIONS? JOSHUA TREE? I THINK THAT ONE'S TAKEN.

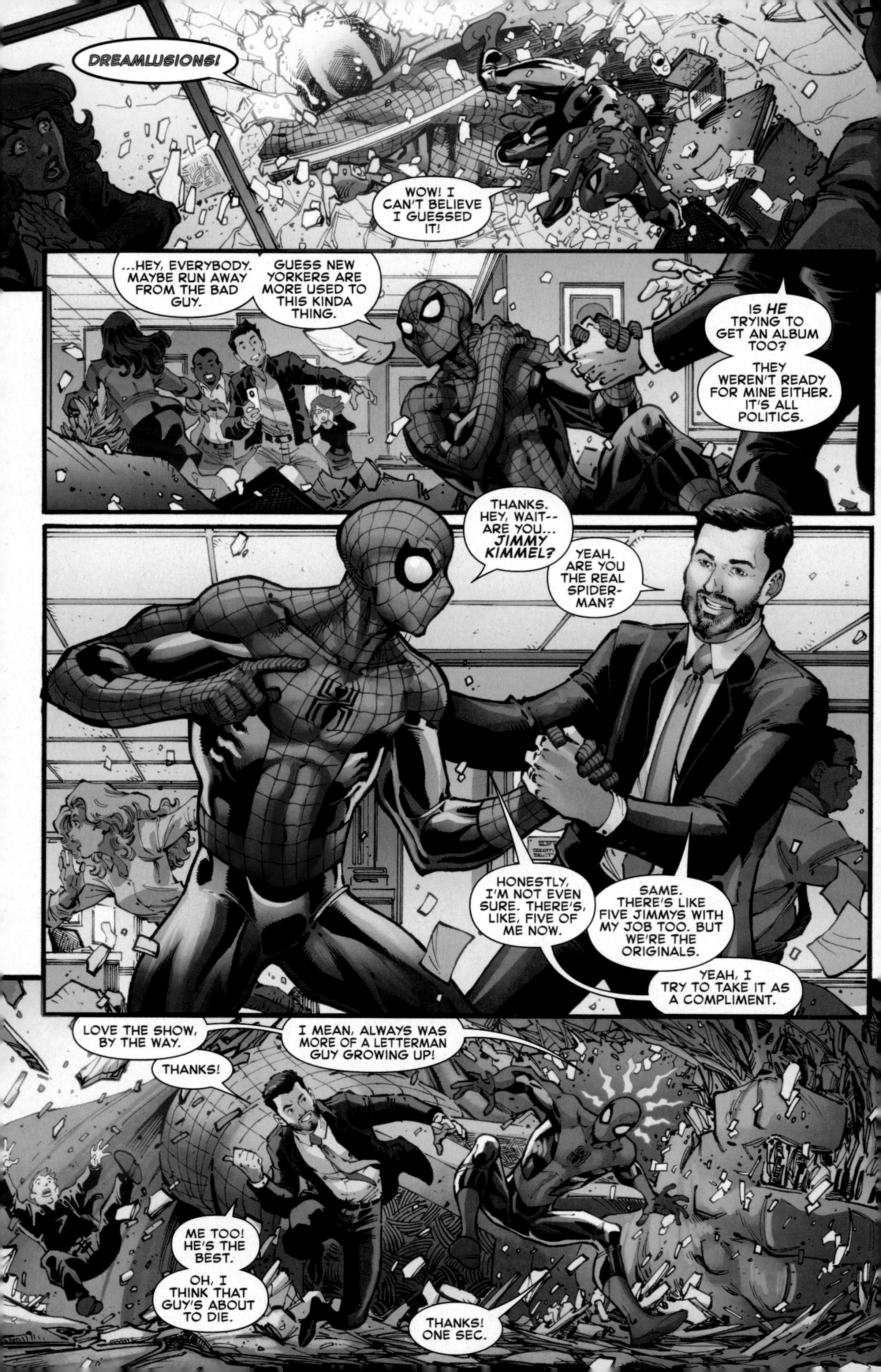
DREAMLUSIONS!
WOW! I CAN'T BELIEVE I GUESSED IT!
...HEY, EVERYBODY. MAYBE RUN AWAY FROM THE BAD GUY.
GUESS NEW YORKERS ARE MORE USED TO THIS KINDA THING.
IS HE TRYING TO GET AN ALBUM TOO?
THEY WEREN'T READY FOR MINE EITHER. IT'S ALL POLITICS.
THANKS. HEY, WAIT--ARE YOU... JIMMY KIMMEL?
YEAH. ARE YOU THE REAL SPIDER-MAN?
HONESTLY, I'M NOT EVEN SURE. THERE'S, LIKE, FIVE OF ME NOW.
SAME. THERE'S LIKE FIVE JIMMYS WITH MY JOB TOO. BUT WE'RE THE ORIGINALS.
YEAH, I TRY TO TAKE IT AS A COMPLIMENT.
LOVE THE SHOW, BY THE WAY.
I MEAN, ALWAYS WAS MORE OF A LETTERMAN GUY GROWING UP!
THANKS!
ME TOO! HE'S THE BEST.
OH, I THINK THAT GUY'S ABOUT TO DIE.
THANKS! ONE SEC.

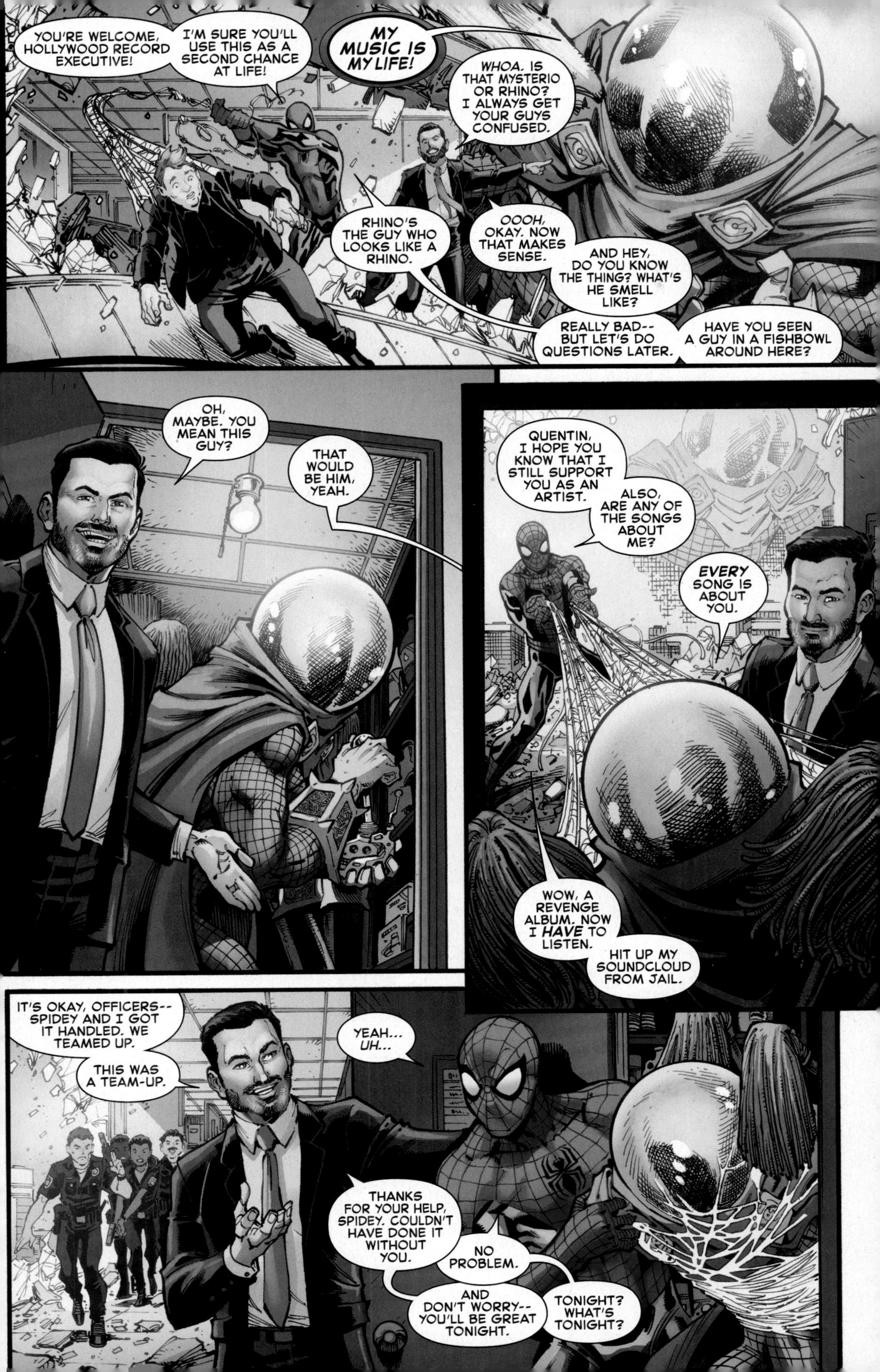

YOU'RE WELCOME, HOLLYWOOD RECORD EXECUTIVE!
I'M SURE YOU'LL USE THIS AS A SECOND CHANCE AT LIFE!
MY MUSIC IS MY LIFE!
WHOA. IS THAT MYSTERIO OR RHINO? I ALWAYS GET YOUR GUYS CONFUSED.
RHINO'S THE GUY WHO LOOKS LIKE A RHINO.
OOOH, OKAY. NOW THAT MAKES SENSE.
AND HEY, DO YOU KNOW THE THING? WHAT'S HE SMELL LIKE?
REALLY BAD-- BUT LET'S DO QUESTIONS LATER.
HAVE YOU SEEN A GUY IN A FISHBOWL AROUND HERE?
OH, MAYBE. YOU MEAN THIS GUY?
THAT WOULD BE HIM, YEAH.
QUENTIN, I HOPE YOU KNOW THAT I STILL SUPPORT YOU AS AN ARTIST.
ALSO, ARE ANY OF THE SONGS ABOUT ME?
EVERY SONG IS ABOUT YOU.
WOW, A REVENGE ALBUM. NOW I HAVE TO LISTEN.
HIT UP MY SOUNDCLOUD FROM JAIL.
IT'S OKAY, OFFICERS-- SPIDEY AND I GOT IT HANDLED. WE TEAMED UP.
THIS WAS A TEAM-UP.
YEAH... UH...
THANKS FOR YOUR HELP, SPIDEY. COULDN'T HAVE DONE IT WITHOUT YOU.
NO PROBLEM.
AND DON'T WORRY-- YOU'LL BE GREAT TONIGHT.
TONIGHT? WHAT'S TONIGHT?

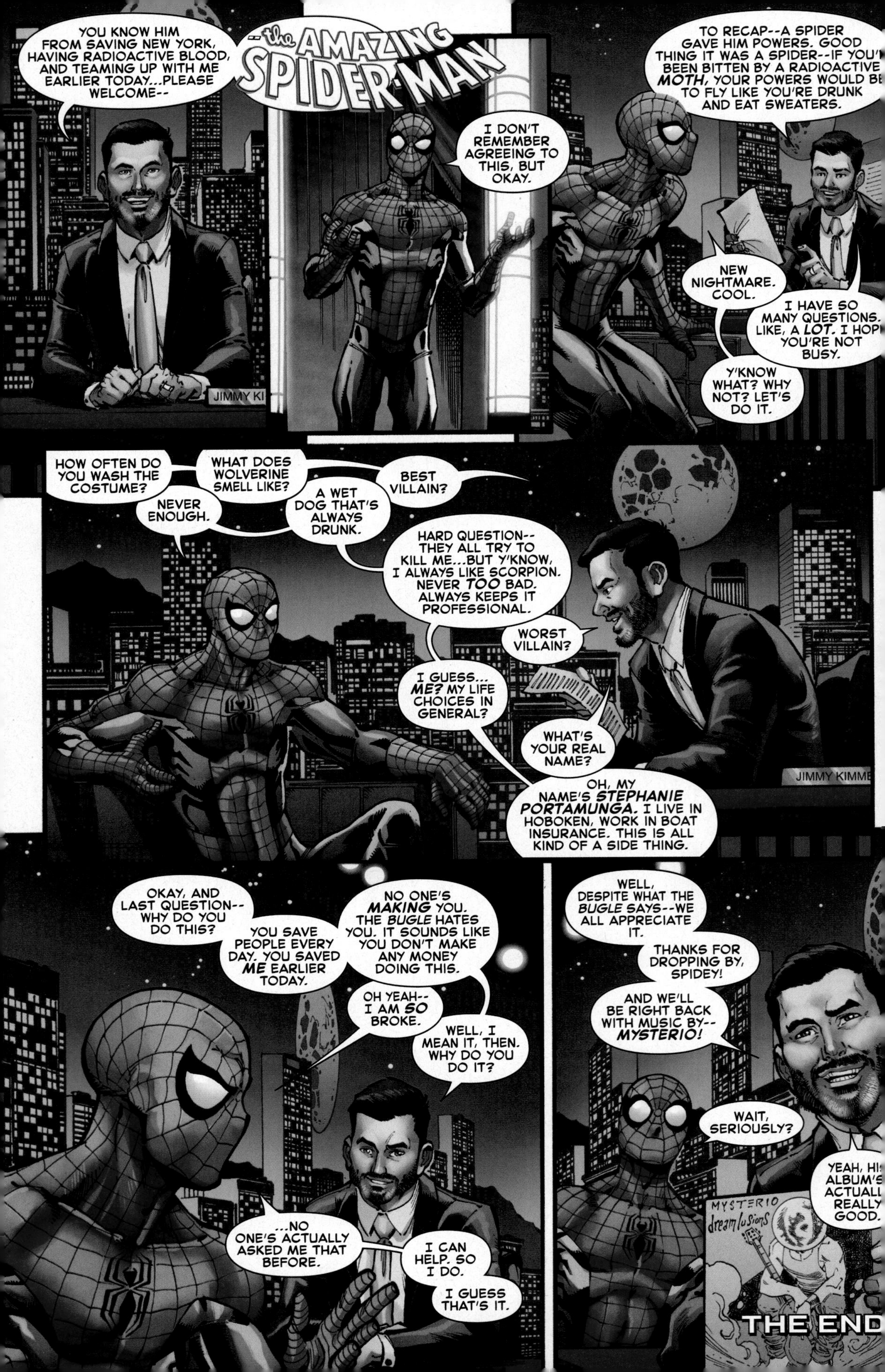
YOU KNOW HIM FROM SAVING NEW YORK, HAVING RADIOACTIVE BLOOD, AND TEAMING UP WITH ME EARLIER TODAY...PLEASE WELCOME--
--the AMAZING SPIDER-MAN
JIMMY KI
I DON'T REMEMBER AGREEING TO THIS, BUT OKAY.
TO RECAP--A SPIDER GAVE HIM POWERS. GOOD THING IT WAS A SPIDER--IF YOU'D BEEN BITTEN BY A RADIOACTIVE MOTH, YOUR POWERS WOULD BE TO FLY LIKE YOU'RE DRUNK AND EAT SWEATERS.
NEW NIGHTMARE. COOL.
I HAVE SO MANY QUESTIONS. LIKE, A LOT. I HOPE YOU'RE NOT BUSY.
Y'KNOW WHAT? WHY NOT? LET'S DO IT.
HOW OFTEN DO YOU WASH THE COSTUME?
NEVER ENOUGH.
WHAT DOES WOLVERINE SMELL LIKE?
A WET DOG THAT'S ALWAYS DRUNK.
BEST VILLAIN?
HARD QUESTION--THEY ALL TRY TO KILL ME...BUT Y'KNOW, I ALWAYS LIKE SCORPION. NEVER TOO BAD. ALWAYS KEEPS IT PROFESSIONAL.
WORST VILLAIN?
I GUESS... ME? MY LIFE CHOICES IN GENERAL?
WHAT'S YOUR REAL NAME?
JIMMY KIMME
OH, MY NAME'S STEPHANIE PORTAMUNGA. I LIVE IN HOBOKEN, WORK IN BOAT INSURANCE. THIS IS ALL KIND OF A SIDE THING.
OKAY, AND LAST QUESTION--WHY DO YOU DO THIS?
YOU SAVE PEOPLE EVERY DAY. YOU SAVED ME EARLIER TODAY.
NO ONE'S MAKING YOU. THE BUGLE HATES YOU. IT SOUNDS LIKE YOU DON'T MAKE ANY MONEY DOING THIS.
OH YEAH--I AM SO BROKE.
WELL, I MEAN IT, THEN. WHY DO YOU DO IT?
...NO ONE'S ACTUALLY ASKED ME THAT BEFORE.
I CAN HELP. SO I DO.
I GUESS THAT'S IT.
WELL, DESPITE WHAT THE BUGLE SAYS--WE ALL APPRECIATE IT.
THANKS FOR DROPPING BY, SPIDEY!
AND WE'LL BE RIGHT BACK WITH MUSIC BY--MYSTERIO!
WAIT, SERIOUSLY?
YEAH, HIS ALBUM'S ACTUALLY REALLY GOOD.
MYSTERIO dreamlusions
THE END

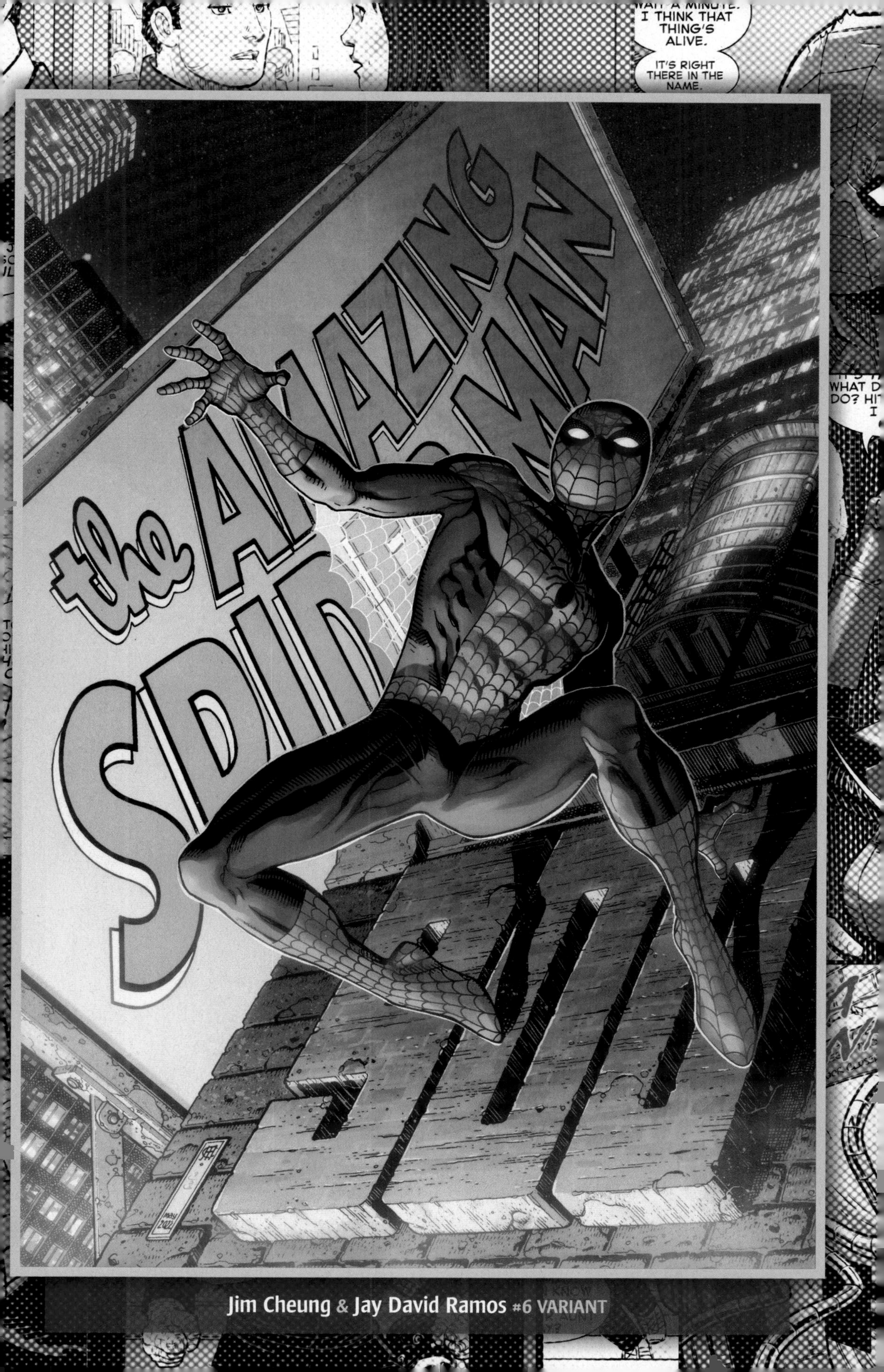
I THINK THAT THING'S ALIVE.
IT'S RIGHT THERE IN THE NAME.

Jim Cheung & Jay David Ramos #6 VARIANT

Mark Bagley & **Edgar Delgado**
#6 VARIANT

Mark Bagley & **Edgar Delgado**
#6 2ND PRINTING VARIANT

Ed McGuinness & **Alejandro Sánchez**
#6 WRAPAROUND VARIANT

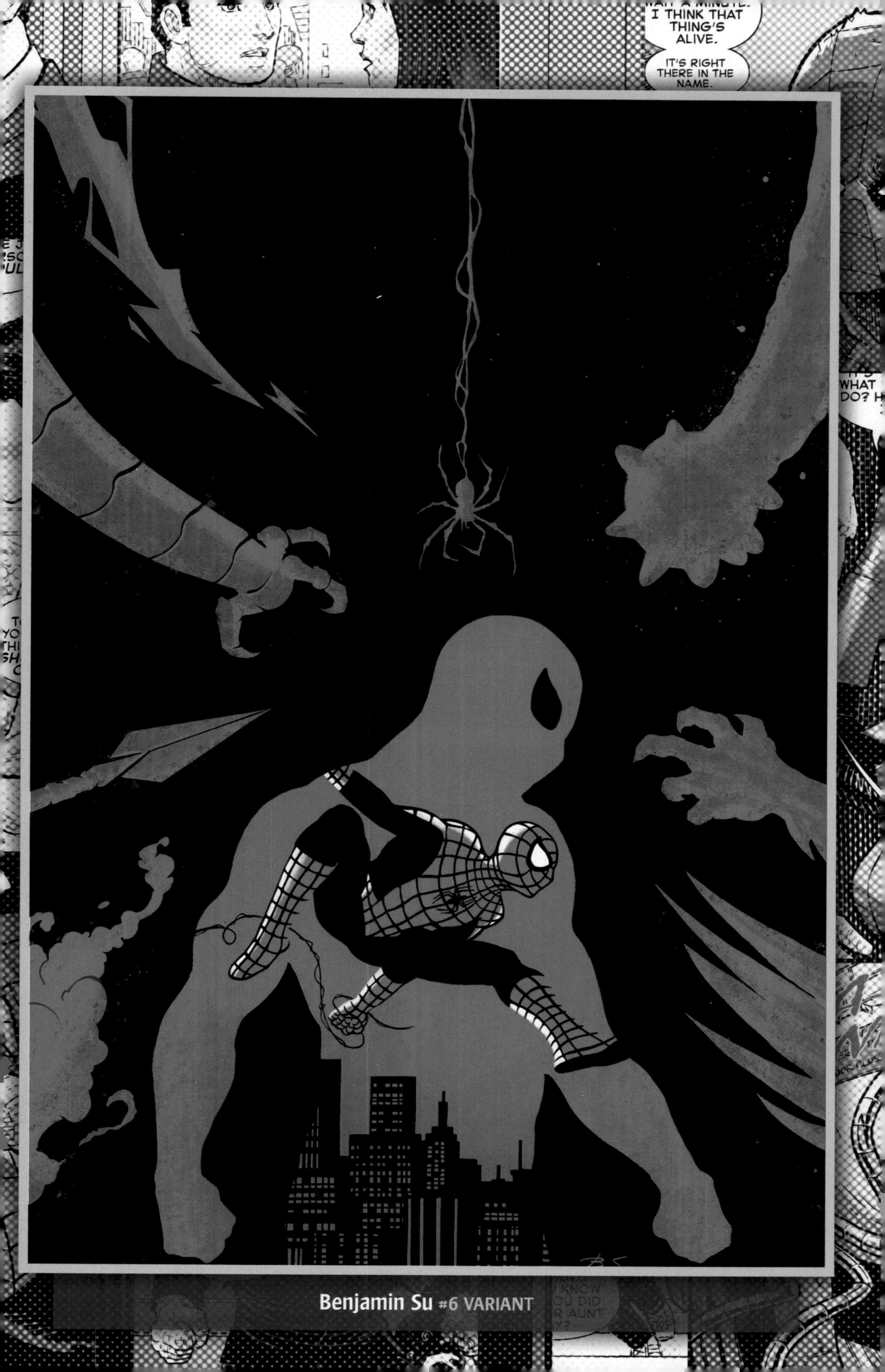
I THINK THAT THING'S ALIVE.
IT'S RIGHT THERE IN THE NAME.

Benjamin Su #6 VARIANT

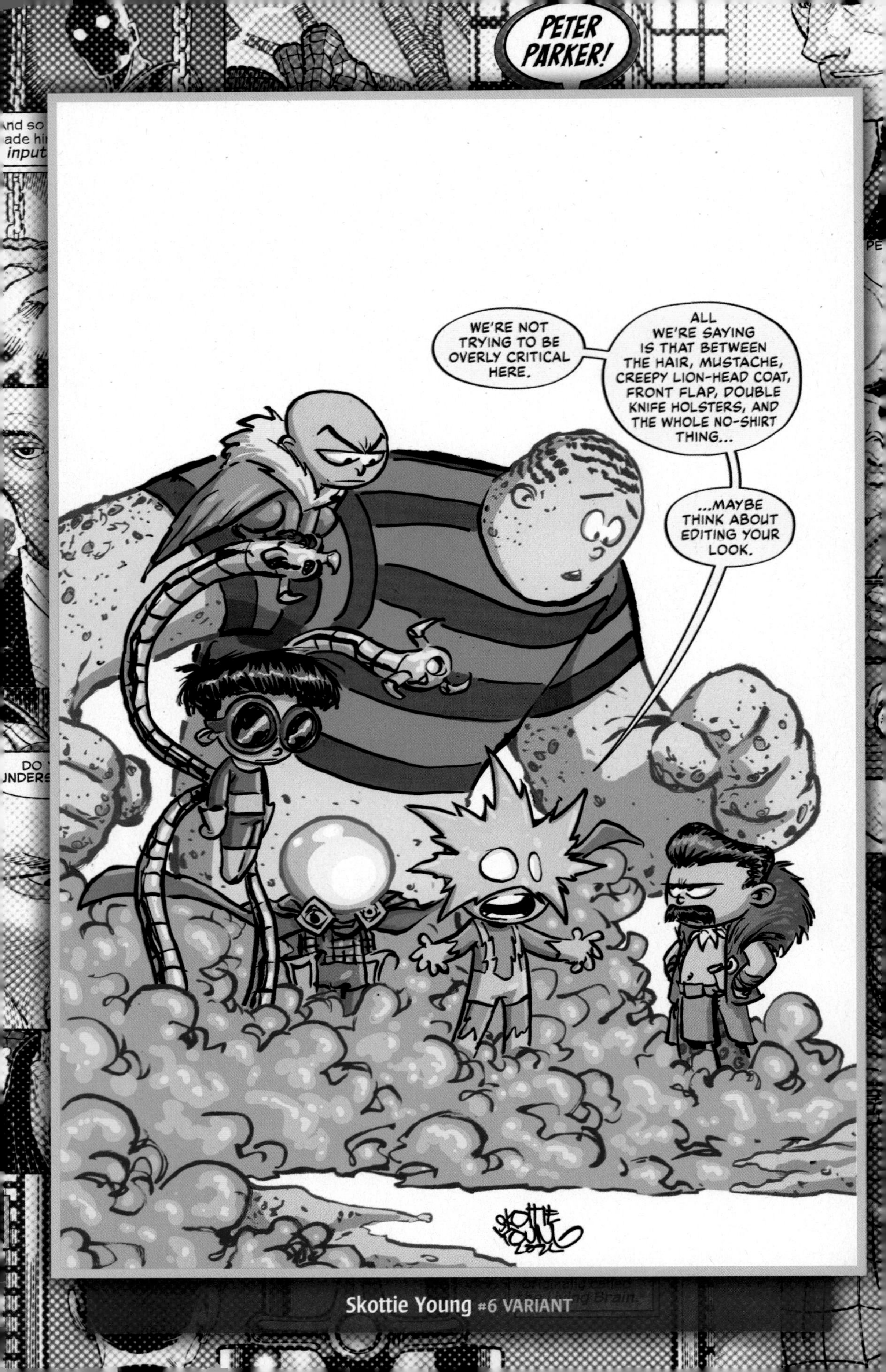
WE'RE NOT TRYING TO BE OVERLY CRITICAL HERE.
ALL WE'RE SAYING IS THAT BETWEEN THE HAIR, MUSTACHE, CREEPY LION-HEAD COAT, FRONT FLAP, DOUBLE KNIFE HOLSTERS, AND THE WHOLE NO-SHIRT THING...
...MAYBE THINK ABOUT EDITING YOUR LOOK.

Skottie Young #6 VARIANT

Humberto Ramos & **Edgar Delgado**
#6 VARIANT

Peach Momoko
#6 VARIANT

Maria Wolf
#6 VARIANT

John Cassaday & **Paul Mounts**
#6 VARIANT

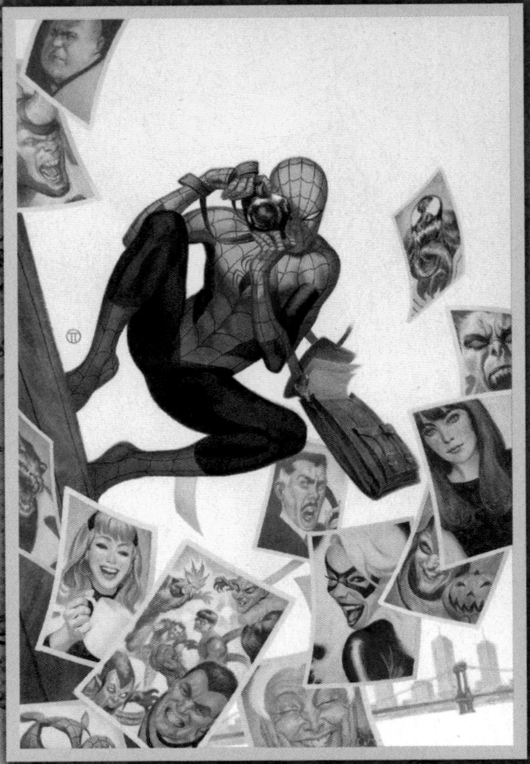

Julian Totino Tedesco
#6 VARIANT

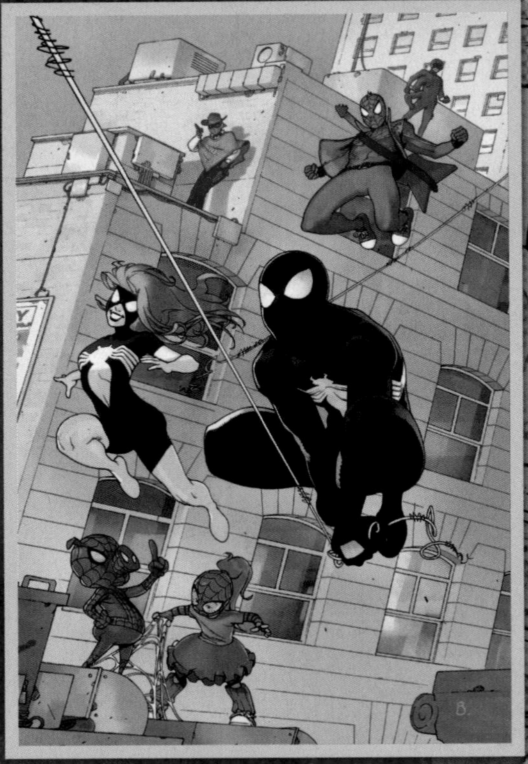

Bengal
#6 CONNECTING VARIANT

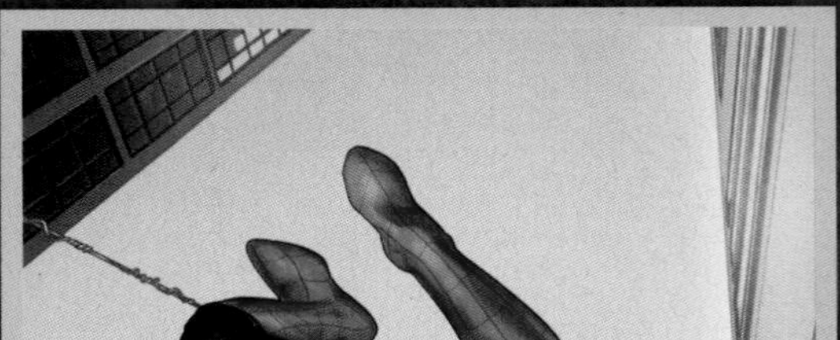

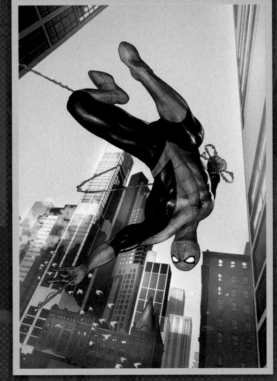

Taurin Clarke
#6 VARIANT

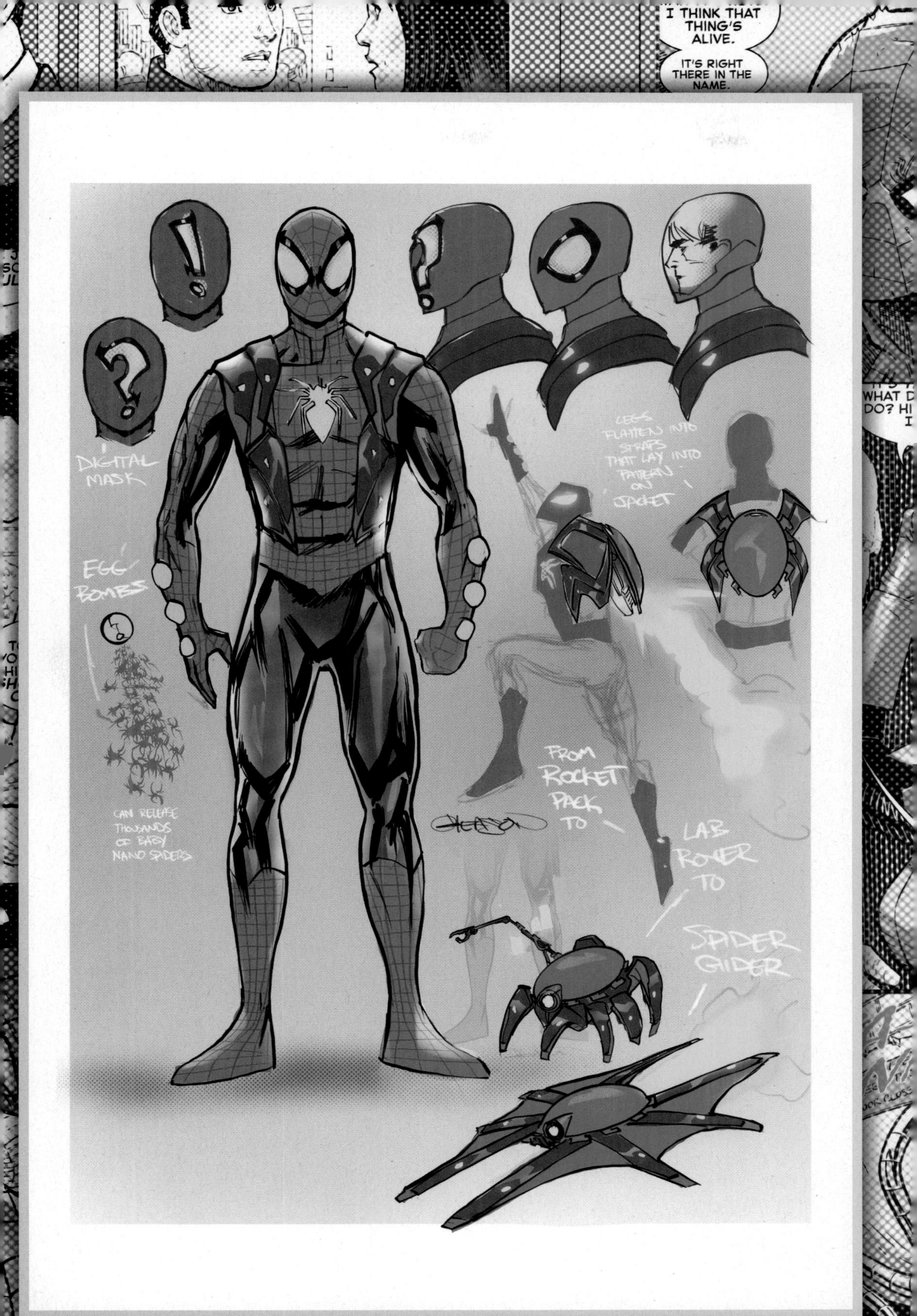
I THINK THAT THING'S ALIVE.
IT'S RIGHT THERE IN THE NAME.
DIGITAL MASK
EGG BOMBS
CAN RELEASE THOUSANDS OF BABY NANO SPIDERS
LEGS FLATTEN INTO STRAPS THAT LAY INTO PATTERN ON JACKET
FROM ROCKET PACK TO
LAB ROVER TO
SPIDER GIDER
GLEASON

Patrick Gleason #7 DESIGN VARIANT

Patrick Gleason & Marcio Menyz
#7 VARIANT

Iban Coello & Jesus Aburtov
#8 STORMBREAKERS VARIANT

Patrick Gleason & Marcio Menyz
#8 VARIANT